MUIRHEAD LIBRARY OF PHILOSOPHY

An admirable statement of the aims of the Library of Philosophy was provided by the first editor, the late Professor J. H. Muirhead, in his description of the original programme printed in Erdmann's *History of Philosophy* under the date 1890. This was slightly modified in subsequent volumes to take the form of the following statement:

'The Muirhead Library of Philosophy was designed as a contribution to the History of Modern Philosophy under the heads: first of Different Schools of Thought—Sensationalist, Realist, Idealist, Intuitivist; secondly of different Subjects—Psychology, Ethics, Aesthetics, Political Philosophy, Theology. While much had been done in England in tracing the course of evolution in nature, history, economics, morals and religion, little had been done in tracing the development of thought on these subjects. Yet "the evolution of opinion is part of the whole evolution".

'By the co-operation of different writers in carrying out this plan it was hoped that a thoroughness and completeness of treatment, otherwise unattainable, might be secured. It was believed also that from writers mainly British and American fuller consideration of English Philosophy than it had hitherto received might be looked for. In the earlier series of books containing, among others, Bosanquet's *History of Aesthetic*, Pfleiderer's *Rational Theology since Kant*, Albee's *History of English Utilitarianism*, Bonar's *Philosophy and Political Economy*, Brett's *History of Psychology*, Ritchie's *Natural Rights*, these objects were to a large extent effected.

'In the meantime original work of a high order was being produced both in England and America by such writers as Bradley, Stout, Bertrand Russell, Baldwin, Urban, Montague, and others, and a new interest in foreign works, German, French and Italian, which had either become classical or were attracting public attention, had developed. The scope of the Library thus became extended into something more international, and it is entering on the fifth decade of its existence in the hope that it may contribute to that mutual understanding between countries which is so pressing a need of the present time.'

The need which Professor Muirhead stressed is no less pressing today, and few will deny that philosophy has much to do with enabling us to meet it, although no one, least of all Muirhead himself, would regard that as the sole, or even the main, object of philosophy. As Professor Muirhead continues to lend the distinction of his name to the

Library of Philosophy it seemed not inappropriate to allow him to recall us to these aims in his own words. The emphasis on the history of thought also seemed to me very timely: and the number of important works promised for the Library in the very near future augur well for the continued fulfilment, in this and other ways, of the expectations of the original editor.

H. D. LEWIS

MUIRHEAD LIBRARY OF PHILOSOPHY

General Editor: H. D. Lewis
Professor of History and Philosophy of Religion in the University of London

Action by SIR MALCOLM KNOX

The Analysis of Mind by BERTRAND RUSSELL

Belief by H. H. PRICE

Brett's History of Psychology edited by R. S. PETERS

Clarity is Not Enough by H. D. LEWIS

Coleridge as a Philosopher by J. H. MUIRHEAD

The Commonplace Book of G. E. Moore edited by C. LEWY

Contemporary American Philosophy edited by G. P. ADAMS and W. P. MONTAGUE

Contemporary British Philosophy first and second Series edited by J. H. MUIRHEAD

Contemporary British Philosophy third Series edited by H. D. LEWIS

Contemporary Indian Philosophy edited by RADHAKRISHNAN and J. H. MUIRHEAD 2nd edition

The Discipline of the Cave by J. N. FINDLAY

Doctrine and Argument in Indian Philosophy by NINIAN SMART

Essays in Analysis by ALICE AMBROSE

Ethics by NICOLAI HARTMANN translated by STANTON COIT 3 vols

The Foundations of Metaphysics in Science by ERROL E. HARRIS

Freedom and History by H. D. LEWIS

The Good Will: A Study in the Coherence Theory of Goodness by H. J. PATON

Hegel: A Re-examination by J. N. FINDLAY

Hegel's Science of Logic translated by W. H. JOHNSTON and L. G. STRUTHERS 2 vols

History of Aesthetic by B. BOSANQUET 2nd edition

History of English Utilitarianism by E. ALBEE

History of Psychology by G. S. BRETT edited by R. S. PETERS abridged one volume edition 2nd edition

Human Knowledge by BERTRAND RUSSELL

A Hundred Years of British Philosophy by RUDOLF METZ translated by J. H. HARVEY, T. E. JESSOP, HENRY STURT

Ideas: A General Introduction to Pure Phenomenology by EDMUND HUSSERL translated by W. R. BOYCE GIBSON

Identity and Reality by EMILE MEYERSON

Imagination by E. J. FURLONG

Contemporary Philosophy in Australia edited by ROBERT BROWN, and C. D. ROLLINS

A Layman's Quest by SIR MALCOLM KNOX
The Elusive Mind by H. D. LEWIS
Indian Philosophy by RADHAKRISHNAN 2 vols revised 2nd edition
Introduction to Mathematical Philosophy by BERTRAND RUSSELL 2nd edition
Kant's First Critique by H. W. CASSIRER
Kant's Metaphysic of Experience by J. H. PATON
Know Thyself by BERNADINO VARISCO translated by GUGLIELMO SALVADORI
Language and Reality by WILBUR MARSHALL URBAN
Lectures on Philosophy by G. E. MOORE
Lecturers on Philosophy by G. E. MOORE edited by C. LEWY
Matter and Memory by HENRI BERGSON translated by N. M. PAUL and
     W. S. PALMER
Memory by BRIAN SMITH
The Modern Predicament by H. J. PATON
Natural Rights by D. G. RITCHIE 3rd edition
Nature, Mind and Modern Science by E. HARRIS
The Nature of Thought by BRAND BLANSHARD
On Selfhood and Godhood by C. A. CAMPBELL
Our Experience of God by H. D. LEWIS
Perception by DON LOCKE
The Phenomenology of Mind by G. W. HEGEL translated by SIR JAMES
     BAILLIE revised 2nd edition
Philosophy in America by MAX BLACK
Philosophical Papers by G. E. MOORE
Philosophy and Illusion by MORRIS LAZEROWITZ
Philosophy and Political Economy by JAMES BONAR
Philosophy and Religion by AXEL HAGERSTROM
Philosophy of Space and Time by MICHAEL WHITEMAN
Philosophy of Whitehead by W. MAYS
The Platonic Tradition in Anglo-Saxon Philosophy by J. H. MUIRHEAD
The Principal Upanisads by RADHAKRISHNAN
The Problems of Perception by R. J. HIRST
Reason and Goodness by BLAND BLANSHARD
The Relevance of Whitehead by IVOR LECLERC
The Science of Logic by G. W. F. HEGEL
Some Main Problems of Philosophy by G. E. MOORE
Studies in the Metaphysics of Bradley SUSHIL KUMAR SAXENA
The Theological Frontier of Ethics by W. G. MACLAGAN
Time and Free Will by HENRI BERGSON translated by F. G. POGSON
The Transcendence of the Cave by J. N. FINDLAY
Values and Intentions by J. N. FINDLAY
The Ways of Knowing: or the Methods of Philosophy by W. P. MONTAGUE

Muirhead Library of Philosophy

EDITED BY H. D. LEWIS

REASON AND SCEPTICISM

REASON AND SCEPTICISM

BY

MICHAEL A. SLOTE

Columbia University

LONDON · GEORGE ALLEN & UNWIN LTD

NEW YORK · HUMANITIES PRESS, INC

LIBRARY OF CONGRESS NUMBER: 75 112502

(U.S.A.) ISBN 0 391 00026 8
(England) ISBN 0 85527 894 3

Reprinted in the United States of America
in 1978 by Humanities Press and in
England by Harvester Press by arrangement
with George Allen & Unwin Ltd.

Printed in the United States of America

TO JENNY

PREFACE

The present work is chiefly concerned with the task of overcoming certain forms of scepticism that have plagued and perplexed philosophers throughout the ages. The focus is on epistemological scepticism; scepticism about moral knowledge or about human freedom, for example, are ignored altogether. My own earliest interests in the area of epistemological scepticism centred around the problem of the external world, and arose from the conviction that previous attempts to refute scepticism about the external world were one and all inadequate. Interest in the other forms of scepticism dealt with in this book—in the problem of other minds, in Goodman's New Riddle of Induction, and in the problem of the existence of God, for example—developed in the course of attempts to deal with the problem of the external world.

Certain portions of this book contain previously published material. I am indebted to the editor of the *Review of Metaphysics* for permission to include parts of 'Induction and Other Minds' (XX, 1966) in the first two sections of Chapter 4; to the editor of *Analysis* for permission to use 'Some Thoughts on Goodman's Riddle' (27, 1967) and 'A General Solution to Goodman's Riddle?' (29, 1968) in the second section of Chapter 5; and to the editor of the *American Philosophical Quarterly* for permission to use a much-expanded version of 'Religion, Science, and the Extraordinary' (*American Philosophical Quarterly Monograph* No. 4) in Chapter 6.

I wish to thank the Columbia University Council on Research in the Humanities for a grant which enabled me to devote myself entirely to the present work during the summer of 1967; and also to thank the Columbia Philosophy Department for providing secretarial assistance in typing the final draft of my manuscript. Those to whom I am indebted for helpful comments and criticisms concerning various parts of this book include: George Boolos, Morris Lazerowitz, David Levin, Sidney Morgenbesser, Ernest Nagel, John O'Connor, Alvin Plantinga, Margaret Wilson, and Robert Wolff. I am particularly grateful to Professor H. D. Lewis for both philosophical and editorial counsel, and to Toni Vogel for aid in preparing the indexes. Bernard Berofsky, David Lewis, Sydney Shoemaker, and Michael Stocker read one or another complete draft of the present work, and saved me from numerous errors and unclarities. I am also greatly indebted to Robert Shope and Roderick Firth who read complete drafts of the manuscript and whose comments brought about much-needed major revisions in Chapters 2 and 5, respectively. Finally, I would like to acknowledge a general philosophical indebtedness to Saul Kripke and Peter Unger, whose ideas and interests in Epistemology have over the years been a source of constant inspiration.

MICHAEL A. SLOTE

New York City
1969

CONTENTS

Preface   13

Introduction   17

1 Some Objections to Scepticism   34

2 The Existence of the External World   65

3 The Nature of the External World   94

4 Induction, Other Minds and Unobserved
   Objects   111

5 The New Riddle of Induction and the
   External World   136

6 Religion, Science and the Extraordinary   188

7 Conclusion   216

Index of Principles   220

General Index   221

INTRODUCTION

What reason or justification is there for thinking that there really is an external (physical) world? What reason or justification is there for thinking that there is not, instead, an immaterial demon who deceptively makes it *appear* to us as if there were real physical objects? What reason is there for thinking that we are not always dreaming, that we ever perceive or remember things correctly, that the humanoid bodies there appear to be around us are the bodies of conscious beings, or that any sort of God at all exists? Questions like these have been raised by philosophers of all kinds over the centuries.

Some philosophers have been, or have claimed to be, sceptical about the possibility of our having or giving good reasons for believing one or another of the above things. There are many kinds of epistemological sceptics and many kinds of epistemological scepticism. There is scepticism about the external (physical) world, about perception, about memory, about other minds, about God, etc. What I shall mean in talking about scepticism about the external world, or about any other matter, can be understood in terms of the notion of a sceptical hypothesis. I shall, in general, call something a sceptical hypothesis about *x* if it entails the non-existence of *x*.[1] Thus the hypothesis that there is a demon who makes it seem as if there is an external world when in fact there is none is a sceptical hypothesis about (the existence of) the external world. By scepticism about *x* I shall (unless I indicate otherwise) mean the claim or view that some sceptical hypothesis about *x* is no less reasonable than its denial, which means that there is no more reason to believe that *x* exists than that *x* does not exist and that it is, consequently, unreasonable to believe that *x* exists. Scepticism about the external world, then, is the view that (*a*) some sceptical hypothesis about the external world is no less reasonable than the claim that there *is* an external world, and that consequently (*b*) it is unreasonable to believe in an external world.

The sceptical problems I shall be dealing with here are several and diverse. Each of them can be dealt with in isolation and has

[1] I am allowing myself the notions of (logical) entailment and logical possibility (and allied notions) without attempting to defend the legitimacy of using them in the light of the recent work of Quine, and others. I think it *is* legitimate to use these notions in philosophy, but shall not *argue* the point here.

been dealt with in isolation by other philosophers. However, a large number of philosophers have thought that the various sorts of scepticism I have alluded to above have much in common. And many of these have thought, in particular, that if one is to overcome scepticism about the external world, memory, other minds, etc., one can do so only on the basis of one's knowledge (or one's reasonable beliefs) about the nature of one's own experience, supplemented by certain valid 'principles of inference'. In the present work, I shall attempt to overcome some of the major traditional forms of epistemological scepticism by showing the reasonableness of belief in an external (physical) world, in the existence of veridical memory and perception of that world, in the existence of other minds, and in the existence of objects that one is not observing, on the basis of a single line of argument based chiefly on premises solely about my experience[1] and on certain valid principles of scientific methodology and of rational thinking in general. I hope to show that, given the sort of experience each of us (has reason to believe he) has, each of us can make use of intuitively reasonable principles of inference to show that the best (scientific) explanation of his having the sort of experiences he does is to be found in the 'hypothesis' of an external world that is pretty much the way it seems to be and to have been. From this conclusion—I hope to show— he can argue for the reasonableness of belief in other conscious beings and in objects that he is not currently perceiving and for there being at least *some* reason to believe in some sort of deity.

In recent years philosophers have objected in many different ways to the sort of enterprise on which I am proposing to embark.[2]

---

[1] Premises solely about my experience are premises that describe my experience and that entail that I am conscious or aware in some way or other, but that do not entail the existence of physical entities or of conscious beings other than myself. Also, premises (or beliefs) about the external world (or about other minds) are ones whose truth entails that there is an external world (or minds other than one's own).

[2] As may already be apparent, this book will involve thought and argument from two different points of view. The first is that of the philosopher who assumes the existence of a community of other philosophers and accepts a large number of (what seem to him) reasonable commonsense, philosophic and scientific beliefs. It is from this point of view that I shall try to show the validity and importance of the enterprise of the present book and the weakness of other attempts to overcome scepticism of various kinds. The second point of view is that of the conscious being who argues from the nature of his experience, via certain principles, but without begging any questions, in an attempt to show the falsity of various forms of scepticism. For purposes of easy exposition the two

Most significantly, perhaps, some philosophers would object to the whole idea of arguing for the external world and for other minds on the basis of claims about experience. Such an enterprise, they would say, presupposes that our beliefs about our own experiences are in some sense *epistemologically prior* to our beliefs about external objects and other minds. And the traditional argument for such priority has been that statements solely about our own experience are certain and incorrigible and indubitable in a way that statements about the external world or other minds are not. Certain contemporary philosophers, notable among them the late John Austin,[1] have thought that statements about immediate experience are neither incorrigible nor indubitable, and have believed, further, that if such statements *are* certain, so *too* are statements that entail the existence of an external (physical) world. I am inclined to agree with Austin and others that statements about experience are not incorrigible, nor indubitable, inasmuch as it is possible for someone to make a genuine mistake, and have reason for thinking that (or wondering whether) he has made such a mistake, about the character of his own (present) experience. But I am not at all sure that if statements about immediate experience are certain, statements about the external world are (at least sometimes) certain. I have argued the point elsewhere,[2] and shall not discuss it further here, since the argument of the present book in no way depends, I think, on the possibility of certainty about our immediate experience or on the impossibility of having certainty about the existence and nature of the exernal world and/or other minds.

In claiming that my experience is a datum that calls for an explanation and enables us to justify belief in an external world, etc., I am not claiming that it is certain that I have the sorts of experiences I think I have. For it is common scientific practice to seek for explanations of data that are themselves not (considered to be) certain—as long as there is *strong reason* to believe in the exis-

points of view will be intertwined in various ways throughout the present work. But it should also be clear that they can be separated when necessary. In particular, when I say that each of us can prove the reasonableness of certain of his commonsense beliefs, I am assuming the first point of view, but committing myself to the claim that an argument for the reasonableness of believing in an external world can be given from the second point of view and, presumably, to producing such an argument myself.

[1] See *Sense and Sensibilia*, Oxford: Clarendon Press, 1962, ch. 10.

[2] See my 'Empirical Certainty and the Theory of Important Criteria', *Inquiry*, 10, 1967, pp. 21–37.

tence of those data. Thus an astronomer may seek to explain an increase in the brightness of a certain star that he believes has taken place in terms of the occurrence of some sort of nuclear reaction in the centre of the star, without wanting to claim that he knows for certain that the star's brightness has increased. He may be willing to grant the *possibility* that his telescope, his eyes, or his other instruments have been defective, and merely claim that there is very good reason to think the star's brightness has increased, that a nuclear reaction in the centre of the star is the most probable cause of such an increase in brightness, if it occurred, and that it is, therefore, in the circumstances, reasonable to believe (at least tentatively) that a nuclear reaction in fact did occur in the centre of the star in question.

All I wish to maintain, similarly, is that we can, for certain purposes of epistemological reconstruction, assume (the reasonableness of belief in) the truth of our beliefs about the nature of our experience. Even if such beliefs are corrigible, dubitable and not (absolutely) certain, it is entirely reasonable for us to accept them. And if one can show that the best explanation of the 'data' constituted by the sort of experiences one has involves 'positing' an external world, that is pretty much as it seems, then one has done a major part of what is required in order to show the reasonableness of belief in an external world, other minds, etc.

It will be replied by certain philosophers that, if I am willing to grant that statements of beliefs about immediate experience are not certain, I have in no way provided a plausible basis for the claim that beliefs (or knowledge) about our own experience are epistemologically prior to beliefs (or knowledge) about the external world, other minds, etc., etc. And if such beliefs are not prior, why is it necessary to argue from them to claims about the external world? Why can't one just assume that there is a world, that other people exist, and forget about proving or arguing for these things?

Of course, I would never want to claim that there is anything necessary about attempting to overcome scepticism about the external world, etc. Ordinary people seem to get on quite well without knowing anything about such scepticism, much less trying to deal with it philosophically. And obviously there are enough other worthwhile areas and aspects of philosophy that not even the philosopher who wants to make a genuine contribution will *have* to spend much time thinking about and arguing against scepticism. But I do believe that attempting to overcome scepticism via a reconstruction of knowledge of the kind to be attempted here is interesting and philosophically worth while, and it is worth considering how such a belief can be defended against the above objections.

In the first place, it is not at all clear to me that one cannot plausibly argue for the priority of claims about immediate experience (claims solely about one's experience) with respect to claims about external objects and other minds, even if such claims are granted to be corrigible, dubitable and only sometimes (or never) absolutely certain. For, surely, most philosophers would be willing to admit that if there is a type of proposition or claim x and a type of proposition or claim y such that it is logically impossible for it to be reasonable for one to believe in (the truth of) some propositions (or claims) of kind y without its being reasonable for one to believe in (the truth of) some propositions (or claims) of kind x, but not vice versa, then propositions (or claims) of kind x are in a significant way epistemologically prior to those of kind y.[1] And this is, I think, exactly the situation with claims about one's own immediate experience and claims about the external world. It is not logically impossible to be warranted[2] in believing propositions solely about one's own experience(s) without being warranted in believing any propositions about external objects (or processes, etc.). This could happen, for example, if there were an intelligent being possessed of the sort of concepts we possess whose (sense) experience was so thoroughly disordered that he could not make any reasonable claims about the nature, or even the existence, of an external world although he had reasonable beliefs about his experiences. (By 'external world' I have meant and shall continue to mean 'physical world'. There is a physical world even if just one's own body exists.) There might also be a case where one's (sense) experience was to some degree orderly, but such as to

[1] Those who are suspicious or wary of (positing) propositions can, I think, rephrase my talk of the epistemological priority of types of propositions so as to speak only of the priority of beliefs. By 'some propositions' I mean 'at least one proposition'.

[2] I shall use 'reasonable', 'justified', and 'warranted' fairly interchangeably (in application to beliefs, etc.), because I think they mean pretty much the same thing (in such contexts). By 'justified belief' philosophers sometimes mean 'belief that can be or has been justified' and sometimes mean 'reasonable belief', but (unless the context makes it clear to the contrary) I shall always use 'justified belief' in the latter sense. Unless it is otherwise stated, I shall use 'justified', etc. to mean 'rationally justified' or 'epistemically justified', etc. On this see Chapter 2, p. 85 ff., below.

warrant one's believing that the sole source of one's experience was a Cartesian demon or spirit and that there was no external world. (I shall have more to say about such a case below, p. 61f., and p. 69f.) On the other hand, without its being reasonable to have some sort of belief about the nature of one's immediate experience, how could one (logically) possibly have good reason to believe (be warranted in believing) any claims entailing the existence of an external world? Of course, to *ask* in dubious tones how something *could* be the case is not to show that the thing in question *is* impossible. But if one examines the matter carefully, one will, I think, be hard put to find a conceivable case where believing in an external world is reasonable for someone for whom no claim (or belief or proposition) about his own experience is reasonable. Those inclined to favour a Coherence Theory of Knowledge (and of the Justification of Beliefs) might at this point claim that one could reasonably believe something about the external world without any belief or claim about experience being warranted for the being in question, if one had a belief about the external world, had no other beliefs or sets of beliefs contradicting that belief, and had no beliefs about one's experience. For according to some Coherence Theorists[1] any belief of a person that contradicts none of his other beliefs, nor any set of his other beliefs, is reasonable and warranted.

But is it so easy, first of all, to imagine someone's having beliefs about the external world but no beliefs about experience? Wasn't it really just because of the difficulty of this sort of thing that some Rationalists wrote of innate ideas as being *virtually* in the mind at birth (before one has had experience), rather than actually or really or fully in the mind at birth? More significant here, however, I think, is the sheer implausibility of the Coherence Theory's principle that beliefs are always warranted if they cohere with one's other beliefs (do not contradict any conjunction of such beliefs). For such a principle implies that a lunatic or paranoiac, whose beliefs about the plots that others are planning and perpetrating against him are coherent, is reasonable in believing the various things he does about the way people are plotting and acting against him. To put the issue in a slightly question-begging way, the Coherence Theory may deny the reasonableness of him

---

[1] Something like this sort of position is held by Bosanquet (*Logic*, Oxford: Clarendon Press, 1911, vol. II, ch. 9, esp. p. 267) and by B. Blanshard (*The Nature of Thought*, N.Y.: Macmillan, 1940, vol. II, ch. 25).

whose beliefs are only partly warped and out of touch with reality, but it affirms the reasonableness of the person whose beliefs are totally warped and out of touch with reality. I can see, then, no reason to think that one could have reasonable beliefs about the external world without having any reasonable beliefs about one's immediate experience, *just* by having consistent beliefs about the former but not about the latter. The mere having of a belief (about the external world) does not ensure its reasonableness. It seems more plausible to imagine, rather, that if one is rationally justified in believing something about the external world, there is always something (that one has good reason to believe) about one's experience that enables one to be thus justified (or, at least, without which this justification would not exist).[1] We have every reason, I think, to hold that claims and beliefs about experience are epistemologically prior to claims and beliefs about the external world.

Note that I have spoken mainly of experience, not of *sense* experience. Many philosophers have thought it natural and correct to divide up our experiences into two kinds: sense (or outer) experiences and inner experiences. Thus Kant in the *Critique of Pure Reason* distinguishes inner and outer sense, and

---

[1] I am not claiming that *knowledge* of the external world is logically impossible without *knowledge* about experience. For someone might have innate knowledge about the external world without having had any experiences (and thus without having *knowledge* about his experiences), as has been pointed out by P. Unger (in 'On Experience and the Development of the Understanding', *American Philosophical Quarterly* 3, 1966, pp. 48–56), and by Don Locke (in *Perception:* London: Allen and Unwin, 1967, p. 207 n.). Locke, however, goes on to propose the following definition of epistemological priority: knowledge *x* is prior to knowledge *y* just in case it is logically impossible to have knowledge *y*, no knowledge *x*, and only normal human ways of knowing. But this definition leaves open the possibility that knowledge *x* and knowledge *y* be prior to each other, and it entails that knowledge *x* is always prior to itself. To amend this, we must add to the definition: but it is logically possible to have knowledge *x*, no knowledge *y* and only normal human ways of knowing. But on the definition thus amended, perhaps no important form of human knowledge is prior to any other. In particular, Locke may be mistaken in thinking, as he does, that knowledge about what we take ourselves to be perceiving is prior to knowledge about (perceived) material objects. For humans may well learn about physical objects (at least) as fast as they learn about their perceptual takings. (I am here assuming, as Locke does not, that learning and knowledge can exist in the absence of justified or reasonable belief. This view is (to my mind) successfully argued in Unger's 'Experience and Factual Knowledge'. *J. Phil.*, 64, 1967, pp. 152–73.) Locke's definition of priority does not make beliefs about experience clearly prior to beliefs about the external world, and so will not help us much in our attempt to justify our present enterprise.

in 'Some Remarks on Sense Perception',[1] Broad speaks of 'ostensible perceptions' as being separate and different from other sorts of experiences.[2] The philosophers who have wanted to make this sort of distinction with respect to experiences have usually thought that sense experiences are relevant to the verification and justification of claims about the external world, while inner experiences are not. In the *Essay Concerning Human Understanding*,[3] for example, John Locke makes it clear that he thinks we can have evidence for or knowledge about external objects only by 'sensation'. C. I. Lewis claims that the existence of objective (physical) realities 'can be verified, or confirmed as probable, only by presentations of sense'.[4] And, in the *Zettel*, Wittgenstein says that it is a 'grammatical' truth that our sensations (or sense experiences) can, but our emotions cannot, give us information about the external world.[5] Many philosophers, then, have wanted to maintain the (presumably, logical) impossibility of evidence or justification for claims about the external world in the absence of (reasonably held beliefs that are solely about) sense experience. And many of them have concluded from this that beliefs (or knowledge) about immediate *sense* experiences are in an important way epistemologically prior to beliefs about the external world, and are, in consequence, the only sort of beliefs from which one can reasonably start in attempts to overcome scepticism and reconstruct human knowledge.

One problem about such a conclusion, of course, is the enormous difficulty of saying just what differentiates sense (or outer) experiences from inner-type experiences or of confidently sorting all kinds of experiences into one or the other of these two classes of experiences. One could try defining sense experiences as experiences that are (in some intentional sense) 'of' entities that seem to be in space or as experiences that (phenomenologically)

---

[1] *Bertrand Russell: Philosopher of the Century*, London: Allen and Unwin, 1967, p. 109 f.

[2] Hume's distinctions in the *Treatise* between impressions and ideas and between sensation and reflexion cut across the dichotomy we are considering. Neither ideas of sensation (e.g. memory images) nor impressions of reflexion (e.g. some emotions) always involve what most philosophers have wanted to call sense experience. (See the *Treatise*, Book I, Part I, section 3.)

[3] Book IV, ch. 11.

[4] *Analysis of Knowledge and Valuation*, Lasalle: Open Court, 1950, p. 203.

[5] Berkeley and Los Angeles: Univ. of California Press, 1967, pp. 84e and 87e. See also Broad's 'Berkeley's Denial of Material Substance', *Phil. Review*, 63, 1954, p. 175.

seem to come from the outside or to be directed inward. On such
definitions as these visual after-images and leg pains would seem
to qualify as objects of sense experience or of outer experience.[1]
But it would still be *difficult* to classify headaches or certain vivid
sorts of waking imaginings (or fantasies) either as inner or as outer
experiences. Nonetheless, there does seem intuitively to be some
difference between the conjuring up of images (or what have you)
in one's mind's eye or ear and the having of thoughts and (non-
bodily) emotions on the one hand, and seeming to see, hear, etc.,
things in space (whether in dreams, in hallucinations or in waking
life) on the other.

Even granting the existence of such a distinction, however, it is
by no means clear that beliefs about outer or sense experience(s)
are epistemologically prior to beliefs about physical entities in the
way so many philosophers have thought. For I think it is in fact
logically *possible* that someone should have good reason to believe
in the truth of certain claims about the external world, without
being warranted in believing anything about his outer experience
(i.e. anything entailing the existence of such outer experiences).
Consider the case of a man (or other form of conscious being) who
is constantly thinking to himself about various matters, but never
has any sense experiences or any beliefs about such experiences.
We can also consistently imagine that he has all (or a large number)
of our ordinary material object concepts, but no actual beliefs
entailing the existence of an external world. (Surely this is consistent, if an amnesiac can, as so often occurs, retain certain concepts while having forgotten whether there is anything to which
they apply.) Imagine, further, that every time he hears the word
'true' faintly in his mind's ear (or has a certain type of thought or
emotion x), his proposed answers to any mathematical or other
conceptual problems he is working on (in his head) and his
current conjectures about the future course of his thoughts and
various other matters he may be thinking of, turn out, in the end,
to be correct in every detail. And every time he hears an inner
'false' (or has a certain type of thought or emotion y), his answers,

---

[1] Actually, what have been called *outer* experiences are not always what one
would clearly want to call *sense* experiences. The having of leg pains or of
realistic dreams, for example. (However, Moore thinks it in order to speak of
visual dream experiences as sensory experiences, and he may be right about this;
see his 'Certainty', *Philosophical Papers*, London: Allen and Unwin, 1959,
p. 248.) This fine distinction, however, can, I think, safely be ignored in our
present discussion.

his predictions, and his other conjectures are gravely mistaken. Such a man might not know why the 'true' or 'false' occurred in his mind's ear when they did, but he would still, I think, after a while have good reason to trust those answers and conjectures accompanied by 'true' *before* checking them out. (Such a man would, I think, be a good example of someone with reasonable beliefs about experience but not about the external world.)

One day the man might begin to wonder about the existence and nature of the external world. He conjectures that there are (or may be) tables (or what have you) in the world, and hears an inner 'true'; when he conjectures that there are unicorns, he hears 'false'. And so on. Surely it would be at least somewhat reasonable for him then to believe in the existence of tables and the non-existence of unicorns. Of course, these beliefs differ greatly from mathematical and other beliefs; and he might wonder whether the 'true' and the 'false' might not be unreliable with respect to external-world conjectures, even though reliable with respect to mathematical and inner-experiential conjectures. But then again, mathematical conjectures are very different from experiential ones, and the 'true' and 'false' were accurate about both of these, so why not also about conjectures very different from either of these? Furthermore, the 'true' and 'false' might always give one consistent answers to one's conjectures if one repeated or varied them in certain ways; and one might, by relying on the 'true' and 'false' as means of learning and gaining warranted beliefs about the world, obtain a highly intricate and detailed, yet at the same time coherent, picture of what the external world was like. Surely in that case there would be good reason to believe those conjectures accompanied by 'true' and the negation of those conjectures accompanied by 'false'. (The fact that certain thoughts or emotions can be substituted for inner hearings of 'true' and 'false' without hurting our example shows that Locke and Wittgenstein were mistaken in holding, respectively, that inner thoughts and emotions can provide us with no information, or evidence for claims, about the nature of the external world.)

Thus it seems to be logically possible for one to have justification for belief in the existence of certain sorts of physical entities without having any justification for beliefs about sense experience. And philosophers have, it seems, been mistaken about the epistemological priority of beliefs about sense experience *vis-à-vis* beliefs about the external world. For many philosophers have thought of the former sort of beliefs as prior to the latter sort in something like our above-defined sense of epistemological priority. What *is* epistemologically prior to the class of claims about the external world is the whole class of claims about one's immediate experience. It is just a *contingent* fact that we humans need *sense* experiences in order to have reasonable beliefs about the external world. It is only a *contingent* fact that we are not able to justify believing in external realities in terms of the sort of argument which the being that we have imagined above could use. But given the sorts of inner and outer experiences *we* all have, any argument *we* could produce to justify our believing in external objects, processes, etc., will have to be based in some way on sense experiences, on assumptions about our sense experiences, or about our *beliefs* about the nature of our sense experiences, etc.

Another fairly common philosophical assumption has been that beliefs about the external world were prior to beliefs about other minds in something like our sense of 'epistemologically prior'. Jonathan Bennett, for example, has claimed that judgments about other minds necessarily depend on judgments about other bodies for their justification.[1] Nor does the possibility of direct telepathic communication between minds show that one *could* have reasonable beliefs about other minds without reasonable beliefs about physical entities. For, as J. Shaffer points out in his 'Persons and Their Bodies', even if one is in telepathic communication with another mind, one may not have reason to believe that this is so unless one does some checking on the correlation of the contents of that mind with those of one's own mind, and this would presumably involve justified beliefs about human bodies and/or other physical entities.[2]

A being without sense experiences of the kind described above, however, might have conjectured that there were other minds and have heard an inner 'true' and conjectured that there was an external world and have heard 'false', and in that case would he not have reason to believe in other minds without having reason to believe in an external world, and perhaps eventually very good reason to believe in other minds, if he were able by conjecturing and paying attention to his inner 'true's and 'false's to gain a detailed and coherent picture of what those other minds were like? (Also, as I mentioned earlier, a case may be possible in

[1] 'The Simplicity of Experience', *J. Phil.*, 64, 1967, p. 658.
[2] *Phil. Review*, 75, 1966, p. 61.

which one has sense experiences and reason to think a demon—another mind—has caused them and no good reason to believe in an external world.) It would seem, then, that claims about the physical are no more prior to claims about other minds, than claims about one's own immediate *sense* experiences are prior to either. It is only because of *contingent* facts about human experience (if it is the case at all) that *we* can justify claims about other minds only on the basis of assumptions about human bodies. And my own argument for other minds in Chapter 4 will proceed along these very lines.

If what has been said above is correct, there is a perfectly acceptable and historically important sense in which the class of claims (solely) about one's own experience is epistemologically prior to the class of claims about the external world and to the class of claims about other minds (minds other than one's own).[1] And once it is clear that it is *possible* to have justification for claims about one's own experiences (even sense experiences) without justification for beliefs about the external world (or other minds), the meaningfulness of scepticism becomes fairly obvious. For we can ask whether (and what reason there is for thinking) this possibility is not in fact the case with us who have the sort of experience *we* do. And if this sort of question is meaningful, then scepticism about the external world (or other minds) and attempts to refute or overcome such scepticism cannot just be dismissed as philosophically unimportant and uninteresting. Even if we have reason—good reason—to believe in the external world and other minds, rather than in any sceptical hypotheses about the external world or other minds, and even if we know and have excellent reason to believe that such good reason exists without having to do any philosophy, we may still be curious to see explicitly stated exactly what those good reasons, say, for believing in an external world rather than in a demon, *are*. Inasmuch as one purpose of philosophy is to seek self-conscious knowledge of things that ordinary people just take for granted or know only in an intuitive,

[1] I should like to add, furthermore, that in talking of one class (or type) of claims being prior to another, certain restrictions should be understood as holding on what is to count as a class or type of claim(s). To avoid certain possible confusions, the claims made by Lyndon Johnson are not to constitute a possible class or type of claim(s). I think we can eliminate such unnatural 'types' of claims by stipulating that k is to count as a class or type of claim only if the claims of type k could not (logically) be claims that were not claims of type k. Claims made by Lyndon Johnson might have been claims not made by Johnson, and so do not constitute a class or type of claim(s) in my terminology.

inarticulate way, an attempt to state exactly what (good) reasons there are for someone with our sort of (sense) experiences to believe in an external world (rather than a demon), etc., recommends itself as a philosophically worthwhile—even to someone—like the present writer—who is not a sceptic and who believes most of what common sense tells him. Even if one believes (and thinks one has reason to believe) that there is something wrong with external-world or other-minds scepticism, it may be a philosophically important task to *show* that something is wrong with such scepticism and to show *what* is wrong with it.

It is my belief, further, that one can grant to such critics of traditional attempts to reconstruct knowledge as Austin that one can support some physical object statements by others (without having to bring in statements about experience),[1] that statements about immediate experience are not as a class incorrigible or indubitable and, perhaps, even that physical object statements can be certain, without having to grant them that such reconstructions of knowledge are philosophically insignificant. And this for reasons just mentioned. Of course, *if* the statements or claims about immediate experience with which one starts are not incorrigible or indubitable, then some sceptic might question those premises, and thereby question our argument against scepticism about the external world and other minds. But it hardly follows that attempting to argue against scepticism on the basis of dubitable (but not necessarily unwarranted) assumptions about experience is philosophically unimportant or jejune. Why should we not try to *reduce* scepticism about the external world and other minds to scepticism about experience (and about certain principles of inference)? We may be less moved or disturbed by scepticism about experience than by scepticism about the external world, and so be interested in seeing how or whether one can justify beliefs about the external world in terms of assumptions about experience.

I am inclined to think, furthermore, that one does not even need to hold that claims about one's own experience are epistemologically prior to claims about the external world, etc., in order to recommend the enterprise on which we are embarking. For if we are scientifically-minded, we wish to explain the existence and nature of the various sorts of things that there are. But, then, why should one not be interested in explaining the fact that we have the

[1] See Austin, *op. cit.*, p. 116 f.

sort of experience we do? And as soon as one considers it worthwhile to seek such an explanation, scepticism and attempting to
overcome scepticism become important; for on the face of it, it
seems hard to rule out *ab initio* the possibility that our experience
is to be explained in terms of the action of a non-material, non-
physical, demon; so if one wants to *show* that the best explanation
of our experience is that it comes from (is caused by) objects,
processes, or events, in an external world, one has to show something wrong or incoherent with the hypothesis of a demon. And
this we shall be attempting here.

The problem of the external world is an old one, but many
philosophers today do not take it seriously. And yet these same
philosophers often profess to believe that science and scientific
reason (or methodology) are the ultimate test of the belief-
worthiness of an hypothesis, and that only scientifically plausible
or reasonable hypotheses are hypotheses worthy of credence. It
seems odd, then, that such philosophers do not take scepticism
about the external world seriously, since no one has ever, as far as
I know, produced a satisfactory argument to show that the external
world provides a better explanation of the existence and nature of
the experiences of each of us than does the demon, better either
by scientific or by other rational standards for the evaluation of
explanatory hypotheses. For many such philosophers (as well as
many scientists) would hold that if one cannot show (or give some
reason for thinking) that some explanation *e* of a phenomenon *p*
is better than certain other explanations of *p* that are incompatible
with *e*, it is scientifically premature and unreasonable to believe *e*.
Such philosophers, then, ought to encourage and seek the com-
pletion of an enterprise like our own, because only by means of
such an enterprise will they be able to reconcile their belief in an
external world with their conviction that one should be scientific
about accepting hypotheses and that one is being unscientific if
one accepts as the explanation of a phenomenon a hypothesis that
one can give no reason for thinking superior to certain other
explanations of that phenomenon. And this is true regardless of
whether claims or propositions about immediate experience are as
a class prior to claims or propositions about the external world as
a class, in the sense of priority defined above.

It might be claimed, however, that if one has in fact already
accepted a certain explanation of a phenomenon and nothing
definite has been found wrong with it, then it is scientifically

reasonable to continue to accept it, even though one cannot show it in any way to be superior to certain newly proposed alternatives to it, because of the validity of some sort of Principle of Scientific 'Conservatism'. If so, accepting the external world might be scientifically reasonable even though one could not fault the hypothesis of the demon. All this may be so; but even if it is, a scientist *qua* scientist would surely rather be able to show something to be wrong with alternatives to his own explanation of a phenomenon than have to justify his adherence to his own explanation by appealing to the length of tenure of that explanation, to the fact that it was accepted before its alternatives were thought up or seriously considered. And so even an adherent of the Principle of Conservatism who already believed in some sort of external world as providing the best explanation of his experiences would have reason *as a scientist* to want to be able to find fault with sceptical hypothesis like that of the demon, and thus to encourage the enterprise of the present work, which seeks to provide him with the means to do just that. Furthermore, one would as an epistemologist prefer to be able to show the scientific superiority of the hypothesis of an external world not only to someone who already believed in such a world, but also to someone who had suspended belief in such matters until he could find reason to believe in the external world rather than in a demon. That is, we want an argument that will have some force *against* the *sceptic*. And we could not produce such an argument, if we argued from the Principle of Conservatism. For then our argument would assume as one of its premises that one already believed in an external world, and, of course, this is precisely not true of the sceptic. And so to overcome scepticism about the external world, we cannot use the Principle of Conservatism, and so must look elsewhere for scientific methodological principles to fulfil the goal of the present work. (Nor, in addition, can we use any assumptions entailing the existence of beliefs in an external world, in order to argue against the external-world sceptic.)

Of course, there have been many previous attempts by philosophers to overcome scepticism about the external world, veridical memory and perception, other minds, etc. Some of these involved trying to discredit various forms of scepticism by showing them to be self-contradictory or incoherent in one way or another. We shall consider some such attempts in Chapter 1 below. Others have sought to overcome scepticism on its own terms, have granted the force and coherence of sceptical doubt and gone on to try to provide reasons for believing those things that can be sceptically doubted. Most notable of these philosophers, of course, was Descartes. Descartes, in the *Meditations*, attempted not only to start from a *single* indubitable premise, but to prove the *existence* of the external world, not just the *reasonableness* of the claim that it exists. But for all its boldness, philosophers have long recognized the failure of his enterprise. For it is not at all clear that he relies on only one, indubitable premise, and his argument for the external world rests on a clearly unsound argument for God's existence.

More recently, Russell, in *Human Knowledge: its Scope and Limitations*, has probed at length the possibility of arguing from assumptions about experience, via certain acceptable principles of scientific thought and methodology, to the (probable) existence of an external world with certain features and of other minds. His argument, of course, does not rely on proving the existence of God, and to that extent his attempt to reconstruct knowledge is more sensible than that of Descartes. But on the other hand, Russell (at least in the work under consideration) does not pay much attention to the possibility of a systematically deceptive demon or of systematically deceptive dreams. Russell's principles all assume that sufficiently orderly experience entitles us to assume the existence of physical entities responsible for that orderly experience. But why not assume that our orderly experience is due to the machinations of some demon? This question Russell does not grapple with. I wish to claim that no attempt to argue for the reasonableness of belief in an external world that ignores Descartes' demon, i.e. does not attempt to show that there is something definitely *wrong* with the hypothesis of a demon as an explanation of our experiences or to show a *contradiction* or *incoherence* in the notion of a demon deceiver, is a philosophically adequate one.[1] That Descartes saw this to be so constitutes part of his enormous importance as a formulator of scepticism and as an innovator (in

---

[1] Hence I think that the attempts of philosophers like Chisholm (*Theory of Knowledge*, Englewood Cliffs: Prentice-Hall, 1966, ch. 3), Price (*Perception*, N.Y.: R. M. McBride, 1933, pp. 185–9), and Ayer (*The Problem of Knowledge*, Harmondsworth: Penguin Books, 1957, ch. 3, esp. p. 132 f.) to provide principles via which one can show the reasonableness of believing in an external world are philosophically inadequate. These philosophers have urged that if one thinks one sees, or seems to see, an object of a certain sensible kind, it is reasonable (or one has at least some reason) to believe that one is seeing such an object, and thus that there is an external world. Such claims, however true they may be,

modern times) of attempts to overcome scepticism about the external world. Inasmuch as Russell, in *Human Knowledge*, does not
cope successfully with the demon, his attempt at reconstructing
our knowledge of the external world is philosophically inadequate.
And, indeed, perhaps one of the reasons why so many philosophers
have considered Moore's 'Proof of an External World' to be so
philosophically beside the point is their feeling that Moore's
argument simply shoves the problem of the demon (and of
dreaming) aside. Even if one wants to say that Moore's proof is
some kind of proof (in the ordinary sense of the word 'proof')—and
something like this ordinary-language point may have been part of
Moore's reason for presenting his proof the way he did—that
proof is at least not *as adequate* a proof of the external world (from
a philosophical standpoint) as one that grapples with demon (and
dreaming) scepticism and overcomes it. We are looking for such a
more adequate proof here.

It is with trepidation that I approach this task; it seems pretty
clear that previous attempts to overcome scepticism have been one
and all unsuccessful. And my feeling is that there is bound to be
much that is wrong with my own arguments against scepticism.
On the other hand, I am not aware of anything clearly wrong with
my arguments. But, of course, many others have written with the
same sense of good faith and adequacy things we would today
consider wrong, absurd, even laughable. So I feel dubious about
what I say in the present work, even though I know of no particular
grievous faults in it. In a way, I think any philosopher approaching
a significant philosophical topic on which there has been continual
disagreement over the ages should have something of this sense of
irony, or tension (call it what you will) about his work on that
topic, a sense of rightness and yet of inevitable inadequacy. At
best, philosophers seem able only to advance towards the truth,
not find it. And perhaps we should limit our aspirations and expectations to just this.

ignore demon (and dreaming) scepticism; it is never shown why the fact that we
think we are seeing, or seem to be seeing, an object of some sort gives more
support to the claim that we are seeing such an object than to the claim that a
demon is making it seem as if we are. They just *assume* the unreasonableness of
demon-hypotheses.

B

CHAPTER I

SOME OBJECTIONS TO SCEPTICISM

In the present chapter, I shall attempt to rebut, as briefly as possible, certain philosophically important objections to scepticism about (the existence of) the external world. Unfortunately, a completely adequate discussion of such objections would require a whole book, and so is impossible within the context of the present work, whose main purpose is constructive, rather than critical. Thus complete refutation of the sorts of objections to external-world scepticism we shall be examining will not always be possible. But an attempt will, in any case, be made to put the burden of proof on those who want to use those objections to undermine scepticism about the external world. I hope, that is, to make it somewhat plausible to believe that previous attempts to cope with scepticism about the external world will not work, and to think, therefore, that it is important to search for other, new ways to deal with that sort of scepticism.

I

The existence of some sort of external world of physical entities is supposed to be the obvious explanation of the fact that people have the sort of sense experience they do. It is the common opinion of educated men that our sense experiences are caused by physical objects and events both outside and inside our own bodies. But surely there are other hypotheses, of a sceptical sort, that might be put forward to explain the fact that we have sense experiences 'of' (certain objects and events in) a physical world.[1] One possible

[1] In speaking of experiences 'of' objects of certain sorts I am using 'of' in an intentional way. We can have experiences that are (phenomenologically) 'of' a house even though there is no such house. (Cf. R. Firth's 'Sense Data and the Percept Theory I', *Mind* 58, 1949, pp. 434–65.) Those who object to my reification of sense experiences can rephrase what I am saying here and elsewhere in Firth's 'looks as if' terminology, without using words like 'experience' at all. (See Firth's 'Phenomenalism', in *Science, Language and Human Rights*, Univ. of Pennsylvania Press, 1952.) Incidentally, I am in no way claiming that it is possible to have the concept of 'sense experience' or of 'looks as if' without having some physical-object concepts like those of 'book', 'apple', etc. I am just saying that it is logically possible for a demon to cause our experiences, give us physical-object and experiential concepts, and trick us into thinking there is an external world. Our problem here, I take it, is to show that there is reason for

such explanation would be in terms of some sort of powerful non-material Cartesian demon or spirit who supplied us with visual, auditory, tactual, etc., experiences in such a way as to make it appear to us exactly as if there were books, rivers, plants, etc. around us, even though in fact nothing physical existed at all. Another possible sceptical explanation of our having the sorts of sense, or outer, experiences we do might be that there really was no external world and no explanation of our experiences. Our experience is, on this hypothesis, a matter of pure chance, a mere accident. Both sorts of hypotheses are mentioned by Descartes in the *Meditations*, and are sceptical inasmuch as they deny the existence of an external, physical world.

us, who have certain concepts and experiences, to think those experiences come from something physical, and *not* from a demon. Furthermore, I am assuming that it looks to us as if there are red boxes, etc.; that what appears is not just colour patches, etc.; that experience comes in meaningful wholes. And its looking to me as if I am seeing a red box may, indeed, logically require my having certain concepts (e.g. that of 'box'). But as I have said just above, it is logically possible to get such concepts and thus the ability to have it look to one as if there is a red box, from a demon, rather than from years of contact with physical objects (like red boxes). 'Looks as if' statements, may, then, say something both about one's 'pure' or 'raw' experience and about the sort of concepts one has; but they are still 'statements solely about one's experience' on the broad definition of that expression stipulated in footnote 1 on p. 18 of the Introduction, and statements of a sort that we are reasonable in assuming in our present enterprise.

Note further that I have not defined 'sense experience(s)' or 'physical (thing)'. The former notion can in part be elucidated in terms of the above-mentioned 'looks as if' locution, and the latter in terms of such specific physical notions as 'table', 'cloud', 'apple', etc. More importantly 'sense experience(s)' and 'physical' are both expressions with whose meaning most educated non-philosophers are acquainted. (Unlike 'sense datum', which I have avoided partly for that very reason, and partly because it is a term whose meaning and application are so ill-understood even by philosophers.) I shall use both expressions, therefore, without defining them, going on the assumption that we can understand and have the right to make use of many terms that we cannot explicitly or exactly define. The same too goes for my use of 'cause' and related terms. I propose to use such terms as they are used by scientists, doctors, and others, even though both they and I cannot define them. (See H. P. Grice's 'The Causal Theory of Perception', *Proc. Arist. Soc. Suppl.*, 1961, p. 144 f., for an example of usage of 'cause' and 'explanation' similar to mine.) Actually, the person arguing for the existence of an external world need not even assume that his usage of 'looks as if', 'physical', 'cause', etc. conforms to ordinary usage of those words *by others*. (If he *were* to assume this, his argument, presumably, would be blatantly circular.) Why can't he know *that* he means something fairly definite by these terms and know pretty well *what* he means by those terms at a certain time, without being able to define those terms and without claiming or knowing that he or others have ever used those terms in the way he is using them? (For a partial defence of this possibility see Chisholm's *Theory of Knowledge*, p. 36 f.; and Lewis's *Analysis of Knowledge and Valuation*, ch. 6.)

Now many philosophers have claimed that there is something inherently wrong with sceptical hypotheses, of the sort mentioned just above, as explanations of our having the sense experience we do. Some Phenomenalists, for example, have seemed to want to say that statements about material objects are entailed by statements about our sense experiences (of those objects), and so have implied that if we assume such experience, hypotheses implying the non-existence of material objects are, logically, ruled out. If this were so, sceptical hypotheses of the sort just mentioned would not constitute even (logically) possible explanations of our sense experience. However, no modern phenomenalists have held that material-object statements (about the external world) follow from statements about the sense experiences anyone *in fact* has; they are, at best, only supposed to follow from statements about the experiences we would have, if certain things were to happen (in our experience).[1] Thus Phenomenalism does not, at least in its modern versions, rule out the hypothesis of a demon as the source of our actual experiences. A phenomenalist might want to claim, however, that we can argue from our actual experiences to what our experience would be like if certain (experiential) events were to take place, and thence to an external world of physical objects. But note that statements or claims about one's actual experience do not entail statements or claims about the experience one would have (had) if certain things (had) happened. Nor is it clear that statements about the experience one would have (had) if . . . logically entail statements about the external world, as even some phenomenalists are beginning to concede.[2] For one thing, it seems to be a logical possibility that one should have a dream about a table or be supplied by a demon (or by scientists controlling one's brain) with sense experiences that seemed to be of, say, a table, in such a way that, no matter what were to change in one's experience, one would still have appropriate table-experiences. The demon, or the scientists, might be such masters of the creation of veridical-seeming experience that no matter what (experiential) tests one might make of the existence of the table, those tests would come out 'positive', even though there was, in fact, no table there at all. It thus seems in no way logically impossible for

[1] Berkeley is generally thought to have held that claims about actual experience entail statements about objects in the external world. I know of no one who gives any credence to his view, and so shall simply ignore it.

[2] See, e.g. A. J. Ayer, *The Foundations of Empirical Knowledge*, London: Macmillan, 1961, p. 239 f.

all appropriate claims about what one would experience or would have experienced if . . . to be true, and yet be true only because of the lawfulness of one's dreaming or of the behaviour of those creating one's sense experience. And in that case, it seems that statements about experiences we would have (had) in certain circumstances—even infinitely many of them, since, for one thing, it seems not to be impossible for there to be an infinitely long lawful dream or an infinitely long succession of experiences supplied by a demon or scientists—do not logically entail statements about the existence of anything physical. Thus Phenomenalism will not help us overcome scepticism about the external world; for even if we could produce some sort of inductive argument, via scientific methodological principles of the kind we shall be using in this book, from assumptions about actual experiences to conclusions about the experiences we would have, if . . ., we have no reason to think such conclusions are ever (even taken jointly) tantamount to statements about the external world. And so we still would not have produced any reasons for belief in an external world and in the falsity of sceptical hypotheses about the external world.

Another way of arguing that sceptical hypotheses are not even *possible* explanations of our having our sort of sense experience(s) has been suggested by John Dewey.[1] According to him, to say that we have sense experience(s) is already implicitly to refer to a physical sensory apparatus, and so to an external world, so that it is self-contradictory for the sceptic to say, as he does, that we may possibly have sense experience without there being any physical world (causing that experience). But is it so obvious that talk about sense experience commits one to talk about sense organs of a physical kind?[2] Is there anything self-contradictory, for example, in the idea that angels, or God himself, might have visual or auditory (sense) experiences of the kind we have without having any physical sense *organs* or other physical means for obtaining such experiences—assuming, for the moment, that unembodied immaterial existence is logically possible? Why should not such beings obtain visual and other experiences by

[1] In 'The Existence of the World as a Problem', *Phil. Review*, 24, 1915, pp. 357–70.

[2] See Russell's 'Professor Dewey's "Essays in Experimental Logic" ', *J. Phil.*, 16, 1919, pp. 20–6; also G. E. Moore's 'Four Forms of Scepticism', in his *Philosophical Papers*, London: Allen and Unwin, 1959, p. 213; and *The Commonplace Book of G. E. Moore*, London: Allen and Unwin, 1962, pp. 267 ff.

some purely mental means, i.e. through some purely mental or spiritual ability?

Furthermore, even if talk of *sense* experiences somehow *did* commit us to the existence of physical organs of sense, we would still possess R. Firth's 'looks as if' terminology for describing immediate experience. Surely a statement like 'it looks to me exactly as if I am seeing (or there is) a red box' seems in no way to say anything about one's physical sense organs. So there is nothing to prevent us from setting up the problem of the external world in a coherent way, even if Dewey is correct, as I very much doubt he is, about the logic of 'sense experience'.

There is, however, a possible objection even to Firth's 'looks as if' terminology as a way of formulating scepticism about the external world. For it might be argued that 'looks as if' statements entail statements not about one's sense organs, but about the nature and lawfulness of the external world. It might be said that a statement like 'it looks to me exactly as if I am seeing (or there is) a red box (over there)' entails something like 'this is the way red boxes normally look (or would look) if there are (or were) any.' Although the latter statement does not entail the existence of any red boxes, it does say something contingent about the nature of such objects if there are any, and is thus very much like the statement of a scientific law. And such statements do not seem to be epistemologically prior in any significant sense to statements that entail the existence of physical objects. Thus, if 'looks as if' and other sense-experiential statements entail statements about the lawful nature and behaviour of certain possible physical objects, we will not, I think, want to maintain that they are as a class prior to statements entailing the actual existence of the physical world, and the enterprise on which we are embarked, which involves an argument from the nature of our sense experiences to the existence and character of the external world, will be less significant than we would like to claim it is.

But such entailments, I believe, do not obtain. Consider the statement: 'Jim acts as if he likes John'. Does this statement entail that Jim is acting the way he normally acts (or would act) if he likes (or liked) John (or somebody)? I think not. For it may well be that Jim (deliberately or neurotically) constantly slaps those he likes on the back when he is with them, and that he dislikes John, but wants, for some ulterior reason, to pretend (to John) that he likes him. He might, then, buy John things, smile at John when he is with him, etc., all for the purpose of making John think that he (Jim) likes him. In such a case, surely an all-knowing external observer might correctly say: Jim certainly acts (is acting) as if he likes John, even though he is not, with John, acting the way he normally does if and when he likes someone (since he is not constantly slapping John on the back when he is with him).

Consider next the statement: 'that creature looks like a dragon'. Surely, something might look like a dragon, because it was huge, firebreathing, green and reptilian, but not look the way dragons normally look, or would look if there were any. For in fact there are no dragons, and if there were any, how do we know that they would not typically go around camouflaged, or in the form of small toads, or perhaps only work up their green colour and formidable breath for special (perhaps festive) occasions? For similar reasons, I think, 'it looks as if I am seeing a red box' does not entail 'red boxes, if there are any, normally look this way'. It is logically possible that there comes a time when there is no more white light (sunlight). Yet even then it might look to me in certain circumstances as if I was seeing a red box, even though red boxes in fact normally looked somewhat different, because of the new lighting conditions. If someone were to reply that, in such a world, conditions would no longer be normal, I would inquire what, exactly, he meant by 'normal'. He cannot mean 'usual', since what is unusual today could become usual in the future, if things changed enough in logically possible ways. Perhaps he means by 'normal' 'optimal for observation'. In that case, he may be suggesting that in the absence of white light, conditions are not normal because only under such light can one make the most accurate colour discriminations with one's eyes. But this is a merely contingent fact; one might (logically) have normal circumstances in the absence of white light, and then it could look to a man (in a dream or a hallucination, for example) as if he was seeing a red box, if his experience was qualitatively like *ours* when *we* in sunlight see a red box, but it might not be the case that red boxes normally looked that way in the kind of world he lived in. One other possible meaning of 'normal circumstances' is 'circumstances in which things look the way they in fact are'. In this sense of 'normal', 'it looks as if I am seeing a red box' certainly does entail 'red boxes, if there are any, normally look this way', since this latter simply means 'red boxes, if they exist, look this way when they look the way they are, i.e. red'. But this last statement is simply a roundabout, redundant way of saying that it looks to me as if I am seeing a red box, and there is no more reason to say it entails non-trivial statements about the lawful nature or behaviour of possible external objects than to say 'it looks as if I am seeing a red box' does. So far, then, we have not been able to find any good reason for thinking that Firth's 'looks as if' statements do anything more than describe one's sensory experience, or thus cannot be used as premises in the sort of reconstruction of knowledge I am attempting here.[1]

Another possible objection to external-world scepticism arises from the claim that an unembodied, non-material conscious being or spirit is logically impossible. For then it would be logically impossible for experiencing beings like us to lack bodies or to have experiences supplied to them by an immaterial demon, and scepticism about the external world would be ruled out from the start unless one wanted to question, as we have not, the very existence of the self and its experiences. What seems to me to be the strongest and most plausible argument against the possibility of unembodied or non-material conscious beings is that based on the claim that there could not (logically) ever be any evidence for or reason to believe in the existence of such beings. This view is typical of the logical positivists, who held that religious claims were not verifiable or confirmable to any degree, and in particular held this to be true about claims entailing the existence of an *immaterial*, all-powerful, etc. God.

But why *would* it be impossible to communicate (perhaps indirectly) with an immaterial being, if one existed, and to gain thereby *some* reason, at least, to believe in the existence of such a being? Such a being might, for example, cause certain physical tablets to be inscribed with a message seemingly directed to *me* and with instructions on how further to communicate with him; and if I followed those instructions, and got more messages, I

---

[1] Chisholm (*op. cit.*, pp. 34 ff., and ' "Appear", "Take", and "Evident" ', in Swartz (ed.), *Sensing, Perceiving, and Knowing*, Garden City: Anchor, 1965, p. 479 f.) also argues for the possibility of descriptions of immediate experience. Incidentally, to say 'looks as if' statements describe sense experience is not to say they entail the existence of such things as sense experiences, or are thus open to Dewey's objection about sense organs. By saying 'this bird is old', I may be describing the last dodo, but I am not committing myself to the existence of dodos, or of a last dodo. When *I* say 'looks as if' statements describe experiences, *I* am committed to the existence of *experiences*, therefore, even though one who just *uses* 'looks as if' statements in a reconstruction of knowledge need not be, and so need not be begging any questions in such a reconstruction.

would have reason to think I was communicating with another being. Furthermore, if his messages (on physical tablets or in the form of a 'voice from the heavens') seemed in no way bound up with other physical phenomena, and if in those messages it was claimed that I was communicating with an immaterial spirit, and if I had no reason to distrust the being who seemed to be communicating with me, it would, I think, be reasonable at least tentatively to believe in the existence of an immaterial conscious being.[1] Indeed, in general, I see no reason for believing we could not, in principle, have something like the same sort of indirect evidence for immaterial beings as we do for electrons or other subatomic particles.

At this point, however, someone might object that it would always be impossible to individuate or distinguish immaterial spirits in the way we distinguish even very similar embodied human beings, because we would lack the bodily criteria that enable us to do this in the latter case. But why could we not tell the difference between non-physical beings in terms of their different cognitive or conative styles? If it is then objected that there might be two spirits, with exactly the same styles, which we could not, consequently, distinguish, it can be replied that the same thing can happen in the case of embodied beings. There might be twins so identical, and so bent on fooling others, that one could never know which one one was addressing; or a given person might be instantaneously (or nearly instantaneously) replaced by another person exactly like him and one might never be able to know it. Surely, we have reason to believe that we can in ordinary cases individuate embodied humans, even though the wild possibilities just mentioned cannot logically be ruled out. And if we believe this, why should we not also believe that one could in most 'ordinary' cases distinguish immaterial spirits by their styles, even though one could not logically rule out being mistaken in one's identifications?[2]

---

[1] If it be objected that even in the situation just described, one should be distrustful, because of all the scientific evidence that points to the impossibility of immaterial existence, then the objector has misunderstood the point at issue. For such evidence need not be available, or exist, in *every* logically possible situation, and we are only trying to show the *logical* possibility of reason to believe in a pure spirit.

[2] Much of this argument for the possibility of individuating spirits come from E. Zemach's 'Sensations, Raw Feels, and Other Minds', *Rev. of Metaphysics* XX, 1966, p. 333 f. My argument here and elsewhere in this chapter is carried on with the assumption of commonsense standards for the confirmation of claims, for reasons adumbrated in the Introduction, p. 18, footnote 2.

Secondly, even if no one could, in principle, verify or confirm the existence of an immaterial spirit *other than himself*, might he not still be able to verify or confirm this *of himself*, and wouldn't this show that claims about immaterial spirits are in principle (logically possibly) confirmable and capable of being reasonably believed, and thus effectively counter the argument of those who hold that such claims cannot (logically) be true because they cannot (logically) be confirmed? Many philosophers have given descriptions of what it would be like to awake one day and find that one was oneself an immaterial spirit, perceiving but not perceivable, capable of thought but not of bodily locomotion, etc.[1] In the kind of situations thus imagined, the spirit in question could presumably verify and come to have reason to believe of himself that he was such a purely mental being. Of course, someone might grant (the bare conceivability of) first-person verification of unembodied spiritual selfhood, but deny the possibility of verifying this of someone else and claim that the possibility in principle of third-person verification is required for the meaningfulness of hypotheses, thus concluding that it is logically impossible for there to be a pure spirit, despite the abstract conceivability of such a being from the first-person standpoint. But is it at all obvious that third-person verifiability is needed in this way? Isn't such a view sheer *prejudice* against the first-person standpoint? I should like then to offer the following Principle of First-Person Verification to the contrary, namely: If one can show the first-person verifiability of an hypothesis (i.e. show that someone could have reason to believe it 'of himself'), then one has shown the verifiability in principle, and the meaningfulness, of that hypothesis. It is my belief, therefore, that we can counter the argument of those who claim non-physical conscious existence is impossible (and talk of such existence meaningless) because unverifiable and unconfirmable, both by pointing to ways in which one could (logically) possibly verify or confirm this of others, and by pointing to ways in which one could verify or confirm this of oneself ('in one's own case'). I have, of course, not proved the Principle of First-Person Verification; but the burden of proof is not on me in this matter. It is, rather, those who wish to *show* the incoherence of external-world scepticism by *showing* the impossibility of a non-physical (conscious) being, who must *show* that third-person verification of

[1] E.g. Ayer (*The Problem of Knowledge*, Harmondsworth: Penguin, 1957, p. 193) and Strawson (*Individuals*, London: Methuen, 1959, p. 115 f.)

such a being is impossible and also *show* either that first-person verification of such a being is impossible or *that it is not enough*. In the light of what has been said, therefore, I do not think that the line of attack on the coherence of scepticism we have been considering is a very plausible one.

It should be noted that at least one philosopher, Strawson, has held that a purely spiritual conscious being *is* logically possible, but that any such being would have to have had a physical body *at some previous time*.[1] If this were so, then scepticism about the existence of a physical world at present would be coherent, but not so scepticism as to whether there had *ever been* such a world. Despite Strawson's arguments to the contrary, however, I think it clearly reasonable to believe that if a disembodied being (being without a body who once had a body) is possible, so too is a being who lacks a body *ab initio*. For if there is a (conscious) being with a certain present character and nature, it is surely always *logically* possible to duplicate that being, create a being exactly like the first being (as it is at present)—in something like the manner described by Unger in his 'On Experience and the Development of the Understanding'. Thus it seems to be logically possible to create a being exactly like one who had but no longer has a body. And this does not involve creating a being with a body who eventually loses it and becomes like the being one is trying to duplicate. For, as I shall argue in Chapter 5, Section II, below, the past history of an individual is not necessarily relevant to what that individual is currently like. Given our notion of alikeness, two individuals can be exactly alike at present despite dissimilar past histories. So it seems possible to create a being *x* exactly like a being *y* who lacks but used to have a body, and to do so without giving *x* a body. For the fact that *y* used to have a body is not involved in what *y* is currently like. Aspects of what *y* *is* currently like include *y*'s present conscious states and mental abilities and beliefs about the past (but not the fact that *y* *correctly* remembers *having done* certain things). So if *x* is exactly like *y* at present and was just created, we have a being who is conscious and able to think and verify things, but has never had a body. But if such a being is possible, if there already exists a disembodied spirit, surely a being just like *x* could have sprung into existence even if *y* had never existed.[2] Thus if we grant the possibility of disembodied spirits and thus of the coherence of scepticism about the *present* existence

[1] *Op. cit.*, p. 115 f.   [2] Cf. Unger's 'On Experience . . .', p. 54.

of matter, we shall, I think, have to admit the logical possibility that there has *never* been anything physical, and, therefore, the coherence of the strong sort of scepticism that admits the existence of conscious beings, but denies that there has ever been any matter.

Some philosophers, however, have wanted to question the logical possibility even of disembodied spiritual existence. They have fastened on the difficulty of verifying the 'fact' that someone has survived death without a body, and argued thence to the impossibility of such survival. The basis of their argument, then, is like that of the above argument against any sort of non-physical conscious existence. All such arguments assume that what cannot be confirmed or verified is not logically possible. And thus far we have not questioned this principle, even though it does not seem an entirely obvious one, or even (to my mind) a very plausible one. But even granting its validity, for the purpose of our present discussion, it does not seem any more difficult to verify or confirm that someone has *passed* from a bodily condition to a non-bodily one, whether that person be oneself or another, than to verify or confirm that there simply *is* such a non-physical conscious being.

There might be circumstances, for example, where one had no scientific evidence for the physical impossibility of pure spiritual non-physical existence and where one made a pact with one's best friend on his deathbed that he should at all costs try to communicate with one after his death if he survived in a disembodied conscious state. Then, if one started getting strange visitations and messages after one's friend's death, would one not have reason to believe he had survived in disembodied form—especially if those messages reflected the 'style' of one's friend and stated that one's friend was conscious and in a disembodied state? Of course, there is the possibility that one's friend is really bodily alive somewhere; but wouldn't this become implausible if one had seen him die (and his body start to disintegrate)? T. Penelhum has argued that even in the sort of case we have just imagined one could not distinguish evidentially between the hypothesis that one's friend had survived, and the hypothesis that a being very much like him in personality but lacking a body had sprung into existence at the death of one's friend.[1] But this fact only shows that one could not be (logically) certain of the survival of one's friend, that other hypotheses are logically compatible with one's evidence. It hardly follows that one

[1] In 'Personal Identity, Memory, and Survival', *J. Phil.*, 56, 1959, 882-902.

does not have any evidence or good reasons in favour of the hypothesis of one's friend's survival as opposed, for example, to the hypothesis that a being similar to him in personality has replaced him. Is the case really very different from that in which we claim to have reason to believe that the person we see today is the friend we saw yesterday, although it is logically possible for that friend to have been replaced by someone just like him, without our knowing the difference? Bernard Williams thinks there *is* an important difference between these two cases.[1] According to him, we always *could* know for certain that a given person (with a body) was the same as one we saw yesterday by strictly applying the identity criterion of spatio-temporal continuity. We could, that is, keep our eye on a given person and thereby make sure that he was the same from one day to the next. But the criterion of spatio-temporal continuity is *ipso facto* lacking in the case of survival of bodily death. Williams thinks this constitutes an important difference, in virtue of which continued existence of one and the same embodied person makes sense, whereas survival of bodily death does not.

But can strict application of the criterion of spatio-temporal continuity really give us the sort of assurance Williams thinks it can? What about the possibility of someone's being instantaneously replaced by a being just like him, or replaced so quickly that no one would ever notice it? Strict application of the criterion of spatio-temporal continuity would seem inadequate to rule out such an hypothesis, and it is no use saying that such things do not, usually, happen, since we might wonder how we can be sure whether this is so.[2] Even if we forget the possibility just mentioned, application of the criterion of spatio-temporal continuity is not quite as straightforward as it might seem. For how does one know, when one is trying to keep one's eye on a thing at all times, that one is continuously conscious? Could one not lose consciousness for a time—in which the object under surveillance was replaced—and then regain consciousness without knowing the difference? Application of the criterion of spatio-temporal identity seems to presuppose the ability to judge reasonably about the continuity of one's own experience, and how does one rule out, with certainty, all alternatives to the hypothesis that one's experience is continuous? But if, as we all assume, we are reasonable in rejecting these sceptical alternatives with respect to the con-

---

[1] In 'Bodily Continuity and Personal Identity', *Analysis*, 21, 1960, pp. 44 ff.
[2] As does Broad in 'Time and Change', *Proc. Arist. Soc. Suppl.*, 1928, p. 183 f.

tinuity of things and of our own experience, on grounds that they are *arbitrary* and/or that our commonsense assumptions about these matters are *simpler*, would we not have at least some reason to do the same thing with respect to the sceptical alternatives to the hypothesis of the survival of our friend, and for similar reasons? Is it not purely arbitrary to imagine him replaced by a spirit similar in personality, rather than surviving himself? Of course, his loss of body *might* destroy him and create a new spirit. But we have no more reason to think this is so than to think that when our friends undergo surgical operations they are destroyed and replaced by similar beings either instantaneously or else while there is a gap in everyone's consciousness. And given our pact with our friend, which no one else, presumably, knows of, other hypotheses can also be ruled out as implausibly complex or arbitrary.

Thus I think that if common sense is right about the possibility of verifying continued existence in general, at least some confirmation of the non-bodily survival of others is possible. But if there remain some doubters, perhaps the following case will help to dispel that doubt. Imagine that one had a magic wand. Whenever one made a wish on it, the wish would come true. One might not know how the wand worked, but frequent enough success with it would surely give one some (inductive) reason for believing one would obtain what one wished for on the wand. One might then wish for the disembodied survival of a friend that one knew was about to die. One would, at that point, have some reason to think the friend would survive, even without having received *post mortem* messages from him or from someone like him. If one then later got such messages, and had no scientific evidence for the (physical) impossibility of non-bodily survival, those messages and the previous reliability of one's wand would presumably give one quite *good* reason to believe in such survival. Thus when we consider whether third-person verification of non-bodily survival is possible, *without assuming* that such survival is logically impossible, such verification does seem possible in principle, so that one cannot plausibly use the claim that it is not possible, in order to show that survival of death in disembodied form is logically impossible.

First-person verification of such survival also seems to be possible. The chief objection to it would seem to come from the fact that when one lost one's body, there might be a time lapse before the experience of a non-physical being similar to oneself in personality started up. So if one were a non-physical being with putative memories of a previous bodily existence, such memories could never prove that one was not a recently created creature instead. But one here needs only good reasons and plausibility, not proof. If it seemed to one that one had had continuous experience since before one's bodily death—that one had been suffering and thinking certain thoughts at the end of one's life and that the thinking seemed to go on in a continuous fashion even when one lost one's sense of one's body and stopped suffering (presumably at bodily death)—then it would be reasonable to assume that one's experience had been continuous and that one had not been replaced. For as we saw above, we could not even verify the continued existence of physical bodies unless our seeming to have continuous consciousness gave us reason to think that our consciousness was continuous and that we were not replacements of earlier beings. Perhaps, then, disembodied existence cannot be verified with any *certainty*, but if there can be good reason for believing in the continued existence of material objects and people, good reason for hypotheses about disembodied survival of one and the same being would also seem to be possible, both from the third-person and from the first-person standpoint. In the light of what we have said, therefore, it seems very unlikely that anyone will ever be able to undermine external-world scepticism by showing the logical impossibility of evidence for the existence of a disembodied spirit, or of a spirit that is non-physical *ab initio*.

Of course, someone might grant the *logical* possibility of survival or existence in an unembodied state, but want to maintain that as a *contingent fact* people are identical with their bodies (or certain states of or processes in their bodies), and that this fact makes it difficult for us to formulate external-world scepticism in any coherent way. One might claim, that is, that if some variety of contingent mind-body identity theory of the sort held by many philosophers in recent years is true, so that people and psychical states and events are contingently identical with physical entities, one cannot use statements involving the concept of 'I' or of 'looks as if' or of 'experience' without implicitly committing oneself to the existence of physical realities. And in that case one cannot consistently put forward sceptical hypotheses about one's own experiences, and external-world scepticism, as we have formulated it, falls apart at the seams. But this line of argument is entirely fallacious. X and y may be identical without my having any reason to believe that this is so, and without my saying that x exists committing me to the existence of such a thing as y. Gagarin may be the first man in space, but I can ascribe existence to Gagarin, without being committed to the claim that men have been in space. 'Gagarin exists' certainly doesn't imply, entail or presuppose that men have been in space. (See footnote 1, p. 40.) Similarly, talk about myself or my experiences does not entail, presuppose or imply talk about my body or its states, even if there is some contingent identity between them. For if this identity is contingent and in fact exists, one may still coherently wonder whether it obtains, wonder whether there are, in addition to oneself and one's experiences, bodily entities identical with them (or any physical entities at all). Even if everything about us is physical, if this is a *contingent* fact, we can always coherently ask what reason there is to think this is so, rather than that our experiences come from a demon and that those experiences and we ourselves are not identical with anything physical. Indeed, mind-body identity of a contingent kind, even if it exists, is *at least* as much open to sceptical doubt as the existence of the physical world, since to establish such identity, one must establish that there *are* physical entities with which mental entities are identical.

II

The contingent fact of mind-body identity, it seems, would not *ipso facto* destroy the force or interest of external-world scepticism; but I think it is worth digressing from our main task for a while to consider whether the whole notion of contingent mind-body identity, on which current identity theorists typically rest their case, has any validity, especially since some philosophers have thought or felt that if mind-body identity *does* obtain, there must be something (though it is hard to say what) wrong with Cartesian-type approaches to reconstructing knowledge (like our own), which are *historically* linked to belief in dualism.

Contemporary mind-body identity theorists often point to statements like 'Columbus is (or was) the man who discovered America' (which we shall, ignoring Leif Ericson and others, assume to be true) and claim that mental and physical states or events can be identical in the same contingent way that Columbus and the man who discovered America are (or were) one and the same. Thus, to use an example of Hilary Putnam's, a statement like 'the pain I am now feeling is identical with the c-fibre stimulation now taking place in my brain' may well be contingently true, according to contingent-identity theorists. And such theorists hold that dualism is false as a matter of contingent fact, but not necessarily.

This whole view of mind-body identity involves, I think, a mistaken notion of the relation of identity. As many philosophers today have come to see, or are beginning to see, identity, even in the case of Columbus and the man who discovered America, is never a merely contingent relation.[1] Because of certain difficulties that arise when one considers definite descriptions (definite descriptive phrases) in modal contexts,[2] it would perhaps be best if we first considered only identity statements involving (only) pure proper names.[3] Once we have done so, we shall be able to say why all true identity statements, even those involving use of definite descriptions, involve a non-contingent 'logical' relation.

Consider the true identity statement 'Cicero is (or was) identical with Tully.'[4] This identity statement is only contingently true,

[1] See, for example, B. Rundle's 'Modality and Quantification' in Butler (ed.), *Analytical Philosophy*, 2nd series, Oxford: Blackwell's, pp. 32 ff.

[2] Cf. R. L. Cartwright's 'Some Remarks on Essentialism', *Journal of Philosophy* LXV, 1968, 615–26, however, where some of the suggestions that have been made as to why descriptions cause problems are very effectively countered.

[3] 'John Smith' is a pure proper name, because it has no descriptive content. Calling a girl 'John Smith', for example, involves no error or untruth, strictly speaking; it is just socially 'not done' and misleading. 'King Henry', however, is, I think, a *mixed* proper name and description, not a *pure* proper name. (Although it sometimes can be *used as* a pure proper name, e.g. when it is the name given to a dog.)

[4] I say 'is identical with Tully', rather than 'is Tully', because I think there is a difference. Most philosophers assume that the 'is' between proper names in statements like 'Cicero is Tully' is always the 'is' of identity. (See, for example, Geach's *Reference and Generality*, Ithaca: Cornell Univ. Press, 1962, p. 42.) But the 'is' between proper names is sometimes like the 'is' between definite descriptions, which *is* conceded by some philosophers to be (at least sometimes) an 'is' of predication, rather than of identity—e.g. by Geach in *op. cit.* Consider, for example, 'Susan is no longer Susan Smith', said of a woman who has divorced Smith and remarried. Such a statement might be true, yet what would it mean to say 'Susan is no longer identical with Susan Smith?' And doesn't this tend to show that 'Susan is Susan Smith' is not always synonymous with 'Susan is identical with Susan Smith' and thus that the 'is' of the former is often more an 'is' of predication than of identity. Notice too that if Susan Smith is now married to Jones, it is natural to say both (*a*) Susan Jones is not Susan Smith (any more) and (*b*) Susan Smith is (now) Susan Jones; and surely this would not be the case if the 'is' involved in (*a*) and (*b*) were one of identity: for if x is identical with y, then and only then is y identical with x.

because it entails, or presupposes, the existence of Cicero and Tully.[1] However, consider the statement: 'Cicero and Tully (tenselessly) go out of existence (or come into existence) at different times.'[2] This statement is, I think, necessarily false. It could never (logically) have been the case that Tully and Cicero came into existence (or went out of existence) at different times. Putting the matter in terms of worlds possible relative to our own: in no world that is possible relative to our own is it the case that Cicero and Tully come into or go out of existence at different times.[3] And we can say this because Cicero was identical with Tully and because 'Cicero' and 'Tully' are pure proper names.[4]

It should be noted that I am not just saying: it is logically impossible for it to be the case *both* that Cicero is identical with Tully *and* that Cicero goes out of or comes into existence before or after Tully. I am saying something that entails this, but that is quite a bit stronger, namely, that what follows from the fact that Cicero and Tully are one and the same is the *logical impossibility* of its being the case that Cicero and Tully come into or go out of existence at different times. That is, given that Tully and Cicero are or were one and the same, one can correctly say *tout court*: it is logically impossible that Cicero and Tully should come into or go out of existence at different times, or that they should *have* done so. Indeed, where 'x is identical with y' stands for any true identity statement involving only pure proper names, it is logically impossible (for it to be the case) that x and y go out of or come into

[1] However, S. Kripke has argued in conversation and lectures that 'if Cicero exists, Cicero is identical with Tully' is a necessary truth. He also points out that such statements may also be *a posteriori*. The possibility of necessary *a posteriori* truths was pointed out by W. and M. Kneale in their *The Development of Logic*, Oxford: Clarendon, 1962, p. 637. But Kripke seems to be the first to suggest that certain identity statements provide specific examples of such truths.

[2] Of course, it may be epistemically possible that Cicero and Tully should have come into or gone out of existence at different times, if the statement that Cicero was identical with Tully is, as Kripke suggests, an *a posteriori* truth of Roman history about which doubt can and often does exist. But *epistemic* possibility is compatible with *logical* necessity, and it is, I think, logically necessarily false that Cicero and Tully (tenselessly) go out of existence or come into existence at different times.

[3] This way of interpreting modal statements comes from Hintikka ('Modality as Referential Multiplicity', *Ajatus* 20, 1957, pp. 49–64) and from S. Kanger (*Probability in Logic*, Stockholm: Almqvist and Wiksell, 1957). The idea is different from Leibniz's conception of worlds that are possible in themselves, and not thought of as possible relative to other worlds.

[4] Cf. Quine's *Word and Object*, Cambridge: M. I. T. Press, 1960, esp. section 41.

existence at different times. And anyone who considers carefully the statement 'Cicero is identical with Tully' can see that that statement is no exception to this claim.

We are now in a position to generalize what we have just said about a specific kind of identity statement to identity statements in general. For any identity statement can be changed so that any descriptions or impure proper names it contains are replaced by proper names with the same referents—if one is in a position to give names to those referents.[1] Consider, then, the following procedure that I shall call *nominalizing*, which can be applied to (true) identity statements involving definite descriptions and/or proper names. Take any description (or impure proper name) on either side of the identity sign (or its ordinary language equivalent) and replace it by a pure proper name that designates (either already, as a matter of usage, or by explicit stipulation) the same entity as is designated by the description (or impure proper name), making sure, at the same time, that no pure proper name is *thereby made* to appear on both sides of the identity sign. The (true) statement resulting from applying this procedure (which will be a null-procedure, if the original statement uses only pure proper names) to a (true) statement of identity will be called the *nominalization* of the original statement. What can be said about true identity statements in general is that their nominalizations will have the same sorts of properties, logically, as those we attributed above to 'Cicero is identical with Tully'. In other words, if '*x* is identical with *y*' stands for a true identity statement involving definite descriptions, impure proper names, and/or pure proper names, then, if '*v* is identical with *w*' stands for any nominalization of the original identity statement, it is a necessary falsehood that *v* and *w* come into or go out of existence at different times. One nominalization of 'Columbus is identical with the man who discovered America', for example, is 'Columbus is identical with Cristoforo Colombo'. And it is clearly logically impossible that Columbus and Cristoforo Colombo should go (or should have gone) out of existence at different times. And the same for coming into existence.[2] Given the truth of what we have just said, there-

---

[1] Cf. Cartwright, *op. cit.*, p. 622.

[2] It *is* possible that *a* Columbus go out of existence before *a* Colombo. But I am not talking about *a* Columbus or *some* Columbus, but about Columbus, *our* Columbus. The statement I am making about what is logically impossible may, then, be true even if similar statements, with different referents or involving less specific reference, are not.

fore, there seems to be a definite sense in which identity is non-contingent.

Now those who have held that mind and body are contingently identical, i.e. that all mental entities are in fact, but not necessarily, identical with physical entities, usually have claimed that this identity is as strict as that between Columbus and the man who discovered America in 1492 or between Cicero and Tully. (I am not interested in arguing against those who have held that only some weaker form of identity holds between mental and physical phenomena.)[1] But consider the sort of statement that identity theorists have held can be true, e.g. 'the pain I am feeling is identical with the c-fibre stimulation now occurring in my brain'. Surely, it may well be the case that whenever my c-fibres are stimulated, I feel pain. But even identity theorists are willing to grant that this is at most a causal or physical, not a logical, necessity. If they are right, then it is indeed dubious that the sort of logical relation that exists between Columbus and the man who discovered America also exists between my present pain and the c-fibre stimulation now occurring in my brain. And if such a relation is necessary to identity, then identity statements relating the mental and the physical will, presumably, not be true in the strict sense of identity which we are considering.

To be more specific, let us (carefully) assign the pure proper name 'Stimie' to the c-fibre stimulation now going on in my brain, and let us call my present pain by the proper name 'Hurtie'. Then, the identity statement 'the pain I am feeling is identical with the c-fibre stimulation now occurring in my brain' will—in the light of what was said above about true identity statements—be true only if Hurtie and Stimie could not (in any logically possible circumstances) go, or have gone, out of existence at different times, because 'Stimie is identical with Hurtie' is a nominalization of the first identity statement. But, I think, if one surveys the matter closely and dispassionately, one will agree that Hurtie *could* (logically) go out of existence before Stimie. If 'Stimie' is the proper name one has assigned to the c-fibre stimulation occurring in one's brain and if 'Hurtie' is the proper name one has given to one's present pain, then it will seem clearly possible that Hurtie should cease to exist (in oneself or in anyone else) without Stimie's

[1] E.g., T. Nagel in 'Physicalism', *Phil. Review*, 74, 1965, pp. 339–58; and also (possibly) H. Putnam in 'Minds and Machines', in S. Hook, ed., *Dimensions of Mind*. N.Y.: N. Y. U. Press, 1960, pp. 138–64.

slackening or diminishing in the slightest. But if such a thing *is* logically possible, then, according to what we have said above, one's present pain is not identical with the c-fibre stimulation occurring in one's brain, no matter how strong a causal connection there is between the two.

And the same argument will hold against the truth of other mind-body identity statements as well. Thus I am not, I think, identical either with my body or with some state of or processes in it. For my pure proper name is 'Slote', and we are in a position to give my body (or certain processes in or states of it) the pure proper name 'Bodio'. Then we can ask whether it is logically impossible for Bodio to go out of existence before Slote. But earlier we saw that there is *no* reason to suppose that disembodied survival of bodily death is logically impossible; and so, given the fact that we seem to be able to imagine, clearly and distinctly, what disembodied survival would be like, I think we have reason to conclude that such survival *is* logically possible. If so, it would seem logically possible for Bodio to go out of existence before Slote. I might lead a disembodied spiritual existence long after my body (Bodio) had disintegrated.[1] It would seem, then, that not all nominalizations of any statement of the form 'I (Slote) am identical with (certain processes p in or states s of) my body' have the properties required in order for any such statement to be a true identity statement.

Those mind-body identity theorists who have claimed that there is a purely contingent, but, none the less strict relation of identity between mental and physical entities are, it would seem, doubly mistaken.[2] For strict identity of the sort obtaining between Colum-

[1] We needn't even assume the possibility of survival of death to prove our point here. As long as a person can instantaneously switch bodies, it is logically possible for Slote to continue to exist (in another body) while Bodio goes out of existence, by disintegration or burning, etc. Incidentally, someone who grants the possibility of disembodied existence after death might argue that what would survive in such a case would (necessarily) only be some psychic aspect or 'side' (or the 'soul') of the original being, not the being himself. I do not think that is correct, but even if it were, mind-body identity would still not obtain. For we could use the name 'Sloto' to refer to that aspect or part of me that *could* survive my bodily death, and for whose survival evidence *could* exist; and for reasons already mentioned, Sloto would clearly not be identical with Bodio, or indeed, with any other physical entity.

[2] And there really is no doubt that identity theorists *have* thought that identity was a merely contingent relation (except for cases like 'nine is the number after eight') and that the relation of identity between mental and physical entities was purely contingent. E.g. Feigl (in 'The "Mental" and the "Physical" ', *Minnesota Studies in the Philosophy of Science*, vol. II, Minneapolis,

bus and the man who . . . is not a purely contingent relation; and mental and physical states, etc., because they are only contingently related at best, and thus do not pass the conditions for identity we have specified, are not, in general, identical with one another. And so some sort of dualism is true.

Of course, someone who already assumed the identity of mental and physical entities might reply that if identity is a logical relation, then mental and physical states must *be* logically related. And he would conclude that Slote and Bodio (or Hurtie and Stimie) could *not* go out of existence at different times. I have no doubt that if one assumes that mental and physical entities *must* be identical at all costs, one will argue this way—or else question what I have had to say about the non-contingency of the identity relation. I am interested, however, only in showing that if one does not assume in advance that mental and physical phenomena are identical and is open-minded about the issues involved, it will be reasonable to believe that some mental and physical entities are not related in the appropriate non-contingent way, and are thus not identical.

In arguing thus for dualism, I have attempted to argue for the logical possibility of the survival of death in disembodied form. And the only positive reason I have given for the claim that such survival is logically possible is the 'fact' that we can clearly and distinctly imagine such a thing occurring. But surely what is clearly and distinctly imaginable may turn out not to be logically possible. Thus one might arrange mirrors in such a way that it looked to a given observer as if he were confronted with two different (and dissimilar) books, one to his left and the other to his right, even though there was in fact only one book present. He might then name the book he thinks is to his left 'Arthur' and name the book he thinks is to his right 'Elsa' and say: 'I can clearly and distinctly imagine Elsa going out of existence without Arthur

Univ. of Minnesota Press, 1958, p. 472) says mind-body identity requires the impossibility of disembodied survival only in the sense that it is impossible both for mental entities to be identical in general with physical ones *and* for such survival to occur. He does not think that it is logically impossible *tout court* for Slote, say, to exist after Bodio, say, is destroyed, and thinks this is compatible with their being identical. Also, there is the fact that identity theorists constantly are saying that mental and physical entities are only empirically related, are correlated only as a matter of empirical fact. Surely if such philosophers believed that such entities were *empirically though also non-contingently* related, they would have said so, since philosophers generally assume that what is empirical is only contingent. There is good evidence, then, that mind-body identity theorists really have thought a strict but purely contingent relation of identity between the mental and the physical to be possible and in fact the case.

going out of existence, and *vice versa.*' But, even granting the truth of what he says, Elsa and Arthur will not be logically separable, as he (let us assume) thinks. For they are one and the same book.

If it is, therefore, possible to be mistaken about the logical possibility even of what one can clearly and distinctly imagine, how can we be certain that this is not, indeed, the case with us who claim that disembodied survival is logically possible on the basis of being able to imagine such survival? The answer, I think, is that we *cannot*. But we still may have *reason* to believe in the logical possibility of something, even if we cannot *prove* that it is possible or in any other way *know for certain* that it is possible. I have every reason, for example, to believe that Elizabeth Taylor could (logically) go out of existence before, or after, Richard Burton. But I cannot *prove* that this is so, What, indeed, would constitute a proof here?

Similarly, I cannot prove that disembodied survival is logically possible. And I do not know for certain that such survival is possible, because I think it cannot be ruled out in advance that someone will someday be able to point out an incoherence in the notion of disembodied survival that we have not been able to detect. In other words, I am not *certain* that I am *not* in *something like* the position of the man in the example described above who is deceived by mirrors into thinking something is possible when it is not. I would like to claim, however, that, if (given that '*x*' and '*y*' stand for proper names) one can clearly and distinctly imagine what it would be like for *x* to go out of existence before *y*, if one has good reason to think that one could imagine this no matter how well acquainted with *x* and *y* one got in the future, and if one has no definite reason to think it is *impossible* for *x* to go out of existence before *y*, then it is reasonable, at least tentatively, to think that *x could* (logically) go out of existence before *y*. If this claim is true, we have reason to believe that survival of bodily death is possible, that Bodio and Slote are logically separable (and also that Hurtie and Stimie are logically separable). We can clearly and distinctly imagine Slote without Bodio, have good reason to think that we could imagine this no matter how much more we learned about each of them, and have found no reason to think Slote and Bodio are not separable. And the same, I think, is true of Stimie and Hurtie. For similar reasons, the man in the mirror example has reason to believe that Arthur and Elsa are logically separable, even though if he does believe this he will be mistaken.[1] In the light of the above argument, therefore, I think we have rendered it (at least to some degree) reasonable to believe in mind-body dualism, to believe, that is, that at least some psychical or mental entities are not identical with physical entities.[2]

III

Let us now put an end to our digression, and consider some other sorts of objections that can be levelled against external-world scepticism as I have construed it.

Norman Malcolm has recently argued that scepticism about the past existence of the world cannot be correct since it implies that all our judgments about the past might be incorrect.[3] And Malcolm would, presumably, want to make the same point about external-world scepticism, claiming that such scepticism cannot represent a valid philosophical position since it implies something that is impossible, namely, that all our present beliefs about (entailing the existence of) the external world could be mistaken. In recent years much criticism has been directed against Malcolm's views on these matters, some of it very convincing.[4] What seems, in general, to be the kind of consideration that lies behind and stands in favour of Malcolm's views on scepticism is the fact that if someone constantly makes mistaken claims in some area, e.g. with respect to the colours things have, the only plausible explanation would seem to be that the person in question is ignorant of the meaning of some of the terms he is using, e.g. is ignorant of the meaning of 'red', 'green', etc. One might in a similar vein argue

[1] However, someone who knows no Roman history is not necessarily justified in believing that Cicero and Tully could have existed at different times. For he may not have good reason to believe that, no matter how much Roman history he learned, he would still be able clearly and distinctly to imagine Cicero without Tully, or *vice versa*. The man in the mirror example, however, has no reason to believe there are mirrors present, so that in the light of his sensory evidence, he has reason to believe that even if he were to learn more about Arthur and Elsa, he would still be able to imagine Elsa existing without Arthur.

[2] An argument similar to that which I have just put forward for mind-body dualism has been arrived at independently by Prof. S. Kripke. Our common indebtedness to Descartes' argument for dualism in the *Meditations* is almost too obvious to mention.

[3] See his 'Memory and the Past' in *Knowledge and Certainty*, Englewood Cliffs: Prentice-Hall, 1963, esp. p. 193 f.

[4] See, e.g. J. Cornman's 'Malcolm's Mistaken Memory', *Analysis* 25, 1965, pp. 161–7.

that if someone constantly makes mistakes about the external world, he does not have the concept of a physical entity (or know the meaning of physical-object words), and so does not really make *judgments*, or have *beliefs*, about the external world. Consequently, since we do in fact, presumably, make judgments (that we understand) and have beliefs (that we understand) about the existence of objects in an external world, at least some of those judgments or beliefs must be correct, and no sceptical hypothesis about the external world can be true.

What seems wrong with this sort of argument is just that there are other possible explanations for why someone always makes mistakes in a certain area besides the hypothesis that that person lacks certain concepts (or is ignorant of the meaning of certain words). If someone constantly makes mistakes about the colour of things, it may be because someone else has been using deceptive lighting (or tampering with his brain) in order to trick him into error, rather than because he lacks colour concepts or is ignorant of the meaning of any colour words. Such deception is not usual, perhaps, but it is always logically possible. And so if we constantly make false statements about the existence of objects in an external world, it may be that we possess the appropriate external-world concepts but are in some way being cleverly deceived, or misled. Thus, given the possibility of constant deception as an explanation of constant error in any given field, Malcolm cannot logically deduce from the fact that we make judgments and have beliefs about the external world the conclusion that there is an external, physical world. And so Malcolm has given us no way of showing the falsity of scepticism about the external world.

A similar sort of proposal for overcoming external-world scepticism has been put forward by Gilbert Ryle in *Dilemmas*.[1] Ryle argues that just as it is impossible for all the coins in a country always to be and to have been counterfeit or false coins, so too is it impossible for all our perceptions always to be and to have been non-veridical (or hallucinatory). And presumably 'impossible' means 'logically impossible' in this context. (If it does not, the whole argument is question-begging, and totally useless in any attempt to overcome external-world scepticism.) But is it really *logically* impossible for there to have been only false coins in a

[1] Cambridge University Press, 1956, ch. 7, *passim*. Also by J. Austin in *Sense and Sensibilia*, p. 11 f.

country? One reason one might assume this is that '*x* is a counterfeit' seems to imply 'there is something *y* of which *x* is a counterfeit.'[1] But consider the following counter-example. It is logically possible that a given government decide for the first time to mint coins (rather than let trade continue to occur by barter), and announce in advance when the coins will appear and what they will look like. Then criminals might obtain means for making such coins themselves, and proceed to make those coins and to circulate them on the appointed day, even though the government's minting machines had broken down in the meantime, so that no coins had been minted or distributed by the government. The coins minted by the criminals would surely be counterfeit and false, and the government, seeing how easy it was to produce false or counterfeit coins, might never go through with its plans to mint coins. But on the appointed day, the only coins in circulation or existence would have been false ones; in fact the only coins ever to exist in that country would all be counterfeit. It would seem, then, to be logically possible for only *counterfeit* coins ever to exist; and '*x* is a counterfeit coin' does not entail '*x* is a counterfeit of some real coin'. The example of counterfeit coins, therefore, gives us no argument for the impossibility of constant non-veridical or hallucinatory perception, gives us no way to overcome external-world scepticism.

The sorts of arguments against external-world scepticism used by Ryle and Malcolm are really variations of the Paradigm-Case Argument, which has come ever increasingly under attack in recent years.[2] The Paradigm-Case Argument, which comes out of the philosophy of the later Wittgenstein, is only one of several ways in which Wittgensteinians have attacked the coherence of scepticism about the external world, however. It has been claimed, for example, that such scepticism is false or incoherent because it entails the logical possibility of a (logically) private language. But I do not see why this entailment should be thought to hold. Why is it impossible for a non-physical being to be given sense experiences by a demon, be thoroughly acquainted with (and only with) the *English* language (or a language exactly like English),

---

[1] Such a claim is made by K. Wilson in 'A Note on Significant Contrast Arguments', *Australasian Journal of Philosophy* 44, 1966, p. 342.

[2] I have attempted myself to show what is wrong with the Paradigm-Case Argument in 'The Theory of Important Criteria', *Journal of Philosophy* LXIII, 1966, p. 223 f.

and come to be deceived about the existence of the external world? If there were no external world or people to talk to or vocal cords or bodies, he might not be able to *speak* English with anyone, but he might still *know* English and think in English. But then scepticism about the external world need only claim that we have no reason to think we are not immaterial spirits in a universe devoid of matter who know English and who could communicate with others in English *if* we had vocal cords, etc. And such scepticism seems in no way committed to the possibility of a private language.[1] Furthermore, even if such a commitment did obtain, it is not at all clear that a private language is impossible. Many interesting arguments for the logical possibility of such a language have appeared in recent years.[2]

Another Wittgenstein-type argument against the coherence of external-world scepticism runs: one who says that belief in an external world is not reasonable must be willing to admit that such belief could (logically) be reasonable, or else stand convicted of abusing ordinary language. For 'reasonable belief that there is a table', for example, is an expression with a use in our language, and any such expression must apply in *some* logically possible circumstances. The external-world sceptic denies the logical possibility of reasonable belief in tables, so his position is incoherent from an ordinary language standpoint.[3] But surely some expressions with a use in ordinary language *cannot* (logically) apply to anything, e.g. 'greatest prime' and 'successful quadrature'. Furthermore, why can't a sceptic deny that *our* sense experience makes it reasonable *for us* to believe in an external world, and simply leave it open whether or not some other set of experiences might warrant such belief? This line of objection to external-world scepticism is not, I think, fully convincing. And, on the whole, I am inclined to think that no crucial objections to scepticism about the external world or satisfactory means of overcoming such scepticism have been provided by philosophers in the Wittgensteinian tradition.

---

[1] A similar argument to this effect is made by A. Plantinga in *God and Other Minds*, Ithaca: Cornell Univ. Press, 1967, pp. 199 ff.

[2] See, e.g. M. Stocker's 'Memory and the Private Language Argument', *Philosophical Quarterly*, 16, 1966, pp. 47–53.

[3] An argument very much like this can be found in M. Lazerowitz's 'Strong and Weak Verification II', *The Structure of Metaphysics*, London: Routledge and Kegan Paul, 1955.

IV

There seems, then, to be no way to rule out sceptical hypotheses at least as *logically possible* explanations of the fact that we have sense experiences that seem to be 'of' physical objects. There have, of course, been other attempts besides those mentioned above to discredit or show the impossibility of sceptical hypotheses about the external world. But a thorough consideration of all such attempts would take us too long away from the task at hand. In the light of the above arguments, in any case, I think the burden of proof is on him who wishes to argue that the problem of the external world is a pseudo-problem and that sceptical explanations of our experience are invalid or inherently faulty. There simply does seem to be a problem of showing why it is more reasonable to believe that our experiences result from something physical than that they are caused by a demon or spirit. And, if that is so, *we* are left with the problem of discovering *just what it is* about sceptical hypotheses that makes them less acceptable or reasonable, by acceptable scientific or other rational standards, than the hypothesis of an external world.[1]

There seem to be only two basic sorts of sceptical hypotheses that could be used to account for our sense or 'outer' experience without postulating an external world. One is the hypothesis of some sort of spirit or demon; the other, the hypothesis that the sense experiences we have and the order they possess are totally surd and inexplicable. There are various other sorts of sceptical hypotheses, of course. There are doubts as to whether we are brains in vats, for example. But such doubts do not involve speculating as to the possibility that the (physical) world may not exist at all. They only involve doubting that the world is as we commonly *think* it is. There is also sceptical doubt that we may at any given moment, or indeed for the entire length of our experience, be, or have been, dreaming. But if we are dreaming, there must be a waking life that we led before we slept, or that we will lead if and when we awake, and that life will involve experience of a real physical world, unless it is the work of some immaterial spirit or demon, or the outcome of pure chance.[2]

---

[1] In talking of the 'hypothesis' of an external world, I do not mean to claim that the existence of the external world is not, in fact, certain. One can, if one wants, replace 'hypothesis' throughout by 'claim' or 'belief' or 'view' or some other expression more neutral with regard to certainty.

[2] In the *First Meditation*, Descartes is well aware of this.

Dreaming-scepticism thus does not alone imply the non-existence of an external world; it does so only in conjunction with one or another of the two sorts of sceptical hypotheses that we have claimed can be used to deny the existence of the external world. We thus need only show that the hypothesis of an external world is not scientifically unreasonable or unacceptable and that these two sorts of sceptical hypotheses are, in order to show that the hypothesis of an external world is at least part of the best (scientific) explanation of our having the sense experience(s) we do.

But this is no easy thing to do. One often goes about verifying an hypothesis by showing it to be compatible with the (experimental or observational) evidence. And normally the easiest way to falsify an hypothesis to show it to be incompatible with such evidence. But sceptical hypotheses of a demon or of chance are just as compatible with our sensory evidence, with our having the sort of sense experiences we do, as is the hypothesis of an external world. And so, on the basis merely of the test of compatibility with the (sensory) evidence, we have no more reason to explain our experience in terms of an external world than in terms of a demon or chance.

At this point, various well-known criteria of the acceptability of hypotheses in science will suggest themselves as possible ways to differentiate the hypothesis of an external world from sceptical hypotheses, with respect to scientific acceptability or plausibility. It is natural to imagine, for example, that what is wrong with demon-scepticism is that the existence of some sort of demon supplying us with sense experiences is unverifiable, whereas the existence of the external world *is* verifiable. But what reason do we have to assume here that the external world's existence can be verified? Our reason cannot be that our sense experience, being compatible with the hypothesis of an external world, serves at least partly to verify that hypothesis; for then the hypothesis of a demon will also be (to some degree) verifiable. Then how can we show that the external world is verifiable, the demon not? Surely we cannot just *assume* that this is so, since that would be to beg the question at issue.

Furthermore, it is not intuitively obvious that the hypothesis of a demon-cause of our outer experiences is to no degree verifiable, even by commonsense standards of what is to count as verification. True, we all believe we have no evidence for the existence of such a demon; but there are logically possible situations in which, I think, we would have what most of us would want to call fairly good, or even very good, reason to believe in such a demon. If, for example, we heard a 'voice' tell us that all our experiences were caused by the owner of the 'voice', and if, to overcome our hesitation in believing this, the 'voice' claimed to be able to change our sense experiences in any strange way we wanted, and soon thereafter our experience was changed in the very ways we requested, we would surely have more reason to believe in a demon (of some sort) than we do now, and most of us would begin to doubt the existence of the external world and to feel that there was a good chance that a demon was the cause of our sense experiences. There seems to be no plausible way, then, in which one can overcome scepticism about the external world by showing that a demon is unverifiable while an external world is verifiable.

Another possible way to argue that the external world is scientifically more acceptable than its sceptical alternatives would be to claim that it is simpler than those alternatives. But by what standards of simplicity? The hypothesis of a demon who makes it seem as if there is an external world and does so by some (non-physical) means *m* and for some reason or motive *r* (or as a result of some cause *c*) is no richer ontologically, it seems, than the hypothesis that our sense experience is due to entities in a physical world. The former hypothesis is committed to a demon-mind containing certain means of and motives for supplying sense experiences, to a mind to which such experiences are given, and, perhaps, to such things as sense experiences. The latter hypothesis is committed to a physical world containing various parts or aspects and various means of supplying sense experiences, to a mind to which such experiences are given, and also, perhaps, to such things as sense experiences. And these seem to be fairly equal ontological commitments. There may be some standards of scientific simplicity according to which the external world is simpler than any demon-hypothesis; indeed later on, in Chapter 5, I shall make an attempt to find such standards myself. But, as far as I can tell, no one has yet turned up any plausible standards of scientific simplicity in terms of which one can successfully differentiate the hypothesis of an external world from sceptical explanations of our sense experiences.[1]

[1] However, see Russell (*The Problems of Philosophy*, N.Y.: Galaxy, 1959, ch. 2) and D. C. Williams ('The Inductive Argument for Subjectivism', *The Monist* 44, 1934, pp. 99–101), both of whom make brief, and to my mind un-

Another possible way of getting around external-world scepticism arises from the claim (made by O. K. Bouwsma,[1] among others) that the hypothesis of an external world as the cause of our experiences and the hypothesis of a demon (or, presumably, that of chance) as the cause (or null-cause) of those experiences are in no sense different hypotheses. Since there is nothing that could favour the one hypothesis over the other, the two are equivalent in meaning. If so, sceptical hypotheses of the kind we have been considering are self-contradictory, since they claim that a demon, *rather than* an external world, is the source of our sense experiences, and there is no reason to worry about external-world scepticism, since that position postulates a false dichotomy between commonsense and sceptical explanations of our experience. This sort of argument assumes, of course, that if there is no way to distinguish between two hypotheses evidentially and no chance of having more reason to believe the one than the other, the two hypotheses are really one. Even granting this none-too-obvious assumption, however, it is by no means obvious that one can so easily prove that the hypothesis of an external world and the hypothesis of a demon are one. For, however hard it may be to show the superiority of the hypothesis of an external world over the hypothesis of a demon, it would seem to be just as hard to show that nothing could ever give us any reason to favour the one hypothesis over the other.

Other attempts to undermine external-world scepticism run into similar difficulties. Carnap, for example, has argued that experience can give us no reason to favour the hypothesis of an external world over that of the demon (or of Berkeley's God) or vice versa, so that all these 'hypotheses' are meaningless and not really genuine hypotheses.[2] In that case scepticism about the external world would be in some sense undermined as an intellectual position. But, even if we grant Carnap the meaninglessness of what is unverifiable—an assumption that I do not find particularly compelling—it will still be hard to undermine scepticism (and show the meaninglessness of the hypothesis of an external world) along his lines. For as I said just above, it is very difficult to show that nothing could distinguish evidentially between the hypothesis

---

successful, attempts to show the greater simplicity of the hypothesis of an external world. Also see A. Plantinga's 'Comments', *J. Phil.*, 62, 1965, p. 586.

[1] 'Descartes' Evil Genius', *Phil. Review*, 58, 1949, esp. p. 149.

[2] *Pseudo-problems in Philosophy*, Berkeley: Univ. of California Press, 1967, p. 334.

of the external world and that of the demon. Even if all possible experience is compatible with either, we might have reasons of simplicity, or other such methodological reasons, for accepting the external-world hypothesis over that of the demon, as the explanation of our sense experiences.[1] Indeed in the next chapter I hope myself to provide such reasons for accepting the external world, rather than the demon. And, if they are good reasons, neither Carnap nor Bouwsma can undermine external-world scepticism by showing that nothing could favour the hypothesis of an external world over its sceptical alternatives.

---

[1] If it be objected that if it is *only* possible to have reasons of *simplicity* favouring hypothesis *a* over hypothesis *b*, or vice versa, there is no genuine distinction between those two hypotheses, what is to be said of competing inductive generalizations—e.g. 'Fewer than half the crows ever to exist are black' versus 'More than half the crows ever to exist are black'—where we can only have reasons of simplicity to favour one over the other? (More on this in Ch. 5, below.) Our samplings of crows will always of necessity be compatible with either of these hypotheses; but if all sampled crows are black, we have, *ceteris paribus*, simplicity reasons to favour the latter hypothesis. If we assume the meaningfulness of these hypotheses and of the distinction between them—which some positivists, e.g. Ramsey, would not have been willing to do—then we will have reason to believe in a meaningful distinction between the hypotheses of the external world and of the demon if we can produce simplicity, or other methodological, considerations favouring one of them over the other.

CHAPTER 2

THE EXISTENCE OF THE EXTERNAL WORLD

I

Science is an open-ended enterprise. It seeks to give explanations of events, processes, etc., but also to give, as far as possible, explanations of all the various aspects of the very things it posits in its explanations. For it is a goal of scientific enterprise to gain deeper and deeper and more and more explanations of whatever things there are in the world, wherever possible. If, for example, a scientist explains why a given bird is black by pointing out that it is a raven and that all ravens are black, the process of scientific inquiry has not thereby come to an end; for science also has the task of explaining why all ravens are black. And, if some genetic structure g is discovered to explain why all ravens are black, the question will still remain why g causes blackness and why all ravens have g, and it will be part of the task of science to investigate these further questions, too, and answer them, if that is at all possible; and so on *ad indefinitum*.

That is not to say that science can never legitimately claim that explanations of certain entities in certain areas do not exist, but only that science tries to allow for more and more explanation of the nature and behaviour, etc., of the things there are in the world, when other things are equal. The positing of a force of *élan vital*, for example, has often been the positing of an occult force or entity whose activity or behaviour cannot in principle be further explained. Those who postulated *élan vital* to explain certain biological phenomena typically did so because they thought those phenomena could not be explained mechanistically or in any other way analysed into or explained by further biological or physical functions. So by its very nature the operation of *élan vital* was supposed to be beyond scientific explanation, i.e. the means by which *élan vital* brought about the phenomena it was supposed to explain were thought to be essentially inexplicable. But then to posit *élan vital* as the explanation of a phenomenon is in effect to prevent oneself from obtaining deeper and deeper and more and more detailed explanations of the phenomenon in question, if such explanations are there to be had, for as long as one continues to

C

posit *élan vital*. And it is at least partly for this reason that *élan vital* has been unacceptable to biologists as an explanatory notion, so that as soon as mechanisms or underlying processes (not thought to be fundamentally inexplicable) have been found to explain what *élan vital* is supposed to explain, explanations in terms of *élan vital* have been generally discarded.[1]

The hypothesis of *élan vital* is what I shall call an inquiry-limiting hypothesis, an hypothesis whose acceptance ensures the impossibility of one's gaining certain sorts of warranted true explanations of the nature and behaviour of things for as long as one continues to accept it. To be more precise, an hypothesis is inquiry-limiting for s[2] as an explanation of certain phenomena at time t, just in case if s at t accepts that hypothesis and holds it to be the best and completest explanation of those phenomena available *at t* (and believes in the existence of those phenomena), he ensures the impossibility of his coming to have rationally justified or warranted belief (consistent with his other beliefs) in more and more true explanations of various aspects of or facts about the phenomena in question (for as long as he continues to accept that hypothesis as true and to believe it to be the best and completest explanation of the phenomena in question that was available at t).

Given the above definition of inquiry-limitingness, it is not hard to see why accepting inquiry-limiting hypotheses is, other things being equal, unreasonable from the scientific standpoint. For one who at some time t accepts such an hypothesis while believing it to be the best explanation available at t of certain phenomena ensures the frustration of certain explanatory goals of science—i.e. makes it impossible, if it is not already impossible, to achieve those goals—for as long as he continues to accept that hypothesis and hold it to be the best. . . . But if one of one's goals or purposes is to do x, then, other things being equal, it is unreasonable—from the standpoint of those purposes—for one to do y, if (one sees or reasonably believes that) doing y during any period of time p

---

[1] The objection against *élan vital* is not that it is unobservable, but that it is in certain ways fundamentally inexplicable. For scientists are perfectly willing to countenance electrons, even though they are not observable (in any direct way). The positing of electrons seems in no way *ipso facto* to preclude the possibility of deeper and deeper explanation of electron behaviour.

[2] A hypothesis may be inquiry-limiting for one being but not for another. Thus I shall argue that the hypothesis of a demon is inquiry-limiting *for us* as an explanation of our sense experiences; but it would not, I think, be inquiry-limiting as an explanation of our experiences *for the demon himself*.

makes it impossible for one to do *x* during *p*. Thus, for example, if one's chief goal in life is to write a novel, then from the standpoint of one having such a goal, it would, other things being equal, be unreasonable and irrational for one knowingly to go and live in a noisy neighbourhood while reasonably believing that one can write only at home and that one cannot write in noisy situations, and thus that in doing what one was doing one was ensuring at least the temporary impossibility of one's attaining one's chief goal in life.

Now if the purposes and goals of science include, among other things the obtaining of more and more explanations of whatever exists, wherever possible, then accepting an inquiry-limiting hypothesis is unreasonable for someone who knows or has good reason to believe that it is inquiry-limiting, at least other things being equal.[1] I should like, then, to propose the principle (*a*) that it is scientifically *unreasonable* for someone to *accept* what (he sees or has reason to believe) is for him at that time an inquiry-limiting explanation of a certain phenomenon, other things being equal; and (*b*) that there is *reason* for such a person to *reject* such an explanation in favour of an acceptable non-inquiry-limiting explanation of the phenomenon in question, if he can find one. This two-part principle I call the *Principle of Unlimited Inquiry*.

I think the Principle of Unlimited Inquiry is a valid principle of rational scientific inquiry,[2] and that its validity can be seen to follow from the fact that science is essentially (i.e. by the very definition of 'science') an intellectual enterprise that seeks (among other things) the completest possible explanation of why things (especially those things it tries to explain in the first place) are the way they are. Furthermore, I think that hypotheses that explain our sense experiences in terms of some sort of Cartesian demon or spirit (and that deny the physical world) are for us at the present time inquiry-limiting as the explanation of those experiences, and

---

[1] Similarly, to borrow and somewhat alter an example from William James ('The Sentiment of Rationality', in *Essays in Pragmatism*, N. Y.: Hafner, 1948, p. 27), if one has to jump a chasm and one realizes that if one thinks one cannot make it, one won't make it, then it is unreasonable to think or not to try to dissuade oneself from thinking that one cannot make it, since one reasonably believes that by doing this one makes the attainment of one's goal impossible.

[2] Inquiry-limitingness seems to be the opposite side of the coin of scientific fertility. Just as fertility (the fact that using a certain hypothesis would enable us to explain things we were previously unable to explain) has been thought to favour the hypotheses that possessed it, inquiry-limitingness is a scientifically unfavourable characteristic of hypotheses.

thus run counter to the above Principle of Unlimited Inquiry (henceforth, for brevity, the PUI), though I do not think that this is true of certain hypotheses that explain our experiences in terms of the existence of some sort of external world of physical processes, things, events, etc. If, for example, we were now to accept the sceptical claim or hypothesis that there was no external world[1] and that some demon supplied us with our sense experiences by certain non-physical means *m* and for certain reasons (or out of certain motives or as a result of certain causes) *r*, and were to hold this hypothesis to be the best and completest *presently* available of our having the particular kind of sense experiences we do, we would *ipso facto* be ensuring the impossibility (for as long as we acccepted the hypothesis in question in the manner indicated) of our coming to believe and to be (rationally) warranted in believing more and more true explanations (consistent with our other beliefs)[2] of various facts about and aspects of the nature and behaviour of our sense experiences (and of their causes). For if an external physical world exists and is responsible (causally) for our sense experiences, we will surely not be able to come to believe *true* explanations about our experiences that are *consistent* with our other beliefs (and all conjunctions of such beliefs) *as long as* we accept the hypothesis mentioned above. And if there is in fact a demon of the kind our hypothesis posits, we will be unable to obtain explanations in which we are *warranted* in believing (or which it would be reasonable for us to believe, or accept) of why the demon exists and has the motives and means of operation that he has or of how he is able to supply us with experiences, and so will be unable to gain *warranted* explanations about certain aspects of our experiences and their causes. For presumably the demon, if he exists, is our sole source of empirical or sensory information, and we will not be able to get such warranted explanations *from him*. Thus, whatever in fact is the explanation

[1] Unless an hypothesis denies the external world, it is not sceptical about the external world. A non-sceptical demon-explanation of our experience is one that posits a demon as the cause of our experience and either admits that there is also an external world, or leaves open that possibility.

[2] The condition of consistency is needed, because one who accepts the demon might also inconsistently come to believe an external world was causing his experiences in certain ways, and, if such an external world exists and he is reasonable in thinking so, believe warranted *true* explanations of his experiences by so doing. Such a possibility does not help inquiry-limiting hypotheses in attaining scientific acceptability, since inconsistency is anathema to science and to rationality in general.

of our sense experiences, if we accept the above sort of demon-hypothesis (or even more complex demon-hypotheses with more built into them about the demon, his motives, and his methods) and hold it to be the best and completest explanation of our experiences now available, we thereby frustrate our purposes as scientists. For it is inherent in science to seek more and more *true* and *warranted explanatory beliefs* about the phenomena one wishes to explain. Thus, for one of us presently attempting to explain the phenomenon of his particular sense experiences, it is, *ceteris paribus*, scientifically unreasonable to accept demon-hypotheses.

But this is to assume that if there is a demon, we cannot obtain warranted explanations of his motives and means (methods) of operation, since there is no one else but him from whom such explanations can be got, and since we would have good reason to distrust anything such an illusion-creating deceiver told us. But this is not self-evident, and requires some argument. After all, someone might object, perhaps the demon might change, and give us warranted (for us) explanations of aspects of and facts about himself, even though he has, if he exists, not done so up till now. And if this is possible, sceptical demon-hypotheses are not inquiry-limiting, and do not contravene the PUI, since it would in no way follow from the fact that we believed in a demon as the cause of our experiences (and in the non-existence of any external world while we were getting those experiences) that we could not gain *warranted* and true explanatory beliefs about the causes of our experiences, in the case where the demon was in fact the cause of those experiences.

We are presumably to obtain warranted explanations from the demon in the following way. The demon announces himself in our experience somehow and convinces us, in the manner described on pages 61 and 62 of Chapter 1, that he is the sole source of our experiences.[1] He then starts to explain to us in great detail all

[1] I am not sure, however, that it would be entirely reasonable to believe a demon-voice's claim that the demon was the sole source of our experiences, no matter how many extraordinary feats one saw performed. For if the demon did not supply all our sense experiences, he is a monstrous liar to say that he did; and, if he is telling the truth, then he is a creator of monstrous illusions; so why should one trust one entirely to any claim he makes, even the claim that he alone is the source of all our sense experiences? Perhaps there are two demons, or perhaps there is an external world that causes some of our experiences while the demon causes others. In any case, though, we would have *some* (substantial) reason, if strange enough things happened, to believe in the demon as the sole cause of our experiences. More reason by far, for example, than *we* have *now*.

about his motives and methods. Even if what he says to us is in
fact true, would we be justified in believing that it was? I am
inclined to think not, considering the deceptive, or at least the
uninformative, illusion-creating way he has acted in the past.[1]
For whether we were actually deceived by him into thinking there
was an external world or always (even in non-philosophical
moments) suspended belief in the existence of such a world, the
demon has, if he exists, made it appear in all respects exactly as
if we were living in a real external world, replete with tables,
apples, pastures, etc. And he has not given us the slightest indication of his own existence or of the non-existence of the external
world until the present.

Furthermore, we cannot rule out the possibility that the demon
was attempting to deceive or mislead us by making it seem as if
there was an external world, even if we are among those who were
not thus deceived or misled. And in order to have justifiable
confidence in what the demon says by way of explanation of his
own motives and methods, would we not have to have justifiable
confidence that he originally did not intend to deceive us or that
he is not deceptive (i.e. attempting deception) *now*, *even if* he
originally was inclined to be deceptive or misleading? And could
we ever have good and sufficient reason to believe that either of
these things was the case? Actually, we do, perhaps, have one
reason for thinking that the demon, if he was originally a deceiver,
is no longer a deceiver. For as we have imagined the case, the
demon has revealed his past illusion-mongering to us, which

---

[1] A demon who creates in us the total illusion of an external world need not be
doing so on purpose. He may, indeed, be attempting, but failing, to give us an
indication that it is an illusion, or he may not know that he is creating this
illusion. And in such cases, he is not acting *deceptively*. It is even questionable
whether the demon-source of our sense experiences has to be acting *misleadingly*.
For to say that something is misleading *may* entail that it tends to mislead or
that it gives one reason for believing something is the case, which is, in fact, not
the case. And for reasons mentioned in the Introduction, I do not, for purposes
of the present argument, wish to rely on any assumptions about our believing,
or tending to believe, in external objects. Nor do I wish to rely, in my argument,
on any causal assumptions about the effects our experiences tend to have on us.
And I certainly also do not want to *assume* that our experiences give us some
sort of reason for believing in an external world *rather* than the demon.

I am not, I think, however, begging any questions by saying that if there is no
external world our experiences have been illusory. I think it follows from the
very meaning of 'illusory' and 'illusion' that, if someone or something makes it
appear just as if there are things of a certain sort when there are no such things,
an illusion (of those things) has been created in someone, and someone's
experience has been illusory.

seems to be a stroke of honesty on his part. And this, perhaps, gives us *some* reason to think he is no longer going to be deceptive, even if he was so before, and so to think that what he tells us by way of explanation of his motives, etc. is true. But notice this. If the demon wished to *deceive* us about the motives and means with which he operated in making it seem (in the past) as if there were various sorts of physical objects, events, and processes, he would first have to reveal his prior illusion-mongering. And so it is not unnatural to imagine that this revelation of the nature of his prior behaviour is simply the first step in an attempt on the part of the demon at a new brand of deception. His revelation can be viewed either as a sign of (new) honesty or as a ruse, intended to make us believe that he is now honest and forthright and constituting a means to new deceptions.[1] And what reason could we possibly have to prefer one of these alternatives over the other?

Well, one might suggest, what if the demon seemed a very decent fellow in what he revealed to you of himself and what if he explained that he had been deceptive (or inclined to supply large amounts of uninformative illusory data) to spirits like us because he had been under orders from an evil demon-superior, but was no longer going to behave as he had in the past because that demon-superior had now passed out of existence? And what if the demon seemed contrite for his past behaviour and did you all sorts of favours, that is, gave you all sorts of pleasant sensory experiences? Wouldn't all this give you at least *some* reason to believe he was telling the truth about his motives and methods? Yes, perhaps it would. But, as I said before, one could still seriously wonder whether it was not all part of a very clever ruse, wonder whether the demon was not lulling one into believing that he had changed in character or tendencies, just in order to perform some new brand of deception. And such doubts have great force, surely, given the sheer enormity of his previous illusion-making and uninformative behaviour, since we have no way of ruling out the possibility that his earlier behaviour was intended by him to cause us to be deceived about the external world, or, at least, to hide the truth about his existence, motives, and methods from us.

Furthermore, and this is crucial, there is no way of making an

---

[1] Or, alternatively, we can see his revelation either as a sign that he is tired of his 'sinful' illusion-making ways, or as a sign that he is tired of one form of deception and interested in trying his hand at another.

independent test of or check on whether the demon originally had deceptive intentions or on whether he is now inclined to deceive us (or thus on whether he has changed from a diabolically clever and powerful deceiver to an honest spirit). If a *man* has deceived us or acted deceptively, we may still come to have excellent reason to believe that he is now no longer deceptive—assuming commonsense opinion about the sorts of reasons we are capable of having for things. For we believe we have other sources of knowledge about the man than what the man *chooses* to tell us about himself. We can consult lie-detectors, run psychiatric tests, or study the man's brain (assuming a more developed state of the science of physiology than exists at present) in order to see whether his character has changed, and, since the man cannot, presumably, control the data yielded by these sources of information, we can use these sources as independent tests of what the man himself tells us about his present character or about his change in character, and gain from them justification for the belief that he has changed. And, if the independent tests show that he *has* changed (with respect to deceptiveness), then no matter how deceptively he may have acted and been disposed to act in the past, we may *justifiably* believe what he tells us, without entertaining any serious doubts about it—even if it is not *certain* that he has changed and that he is not trying to deceive us once again. Similarly, if a man does things that *may* be part of an attempt to deceive us, we can use tests that are presumably independent of his control to justify the view that he was and is, in fact, not trying to deceive us—again assuming commonsense views of what we can verify.

But no such independent verifying tests of non-deceptiveness or of character change with respect to deceptiveness are possible concerning the demon, if we believe that he has supplied us with sense experiences in the past. For, either the demon will continue to supply us with sense experience in the future, so that any check on his present or past veracity will involve getting information from him, and thus not be independent; or he will allow us to see certain material objects (which have somehow come into existence since he began his revelation). Let us imagine, for example, that he shows us real material objects on which are written descriptions of the motives and means by which he operates, and tells us that these are objects, whose existence and nature are independent of his will, and which prove, by virtue of what is written on them, that he was never deceptive, or that what he is now saying about himself is true. We would not be justified in believing that we were seeing objects, rather than still getting our sense experiences from the demon, and that what was written on those objects was independent of the demon's will, unless we were already justified in believing that the demon had never intended deception, or was not, at least, presently inclined towards deceptiveness.[1] So surely we could not use what seemed to be written on those objects to verify the earlier honesty or present honesty of the demon, or to gain warranted beliefs about his motives, etc. In other words, if we rely on sense experiences that the demon claims (or we think) that he is giving us, for our decision about his honesty or non-deceptiveness now or in the past, we must assume that he is not trying to use those sense experiences to deceive us (about himself), and so beg the question at issue. And, if we rely on what he claims are (or what seem to be) independent objects that are inscribed with putative information about the demon, we can never be confident that they are either objects or independent, unless we trust him. Thus whether the demon continues to supply us with sense experience or not, there is no way of checking on his honesty, or on the truth of what he says, that does not already presuppose his honesty, i.e. that is genuinely independent and not question-begging. And so, no matter what the demon does to convince us that what he says about his motives and methods is true, there will always remain serious doubt that he is and has been trying to deceive us, doubt of such a sort that belief in what he says will never really be warranted or justified.

Of course, it *might* be claimed that it was possible to gain warranted explanatory beliefs about the demon's motives and methods *without* getting explicit putative explanatory information from the demon or some other source about those motives and methods. But it is hard for me to see how this *would* be possible, if, as we have just argued, it is impossible to get warranted explanatory beliefs about the demon's motives and methods from any source of *explicit putative* information about those motives and methods. Surely, ordinary experiences of tables and books, for example, can in no way be reasonably interpreted as indicative of

---

[1] Also, *even if* we believe that what is on the tablets is independent of the demon, why should we believe that the tablets contain the truth about the demon rather than total (or partial) falsehood?

the correct explanation of why the demon has the motives he does or of how he creates experiences in us. And surely, even if certain complex facts about one's experience might be thought to indicate something about the demon's motives and methods, one could always seriously wonder whether the demon was responsible for those facts about one's experience and hoping thereby to deceive one in certain ways about his motives and methods.

It seems to me, therefore, that the following principle, which I shall call Principle A, is a highly specific, but none the less valid principle of rational thinking (epistemic principle):

If (a) one (reasonably) believes that P has in an extraordinarily complete way made it seem or appear as if certain things, that in fact did not exist, did exist, without giving one any positive indication of his existence, of what he was doing, or of the fact that one's experiences were illusory; and if (b) P's prior illusion-making is then revealed to one in some way and one begins to get putative explanatory information about P's motives for and methods of creating illusions (or any other data one might attempt to interpret as clues to the why's and how's of P's motives and methods); and if (c) it is clear that revelation, or knowledge, of P's prior illusion-making is necessary for P to be able to deceive one about his motives and methods; and if (d) there is no way independently to verify that P is not trying to deceive one about his motives and methods by means of the putative information (or the data) one is getting, or that P did not create the illusions he did in order to deceive us into believing in the existence of the sorts of things he was creating an illusion of, then it is not rational or reasonable for one to believe the putative explanatory information one gets about P's motives and methods (or to trust any other data one gets as giving one clues to the why's and how's of P's motives and methods)—whether that putative information comes (or those data come) in fact from P or from some other source.

If Principle A is valid, then demon-hypotheses run counter to the PUI. For there will be no (logically) possible case where we will be rationally warranted or justified in believing any new explanation the demon or any other source of purported information gives us of the demon's motives for or methods of giving us sense experiences. Nor will there be any possible case where we are justified in trusting data that are *not* explicitly informative about the demon as giving us clues as to the proper explanation of his motives and methods. And so the hypothesis of the demon is inquiry-limiting for us as an explanation of the sort of sense experience we have had up till now. The argument of the present section, therefore, gives us reason to think demon hypotheses are inquiry-limiting, and thus shows that such hypotheses are scientifically unacceptable for us—assuming that the PUI is valid.

II

But do all demon hypotheses that might be put forward to explain our sensory experiences conflict with the PUI? This is, of course, true of the sort of demon hypotheses we have been considering, which straightforwardly posit a demon who supplies sense experiences for certain reasons and by certain means (which in turn exist and function as they do because . . ., etc.). But consider the sort of sceptical hypothesis that says that there is a demon who (in the absence of an external, physical world) supplies us with experiences of the sort we have for reason r and by means m and who will in fact soon reveal himself and his illusion-mongering to us, and then will truthfully tell us as much as we want to know in explanation of his motives and methods for giving us sense experiences. Someone might want to claim that accepting this hypothesis does not in any obvious way ensure the impossibility of our gaining more and more warranted true explanatory beliefs about the motives and methods of the demon, or thus about our sense experiences. For our accepting such an hypothesis would seem to *commit us to believing* that we probably *will* gain more and more warranted true explanatory beliefs about these matters *from the demon*. And surely in some logically possible circumstances it would be reasonable to accept such an hypothesis and so to believe that we will get more and more warranted true explanatory beliefs about our experiences from the demon. And then, if the demon proceeds to give us putative information about his motives and methods, we will presumably be justified in believing what he says, so that, if what he says is true, we will have obtained warranted true explanations about our experience.

This whole argument rests on the assumption that the above hypothesis could in certain circumstances be rationally warranted. And this assumption is, I think, extremely doubtful. For the very things that make it unreasonable for one to believe any putative explanatory information one gets about the demon if one is in the situation described in Principle A would, I believe, make it unreasonable ever to believe the above hypothesis. In particular, any source of putative information to the effect that the demon would soon make truthful revelations about himself would be open to reasonable mistrust that could not be allayed by independent verification of its reliability (or veracity). So I think that if Principle A is valid, the hypothesis currently under consideration is inquiry-limiting. Furthermore, even if this hypothesis is not inquiry-limiting, and unacceptable for that reason, there is another principle that immediately recommends itself as a clear means of ruling it out as (scientifically) unacceptable.

This principle, Principle B, says: it is (scientifically) unreasonable to hypothesize (accept an hypothesis to the effect) that something has acted or operated one way in the past, but will act or operate in a different way in the future, unless one has a definite reason that justifies thinking this change will occur. This seems to be a valid methodological scientific principle, and one that scientists in fact adhere to. The hypothesis of a demon who has been supplying us with illusory sense experiences without giving us any indication of his motives and methods and later will communicate with us and give us putative information about his motives and methods clearly offends against B. Right now we have no definite reason to think that such a change will occur in the demon, if he exists. And so the hypothesis in question can be ruled out as (scientifically) unacceptable.

Consider next the hypothesis of a demon who (in the absence of an external world) gives us illusory sense experiences for motives r and by means m, and is such that, if he communicates with us directly and overtly about his motives and means, he never tells anything but the truth about them. This hypothesis is inquiry-limiting if the hypothesis just considered is inquiry-limiting; but unlike that hypothesis, the hypothesis that we are now considering does not contravene Principle B. For it does not say that the demon, who has not informed us of his motives and methods in the past, will do so in the future; it only leaves open that possibility. The hypothesis we are considering clearly does, however, offend against another principle, Principle C, which runs: it is (scientifically) unreasonable to hypothesize that something acts or operates in one way if certain conditions or circumstances obtain and in another way if other conditions or circumstances obtain, unless one has a definite reason that justifies belief in such a difference. The present hypothesis offends against C, because it is committed to saying that the demon has not been truthfully self-revealing in the circumstances that have obtained up until now, but will be truthfully self-revealing if circumstances arise in which he explicitly makes his presence known and gives us putative information about himself. And at present we have *no* justification for thinking that a demon will act thus differently in these different circumstances.[1] Principle C, like Principle B, seems to be a valid principle of rational scientific inquiry, one to which scientists implicitly adhere in their inquiries. We often do postulate differences in the way a given thing acts, will act, or is disposed to act, in different circumstances, but, when we do, it is always because we think we have some particular positive reason that justifies thinking these differences obtain. Thus, if I know that my dog drinks a great deal of water when he is in New Haven and have no definite reason to think he will act differently if he is in Hartford, it is surely unreasonable for me to believe that he will drink *very little* water if and when he goes to Hartford.

We have developed principles, therefore, that will, I think, suffice to show the unreasonableness and unacceptability, from a scientific standpoint, of any demon hypothesis.[2] But what about the hypothesis of chance or accident as the null-explanation of our sense experiences? I think that, if we construe the notion of 'explanation' used in our definition of inquiry-limitingness broadly enough so that it applies to the hypothesis of chance or

[1] The fact that the demon will have to be truthfully self-revealing *about his own existence* if he communicates with us explicitly does not *justify* believing that, even though he has not been truthfully self-revealing so far, he will be if and when he communicates explicitly and overtly about his motives and methods, for the same reason that it does not *justify* belief in what the demon says about his motives and methods on the part of one who has been given illusions by the demon (and no indication of the demon's doings), has then been informed of this illusion-making, and is currently being told about the demon's motives and methods by the demon himself. And that reason is encapsulated in Principle A, and in the argument that preceded and justified the introduction of that principle.

[2] One might try to patch up the hypothesis that the demon will be truthfully self-revealing if he communicates with us although he has been totally uninformative up till now, so that it does not offend against Principle C, by assuming as a further part of that hypothesis some reason to think, e.g. that the demon will be willing to reveal his true nature if and when he communicates with us directly, even though he has been anxious to hide that true nature at all times up to the present. We might hypothesize, for example, that a demon-superior has commanded him to stay hidden from us until now, but to say only true things if he wants to communicate openly with us in the future. But one cannot, by building into an hypothesis that posits certain differences an *assumption* as to

accident, i.e. to null-explanations, then the hypothesis that the existence, nature and order of our sense experiences is a matter of mere chance or accident is inquiry-limiting as an explanation of our having the sort of sense experiences we do. (And if one wishes to insist that null-explanations are *not* explanations, we can use the notion of an 'explanatory account', rather than that of an 'explanation', in our definition of inquiry-limitingness, without in any way affecting the scientific relevance of the notion of inquiry-limitingness. Since the hypothesis that a given phenomenon is a mere accident is surely in some sense an explanatory account of that phenomenon, we will be able to say that the hypothesis of chance or accident is inquiry-limiting (as an explanatory account of our experience).) The hypothesis of chance is inquiry-limiting because anyone who at some time *t* accepts such an explanation (or explanatory account) of his experiences and holds it to be the best . . ., makes it impossible for himself to gain more and more warranted *true* explanatory beliefs about his experiences (if there are any to be got) for as long as he accepts that explanation in the manner indicated. Thus if one accepts the hypothesis of chance with regard to a given phenomenon, and that phenomenon *has* an explanation, one believes a falsehood; and if one accepts a positive (non-null) explanation of that phenomenon, and that phenomenon has *no* explanation, then one will also be believing a falsehood. But, of course, if there is an explanation of the phenomenon in question, there may be true explanations of that explanation, and so on *ad indefinitum*, and one bars oneself from believing these truths by accepting the hypothesis of chance in a consistent way. So it would seem to be more undesirable scientifically to accept the null-explanation of chance than to accept positive explanations, other things being equal, because of the inquiry-limitingness of the former.

But note one very important fact. If one accepts the hypothesis of chance with regard, say, to one's experiences, one may bar the possibility of one's believing indefinitely many true explanations, but one is also ensuring that one will make *no further mistakes* in explaining the nature of one's experiences (as long as one holds to

the reason for those differences, actually create a *reason* for believing in those differences. We have in fact no reason to think that the demon, if he exists, is under orders from a demon-superior, and so have no reason to posit the differences posited in the hypothesis under consideration. And any hypothesis that posits such differences offends against C, no matter what assumptions we tack on to it, as long as such a reason does not exist.

the hypothesis in a consistent manner). So by 'explaining' our experiences via the hypothesis of chance or accident, one achieves or ensures one scientific goal (the avoidance of further mistaken explanations) at the expense of another (the obtaining of true explanations). And if these goals are equally important from the standpoint of science, then there is nothing (on balance) wrong with or undesirable about the hypothesis of chance from that standpoint, at least as far as *we* have shown *here*.

But are they equally important? The very fact of an existent enterprise of science that makes it its business to explain various phenomena shows, I think, that they are not. For, in attempting to explain the nature of various things, scientists frequently (tentatively) accept (or find plausible or just test) hypotheses that they later reject as faulty. Indeed, is there any *a priori* guarantee that science *qua* science, or scientists *qua* scientists, will be involved more with truth than with error in the long-run process of trying to explain various phenomena? If anything, the contrary would seem to be much more likely. But, then, if truth were no more important for scientists than avoiding falsehood, would it not be perfectly reasonable for the scientist to give up trying to explain things altogether? For this would assure his freedom from erroneous explanations at the same time that it ensured his lacking true explanations of various phenomena. But scientists would never give up explanatory science for this sort of reason; and that is, I think, because they value or emphasize the pursuit and attainment of truth much more than the avoidance of error. In other words, since scientists would not be willing to give up the pursuit and (possible) future attainment of indefinitely many explanatory truths in favour of the future avoidance of explanatory error, they would seem to be committed to the greater value and importance of the former as a goal of science. And, in that case, there really is something wrong with accepting inquiry-limiting hypotheses like that of chance or accident (or like the inquiry-limiting demon hypotheses examined earlier), even though such hypotheses prevent certain mistakes if held to in a consistent and rational manner. And we need only maintain the claim that truth and its pursuit are more important for one who seeks a scientific explanation of things (and for the enterprise of science in general) than is the eschewing of error, a claim implicitly accepted by scientists, in order to show that this is so.[1]

[1] Cf. James's 'The Will to Believe', in *Essays in Pragmatism*, p. 99 ff.

Thus if the PUI is valid, the following Principle D seems also to be valid: it is (scientifically) unreasonable to believe that a given phenomenon has no explanation, unless one has very strong reason for thinking so, and so unless other things are *not* equal. D is a principle that scientists do in fact adhere to; scientists never assume there is no explanation for a phenomenon unless they have very definite and overpowering reasons to do so. Indeed, D recommends itself as valid even independently of its justification via the PUI. Anyone who undertakes the *scientific* investigation of some phenomenon *x* in a rational manner will, I think, tend to assume that *x* has some explanation, and will conclude that it cannot be explained only as a last resort or for overwhelming methodological reasons.[1] It would seem, then, to be unreasonable from a scientific standpoint to accept a null-explanation of our experiences, unless all the other explanations of those experiences we had considered had been shown to be implausible or in some other way unacceptable. (And it should be clear that D and the PUI also enable us to eliminate hypotheses that explain the demon's behaviour in terms of certain motives and methods, but claim that those motives and methods cannot themselves be explained.)

The PUI and Principles A, B, C and D are, I think, sufficient to cast grave doubt on the scientific acceptability of any explanation of our particular sense experiences that does not posit an external world. We have seen reason to think that demon hypotheses are inquiry-limiting, and thus unacceptable *other things being equal*. But are other things equal? A doubter might, at this point, argue as follows. It is scientifically unreasonable, perhaps, to do something if one (reasonably believes that one) is thereby *ensuring* the impossibility of attaining some intrinsic goal of science, but this is only true when the attainment of that goal is *not already* im-

---

[1] For support of Principle D see A. Kaplan's *The Conduct of Inquiry*, San Francisco: Chandler, 1964, pp. 351–4. One kind of situation in which it might be reasonable for methodological reasons to think certain facts or phenomena could not be further explained would be one in which physicists discovered that all physical phenomena could very neatly be explained in terms of a unified set of laws governing the behaviour of one 'fundamental' kind of particle. (In fact, many elementary particle physicists are seeking or hoping to find laws of just this kind.) In such a situation, considerations of simplicity and/or elegance might dictate the assumption that the laws one had arrived at were ultimate, i.e. incapable of further explanation. Cf. S. Morgenbesser's 'Explanation and Prediction', in B. Baumrin (ed.), *Philosophy of Science: the Delaware Seminar*, vol. 1, N. Y.: John Wiley, 1963, pp. 53 ff.

possible. For, if the attainment of that goal *is* already impossible, then one is not in any way frustrating scientific purposes *by one's act*. But it already *is* impossible, it might be claimed, ever to have any *warranted* true explanatory beliefs about one's sense experiences (or about certain *explanantia* of those experiences). So accepting demon-hypotheses does not frustrate our scientific endeavours, despite our claims earlier to the contrary. And in that case other things are not equal, and there is nothing wrong, from a scientific standpoint, with accepting (certain) demon-hypotheses.

I do not think, however, that this gambit will really work. For one thing, it is a mistake to think that it is never unreasonable to do something that one reasonably believes will *ensure* the impossibility of doing what one wishes to do *if doing that latter thing is already impossible*. If doing a thing x is *in fact* impossible, but one does not *know for certain* that it is, then it surely *is* unreasonable to do y, if one realizes that by doing y one is ensuring the impossibility of doing x and realizes that one wants to do x. Thus, even if it is in fact impossible to obtain *more and more warranted* true explanatory beliefs about one's experiences (or even to obtain *any* warranted explanations of those experiences, or of anything else, for that matter), as long as we do not know for certain that this is so, it is scientifically unreasonable to accept inquiry-limiting demon-explanations of our experiences. And, even if we do not have the right, in an enterprise such as ours, to assume the possibility of more and more warranted true explanations about our experiences, I think we *can* claim that we do not *know for certain* that such explanations are impossible. For, if we examine our sensory (and memory) evidence or any other evidence we have reason to think we have, and do so in a rational way, we are able to find no conclusive reason or argument for thinking, e.g. that it is impossible to get more and more warranted true explanatory beliefs about our experiences, if there is an external world causing them, or for thinking that it is impossible for external entities to cause those experiences. Of course, if we assume the validity of certain sceptical principles or conclusions, such an argument will, presumably, be forthcoming. But in the present work we are only assuming principles that recommend themselves as valid from the point of view of scientific or other rational inquiry. Sceptical principles (e.g. the blatant claim that warranted explanations are impossible) do not recommend themselves to rational scientific explanatory thinking and are thus not being *assumed* by us here. And, furthermore, one surely does not *assume* sceptical principles in an attempt to undermine scepticism of the sort we are making.

We have no way, then, given our present evidence, to show that we could not obtain warranted true explanatory beliefs about the causes of our sense experiences if those experiences were caused by physical processes, events, etc.[1] And so we have no way to *show* that more and more warranted true explanations of our experiences are impossible. But, then, we do not *know for certain* that such explanations of our experiences are impossible, for we surely cannot reasonably claim to know for certain of this impossibility by intuition, or hunch, or some sort of 'illative sense'. And in that case, it is unreasonable for us as scientists to accept inquiry-limiting sceptical demon-hypotheses. For in doing so we have every reason to believe that we *may well* be *making* it impossible, and that we are *definitely ensuring* that it is impossible, for us to accomplish something that as scientists we wish to accomplish.

Of course, if we explain our experience in terms of the external world, we *may* be making warranted *true* explanatory beliefs about our experiences impossible, *if* in fact the demon is causing them. But we have no argument to show that accepting the external world as an explanation of our experiences *ensures* the impossibility of warranted. . . . And we *have* provided such an argument with respect to various demon-hypotheses. And this makes a great difference with respect to the acceptability of the two sorts of hypotheses. For consider a situation where there are two buttons and where one reasonably believes that if one does not push a button, death by explosion is unavoidable, but that one of the two

---

[1] Making this claim, and others like it, involves us in assuming that we are capable of rationally considering and weighing evidence. But anyone who seeks to justify a certain explanation of a phenomenon presupposes his own ability rationally to consider and weigh evidence. Similarly, anyone who seeks to justify a conclusion via an argument presupposes his own ability to see the rational validity of the principles of inference he uses and the soundness of his argument. Since we are in the present work attempting to justify a certain explanation of a phenomenon via an argument, we too are involved in these presuppositions, which are presuppositions every scientist has frequently to make. It would, of course, be impossible to justify those presuppositions via an argument. Such an argument would inevitably be circular, as circular as attempts to justify induction inductively. Since these presuppositions, or assumptions, are as fundamental to the doing of science as any principles of induction, we are justified in accepting them in our present enterprise, which seeks to base itself on principles of scientific methodology and thought.

buttons may be such that, if one pushes it and it alone, one may prevent this catastrophe. Then, if one does not push a button, it is reasonable for one to believe that one is *ensuring* one's own death, and also to believe that one may be making it impossible to go on living (depending on whether pushing one of the buttons would be effective). But, if one pushes one of the buttons, it is not reasonable to believe that one is ensuring one's death (because for all one knows, pushing the button in question may save one's life); it is only reasonable to believe that one *may* be making it impossible for oneself to go on living (because the other button was the one to push in order to prevent an explosion). And in this situation, obviously, the reasonable thing to do is to push a button, and not to do nothing. Similarly, when we accept the external world, or the demon, we may be making true explanatory beliefs impossible (depending on what or who is in fact causing our experience). But we have produced a reason to think that accepting the demon ensures the impossibility of gaining warranted true explanatory beliefs about our experience, but no such reason with respect to the hypothesis of an external world.

We thus have reason to reject sceptical demon-hypotheses, as well as the hypothesis of chance, as explanatory accounts of our experience. Of course, if the demon who supplies us with experiences had in the past always let us know of his existence in some way (rather than hiding himself from us, as he has done up to now, if he exists), Principle A would not apply and we could not, I think, show that sceptical demon-hypotheses about our experience were inquiry-limiting. And, presumably, in such a case it would be reasonable to believe our experience had been supplied by a demon. Or if a demon-voice began *now* to speak 'in' our experience, we would have some reason, perhaps good reason, to prefer certain inquiry-limiting demon-hypotheses to the hypothesis of an external world. In such a situation, other things (besides inquiry-limitingness) would *not* be equal inasmuch as there would be something definitely wrong with accepting the hypothesis of an external world: it would not plausibly account for all the facts of our experience. But as things stand at present, we have not heard any demon-voice or seen any demon-wonders worked, so that other things (besides inquiry-limitingness) *are* equal as between the hypothesis of an external world and inquiry-limiting demon-hypotheses. (Unless, of course, there are *other* things wrong with demon-hypotheses that we have not mentioned.) And, in that case, it is unreasonable for us now to explain our sense experiences in terms of chance or a demon (and at the same time deny the existence of the external world), given the existence of definite scientific methodological reasons for not accepting such sceptical explanatory hypotheses about our experiences and given the existence of alternative hypotheses (positing an external world) which, after rational consideration of our evidence, we can see no reason to think to be inquiry-limiting, or otherwise unacceptable, on the basis of the principles we have proposed, or, indeed, on the basis of any other valid principles of scientific, or rational, thought. It would seem, then, that the hypothesis of some sort of external world is more scientifically acceptable and reasonable than any sceptical hypotheses that imply the non-existence of such a world, as a means of (at least) partly explaining our having the kind of sense experiences we have every reason to think we have. And, if it has been shown that all alternatives to a given explanatory hypothesis about certain data are in some way scientifically unacceptable,[1] and nothing has been found wrong with the hypothesis itself after rational consideration of it in the light of one's evidence, and if one is justified in believing that the data one is trying to explain do exist, then it is scientifically reasonable for one to accept the hypothesis (believe it) at least tentatively. Thus, I think we have shown that it is scientifically reasonable to have tentative belief in an external world (as part of the explanation of our having the sorts of sense experiences we do),

---

[1] One sort of hypothesis we have not yet eliminated is the sort that says that it is unconscious ideas or mental processes *of our own* that cause our experiences. Descartes mentions something like this sort of hypothesis in the *Second Meditation*. I think such hypotheses could be eliminated in the way we have eliminated sceptical demon-hypotheses. (On this point, and others in the present section, I am indebted to discussion with Prof. R. Shope.) We have also not eliminated any *non-sceptical* demon-hypotheses about our experience, e.g. that there is an external world but that a demon with certain motives *r* and methods *m* is giving us our sense experiences. Such hypotheses are, I think, inquiry-limiting, but they cannot be shown to be so via Principle A, since they do not entail that the demon made it appear as if there were certain things when there were no such things. But, if a demon tells us he is the source of our experiences, but that there are objects of the kind there appear to be, one will wonder why he bothers giving us experiences 'of' objects that already exist and one will have no means of independently checking on what he says (of finding out, for example, that the experiences he gave us really were not illusory) So, even if there *are* such objects as he says, and he is *not* creating illusions, we have no more reason to trust him than if there *were no* such objects and he *were* creating illusions, and so cannot get warranted explanations from him. So surely non-sceptical demon-hypotheses are inquiry-limiting as explanations of our experiences.

and have done so by the use of valid scientific methodological principles.

Note that we have so far only shown the *scientific* reasonableness of tentative belief in an external world, not the *epistemic* reasonableness (i.e. *rational* justifiedness) of such belief. However, this latter might be argued in the same way we have conducted our whole argument up to now, that is, by appeal to principles that are presupposed or assumed in scientific inquiry and explanation. For it is surely a principle of scientific thinking accepted by scientists of every kind that one who investigates, accepts, and rejects beliefs and explanations in accordance with valid scientific principles and standards is rationally justified or warranted in so doing. Scientists generally assume that their ways of and standards for investigating phenomena are rational (epistemically reasonable) ones—even if not the only rational (epistemically reasonable) ones. It is, then, an accepted principle of scientific thought that beliefs and explanations that it is scientifically reasonable to accept are, at least in the absence of other sorts of epistemic reasons to the contrary,[1] epistemically reasonable, i.e. beliefs and explanations that one is rationally warranted or justified in accepting. It would seem then that we can make use of principles of scientific thought, not only to show the scientific reasonableness of belief in an external world, but also to show that such belief is rational in general.

If someone were to question the rationality or epistemic reasonableness of accepting what is scientifically reasonable, however, the following further points could be made. The only half-way plausible definition of epistemic reasonableness that has, as far as I know, been made is that of Chisholm, who defines 'p is epistemically reasonable in believing q' as 'if p were a rational being, and if his concerns were purely intellectual, it would be reasonable (i.e. a good thing) for him to believe q'.[2] The point of this definition is to separate aesthetic, moral or religious, etc. reasons for believing something from intellectual ones. What is *epistemically* reasonable can be justified as reasonable from the point of view of strictly intellectual considerations. But which intellectual considerations? What if a man has only one intellectual or theoretical concern, say, the desire to understand the nature of comets, and no non-intellectual or non-theoretical concerns at all?

---

[1] See Ch. 6 below for a discussion of some such possible reasons.
[2] *Theory of Knowledge*, p. 21 f.

He might be rational too, and thus be the kind of man mentioned in Chisholm's definition. But, if he were given some good evidence for the existence of dinosaurs, it might not be reasonable (a good thing) for him to believe in the existence of dinosaurs *solely on the basis of his narrow intellectual concerns.* And yet surely it might be epistemically reasonable for him to believe in dinosaurs in such a situation, because in that situation it would be reasonable (a good thing) for someone whose concerns or interests were those of *intellectual understanding in general* to believe in dinosaurs. There will, therefore, be counter-examples to Chisholm's definition unless one understands 'his concerns were purely intellectual' to mean 'his concerns were those of intellectual (or theoretical) understanding and knowledge *in general,* and included no other concerns or interests'. Thus understood, Chisholm's definition seems plausible. And if it is, we can use the argument hitherto given in this chapter to show the epistemic reasonableness of tentative belief in an external world. For our previous argument presupposed only the intellectual (or theoretical) concerns of science. The PUI, for example, presupposes only the strictly intellectual concern for or interest in further and further explanations of phenomena. Indeed, the scientific concern with explaining things in general is a purely intellectual one. Inasmuch as we have shown that people with such intellectual scientific concerns are justified from the point of view of those concerns in believing in an external world on a tentative basis, we have shown that people whose sole interests are those (and only those) of intellectual understanding and knowledge in general would be reasonable in believing tentatively in an external world—in the absence of any other intellectual interests or concerns that are frustrated by such belief. Inasmuch as rational scrutiny seems to provide us with no reason to think we *are* frustrating any other intellectual interest when we believe tentatively in an external world, our argument shows, I think, that it is *epistemically* reasonable to have tentative belief in an external world. Of course, one might then ask why it is reasonable to have all the interests and goals of intellectual understanding, or why one should accept or reject beliefs in the way that someone with solely intellectual interests would do so. After all, we are men, not pure intellects, and as such often have interests and concerns that we emphasize far more than any of our strictly intellectual interests. And indeed there is a sense of 'justified' in which one may be justified in believing something though it is not scientifically or in any other way epistemically reasonable to do so. As Firth has quite convincingly argued, it may well be that some people are justified in having (and ought to have) certain religious or moral beliefs, even though those beliefs are not and cannot be scientifically or rationally justified.[1] Thus it is by no means clear that we should accept and reject beliefs in the way that a purely theoretical rational being would.

Nor is it my purpose here to show that tentative belief in an external world (or in certain things about that world) is justified *ueberhaupt*, all things considered. Philosophers who have been interested in combatting scepticism have generally been interested *just* in showing that there are rational or epistemic reasons for rejecting scepticism and believing in an external physical world. Or they have at least felt that showing this was the most important part of overcoming scepticism. It is my purpose here, similarly, simply to show that belief in the external world can be rationally justified, can be shown to be reasonable for one who seeks purely disinterested intellectual understanding and knowledge of the nature of things. Showing this is clearly of great epistemological importance, and I shall be quite content if I can do so.

III

Up to now I have been talking about actual scientific practice and about what 'we' experience and have reason to think, in order to point up the validity of the principles I have used to show the (epistemic) reasonableness of believing in an external world. But one does not need to assume that there is an external world or that there are other persons in order to see the validity of these principles. And so we need not beg the very question at issue here by using as premises in our argument for the reasonableness of belief in an external world (on which our argument for the reasonableness of belief in other minds will eventually depend) principles that can only be shown or seen to be true or warranted if one already assumes (the reasonableness of belief in) an external world or other minds.

Of course, it is and has been helpful, in order to point up the

---

[1] 'Chisholm and the Ethics of Belief', *Phil. Review*, 68, 1959, pp. 493–506. Also 'Ultimate Evidence', in Swartz, ed., *op. cit.*, p. 489 f.

validity of these principles, to refer to actual scientific practice and thus to the external world. But one can see their validity, I think, merely on the basis of the fact that one has had certain sense experiences of what seemed to be the activities of scientists in a real external world. Upon having such experiences one can see that certain principles of scientific inquiry make good sense and others do not, and if one then comes to wonder whether the external world and the on-going enterprise of science really exist, or even to believe that they do not, that will presumably not cause one to doubt that, *if* there is (were) a physical world with scientific activities going on within it, it is (would be) rational for scientists to adhere to those principles. Thus, while we assume the existence of a physical world with scientific activities occurring within it, the principles proposed in this paper come to recommend themselves as valid; and when and if we doubt the existence of such a world, we will still be able to recognize those principles as valid for scientific enterprise, *if* it exists, for any possible (rational) scientific enterprise whose aims are those of science in general. For, I wish to claim, those principles will seem intuitively clear and reasonable to those who consider them carefully and thoughtfully.[1] That is not to say that those principles are known for certain to be true. For all I am claiming, they might lose their plausibility and intuitive appeal for us or for others in the light of future knowledge. But this *possibility* is no reason for not accepting these principles now or for thinking that they are not now rationally warranted for us, even if it may mean that these principles are not certain or indubitable. Since, therefore, each of us can be rationally justified in believing the principles proposed in this chapter independently of any assumptions about the (reasonableness of belief in an) external world or scientific enterprise going on within it, it is possible for each of us to construct for himself a sound argument, making use of these principles and of facts about his own sense or

[1] My use of principles that I claim are intuitively clear and plausible 'truths of reason' and stand in need of no defence through argument or evidence relies on Aristotle's view (*Posterior Analytics*, Book I, ch. 1 and 2; Book II, ch. 19) that there is a need for unreasoned but intuitively reasonable first principles in any theoretical discipline. Furthermore, in both *Human Knowledge* and in *The Problems of Philosophy*, Russell has argued quite convincingly that justification for belief in an external world or in the orderliness of nature rests on *a priori* principles not susceptible of proof that one is justified in accepting. I do not think anyone has ever shown that there is something wrong or even doubtful about principles that cannot be proved or that we can avoid such principles in philosophy or in any other theoretical discipline.

outer experience, for the scientific and epistemic reasonableness of believing in an external world.

Of course, I am still talking about 'us', about what 'we' can prove. But this is only a rhetorical device that makes for easy exposition of the points I am trying to make; and it can be used without begging any questions, because such use in no way affects the fact that the present chapter presents any reader who understands it with the means of arguing for the reasonableness of the claim or hypothesis that an external world exists and is responsible for his sense experiences *without* talking about 'us' or making any sorts of assumptions about other people. The principles we have adopted can be adopted by rational beings in the solitude of their own thoughts to argue in the manner indicated here for the existence of an external world, and to do so without begging any questions.

In the present chapter we have not answered every possible form of sceptical doubt about the external world. For an entrenched sceptic might question the principles we have proposed, or even various of our assumptions about our immediate sense experience. (Actually we are only assuming the rational warrantedness of various claims about such experience, but this too could be called into question by the sceptic.) The fact that a sceptic can call something into question, however, does not entail that the thing in question cannot reasonably be believed. And I would want just to state that the assumptions made here *are* rationally justified, even if a sceptic might not think so. There is one result of the argument of the present chapter, furthermore, that even a sceptic would have to accept (if the argument we have given is valid), namely, that scepticism about the external world *reduces* to scepticism about certain aspects of scientific and other forms of rationality. One can be sceptical about the existence of the external world only if one is also sceptical about the principles I have put forward or about the reasonableness of believing in the data they are used to interpret or about the validity of my argument.

Up to now I have been assuming that we wish to find the best explanation of the sense experiences we have had up to now. I have thus been assuming the existence of experiences in the past, and since one needs to assume the validity of memory to justify this assumption, we have implicitly relied on the validity of memory, on the belief that our purported memories of past sensory events,

qualities, etc. are generally reliable. Indeed the problem of the
external world is frequently set up with the tacit assumption of the
validity of memory. But it need not be. We need assume only a
specious present (or what C. I. Lewis aptly calls an 'epistemological present')[1] in which we have certain memory impressions about
the past nature of our sense experience and certain sense experiences (that seem to be 'of' objects in an external world).[2]
However, the principles we have proposed can be used by each of
us to eliminate all but the hypothesis of an external world as
epistemically reasonable explanations of his present sense experiences and memory impressions. For, whether or not the
demon has supplied us with 'false' memory impressions of certain
sense experiences, the demon is an extraordinary creator of
complete and detailed illusions and totally secretive and uninformative about his illusion-mongering, and so, because of the
validity of Principle A, we will have no chance of gaining more
and more warranted explanatory beliefs about his motives and
methods. And whether the demon is creating illusions now for the
first time, or has done so in the past, it still offends against Principles B and/or C to hypothesize that he will be truthfully self-
revealing in the future if or when he communicates with us openly
in the future. Thus the validity of memory need not be assumed in
order to prove the reasonableness of the hypothesis of an external
world. Our whole argument can be made to rest on assumptions
about the reasonableness of certain claims or beliefs about one's
present sense experiences and memory impressions.

It is interesting to note that the principles adopted here can
actually be used to show the reasonableness of certain claims
about the past and the reasonableness of trusting certain memory
impressions. For consider the attempt to explain our current sense
experiences and memory impressions in terms of an hypothesis
that entails that the physical world sprang into existence five
minutes ago 'complete with memories and records'. Such an
hypothesis would say either that this springing into existence had

[1] *Analysis of Knowledge and Valuation*, p. 331 f.
[2] One might object that we cannot assume just a specious present and also
assume that it looks as if we are seeing a red box, e.g. because it cannot look as
if there is a box unless we have the concept of a box and unless we have the
ability to see something *as* a box, and because the possession of this concept and
this ability logically entails *past* experience. But this latter assumption, at the
very least, is very implausible in the light of Unger's 'On Experience and the
Development of the Understanding'.

no cause and came about by accident, or that some demon or spirit brought it about. The former alternative offends against Principle D and the PUI. And the hypothesis of a demon who five minutes ago brought the world into existence and gave us the memory impressions we have (or most of them) can be formulated in various ways, but will, in any of those formulations, offend against B or C or the PUI, because it involves the assumption that the demon has been an extraordinarily secretive illusion-monger, etc. For all of us have memory impressions of having had certain sense experiences ('of' external objects) more than five minutes ago. And, if a demon has given us these memory impressions and they are not veridical (because we were not having those sorts of experiences more than five minutes ago), then he is a creator of monstrous memory-illusions. On the other hand, if they are veridical, the demon will also have been a creator of monstrous illusions, since he will have made it appear to us (more than five minutes ago) as if there were external objects when in fact there were none. Thus, on any formulation, the hypothesis that the external world is only five minutes old could be shown to be unreasonable via the principles proposed and used in the present chapter. We are left, then, with the hypotheses that there is no external world at all, or that the external world is more than five minutes old, and since the former can be eliminated by our principles, those principles can be used to justify the claim that the external physical world is more than five minutes (or even more than five years) old as part of the best explanation of our present sense experiences and memory impressions, and thus to justify at least this one claim about the past.[1] Furthermore, we all

[1] We could show the reasonableness of believing in the past existence of an external world by an argument different from that just used, if we made use of a Principle C' very similar to C that runs: it is scientifically and epistemically unreasonable to hypothesize that something exists at one time but does not exist at another, unless one has a definite reason that justifies thinking so. Then since we have shown the reasonableness of belief in the external world's present existence, and have no definite reason that justifies thinking it did not exist more than five minutes ago, we could show the greater reasonableness of thinking that the world did exist five minutes ago than that it didn't. Actually, however, we haven't really even shown the reasonableness of believing in the *present* existence of the world. All we have shown is that (it is reasonable to believe that) something physical caused our present sense and memory experiences; but perhaps that physical something went out of existence long before the sensory effect of it took place. However, given that something physical has existed at some time in the past and was the cause of our present sense experiences and memory impressions, we can again use C' to argue that something physical exists at present too (as well as five minutes ago).

have memory impressions of there having been certain sorts of physical objects more than five minutes ago, and so of there having been a physical world more than five minutes ago. Thus we have shown the reasonableness of trusting at least one of our memory impressions, and thereby shown the falsity of that sort of scepticism that claims that it is impossible to have warranted beliefs about the past and unreasonable ever to trust our memories, i.e. our memory beliefs or our memory impressions.[1]

Almost every philosopher who has considered the matter has held that any attempt to justify certain memory beliefs or certain claims about the past *inductively* must of necessity rely on premises about the past and thereby presuppose that we can sometimes trust our memories and have reasonable beliefs about the past. Thus they have believed that any attempt to overcome (general) scepticism about the past or about the validity of memory on an inductive basis is bound to be circular and question-begging.[2] And, indeed, it is obviously futile to argue that it is epistemically reasonable, at least sometimes, to have certain beliefs about the past (or to trust one's own memory) because in the past it was reasonable to do so, or because one's present beliefs and memory impressions about the past cohere with those one had in the past, or with certain present records that accurately reflect what happened in the past. But if the argument of the present chapter is correct, it *is* possible to give some sort of sound inductive argument against scepticism about the past and about the validity of memory. For (most of) the principles we have employed are surely in some sense inductive ones,[3] and the argument we have based on those principles does show the reasonableness of belief in the past

---

[1] Note that our argument against scepticism about memory and about the past in no way begs any questions about the demon, and thus has a genuine claim to be a philosophically adequate argument against such scepticism, according to the standards of adequacy proposed in the Introduction. This is not, however, true of Coherence-type justifications of memory-beliefs and beliefs about the past (see, e.g. R. Brandt's 'The Epistemological Status of Memory Beliefs', *Phil. Review*, 64, 1955, pp. 78–95) or of the sort of justification for such beliefs offered by Chisholm, *op. cit.*, ch. 3.

Note too that memory impressions are not the same as memory beliefs. I can seem to remember doing something (memory impression) that I know I did not do (memory belief).

[2] Examples of such philosophers are J. Bennett (*op. cit.*, p. 205), S. Shoemaker ('Memory', in Edwards (ed.), *The Encyclopedia of Philosophy*, N. Y.: Macmillan, 1967, vol. 5, p. 273), and C. I. Lewis (*Analysis of Knowledge*, ch. 11).

[3] They are inductive principles in a broad sense of the term. For an example of such use of 'inductive' see R. B. Braithwaite's *Scientific Explanation*, Cam-

existence of the external world and thus of trusting our memory belief (or impression) that there was an external world more than five minutes ago. Total scepticism about the past and about the validity of memory can, therefore, be undermined via inductive reasoning, but it is inductive reasoning of a sort different from any used previously in attempting to overcome these forms of scepticism. (In Chapter 3, furthermore, we shall use certain further inductive principles, as well as some already used, to argue for the reasonableness of trusting one's memory *in general*, not just in the one case mentioned in the present chapter.)

If the argument of the present chapter is a sound one, each of us can justify his believing in an external world, in the past existence of such a world, and in the (at least) occasional trustworthiness of memory, on the basis of reasonable assumptions about experience and reasonable principles of rational thought and inquiry. Someone might, however, question the soundness of our whole technique of argumentation on the grounds that our argument rests on premises that are less certain, less warranted, than the claims (e.g. that there is something physical) that they are used to establish. But an argument for a conclusion c based on premises x, y, and z can be sound, even if c is in fact more warranted than any of x, y, and z, as long as one can be warranted in assuming x, y, and z each independently of the assumption of c. And this, I think, is true of the argument given here for the external world, etc. Thus what we have done in this chapter perhaps resembles what Whitehead and Russell attempted to do in *Principia Mathematica*, where an attempt was made to show that two and two make four on the basis of premises some of which were less warranted than that conclusion.

bridge, 1953, p. 257. There is, of course, a narrow sense of the term in which the method of hypothesis, abduction, is not inductive, and in this narrow sense I have not given an inductive vindication of memory and of claims about the past.

CHAPTER 3

THE NATURE OF THE EXTERNAL
WORLD

In the last chapter, I argued that the 'hypothesis' of an external world is (and can be shown by any person for himself to be) superior to sceptical hypotheses that deny the existence of such a world. I argued that it was reasonable to believe (at least tentatively) in the existence of an external physical world (as the cause of our sense experiences and memory impressions), given the argument that was provided, but I did not attempt to show that we have any reason to think that the external world is anything like the way we think it is or the way it visually, tactually, etc., appears to us to be. That is because I in no way attempted to deal with and overcome certain forms of scepticism which call into question the veridicalness of our sense experiences and memory impressions, and thereby deny the accuracy and correctness of our putative information about the kinds of objects and events there are and have been around us.

We have not, for example, dealt with the sort of scepticism that claims we have no reason to believe we are not presently, or even always, dreaming. And, if we are dreaming, then our outer experiences and memory impressions of things may bear no relation to reality, to the way things are in the external world; they may be (almost) all illusory. For there is no logical impossibility in there being dreams of fields and rivers, dogs and people, etc., caused by certain physical mechanisms and/or processes in a world where none of these things existed. (Indeed, it is a common assumption of mankind that dreams *in fact* often bear little relation to reality.) And there are other ways of calling into question our common assumptions about the past and present nature of the external world—without mentioning dreaming-scepticism.[1] There is, for example, the hypothesis that our present sense (or outer) experiences and memory impressions have all been induced in us by scientists working, with electrodes and fine wiring, etc., on our

---

[1] By 'dreaming-scepticism' I shall mean the view that there is no more reason to think we are not dreaming than to think we are, and that, in consequence, it is unreasonable to think we are not dreaming. By 'sceptical dreaming-hypotheses' I mean hypotheses that entail both that we are dreaming and that those dreams are illusory (i.e. do not reflect the way things are).

brains, who wish to mislead us in various ways; or the hypothesis
that all there is to our bodies is our brains and that our brains are
in vats whose contents are causing us to have the various (illusory)
sense experiences and memory impressions we do. In the present
chapter I shall consider and argue against hypotheses like these
that are sceptical about the nature (but not the existence) of the
external world.[1] In doing so, I shall first consider what can be said
against sceptical dreaming-hypotheses of the sort that explain
one's present (or present and past) sense experiences and memory
impressions as being due to physical events, processes, etc., x, y,
and z, occurring inside and/or outside one's body while one is
asleep (so that the experiences thus caused are all dream-experiences) and in a world where (almost)[2] none of the things
dreamed about in fact exist or are as they are imagined to be in the
dream. If something can be said to overcome sceptical hypotheses
of this sort, it can perhaps also be used to overcome the various
other kinds of sceptical hypotheses that claim that our sense
experiences and memory impressions are hallucinatory and
(almost) entirely non-veridical.

One traditional answer to scepticism about dreaming is that we
have reason to believe and indeed know that we are not dreaming,
by virtue of the order and cohesiveness of our memory impressions
and sense experiences. Such a line is taken by Descartes in the
Sixth Meditation, and is ably and amply criticized by Norman
Malcolm in his *Dreaming*.[3] Malcolm's point—and it is a point
that has been made by many other philosophers as well—is that
one can always have dreamt any given order and cohesiveness of
experience that there might be, and that in a dream, anyway, one
might think (or dream that one thought) that one's experience was
orderly, etc., and that one was able to bring one's memories
together in an orderly way, without either of these things being the
case. Thus the argument from orderliness and coherence leaves
the problem of dreaming-scepticism unsolved. Even if it is
impossible to dream in an entirely orderly way and to reconstruct

[1] By 'hypotheses sceptical about the nature of the world' I mean 'hypotheses
that say that the world is not as it (in fact) appears to us to be'.

[2] The 'almost' is necessary, because to dream, e.g. about dragons, is also to
dream about the external world, so, even if there are no dragons, one's dream
is not *totally* non-veridical *as long as* there are *other* sorts of physical things
around in the world. At least one thing one is dreaming about, namely, the
physical world, does in fact exist.

[3] London: Routledge, 1959, ch. 16–18.

an orderly past life in the course of a dream, it is still possible, even when we are awake and having orderly sense and memory experiences,[1] to wonder whether we may not just be dreaming that we are having the orderly and coherent sort of experience that we are, in fact, having. No non-question-begging argument can, I think, be provided along these lines to overcome dreaming-scepticism.

Nor are the sorts of Wittgensteinian arguments mentioned and discussed in Chapter 1 any more capable of providing a way to undermine such scepticism than they are of providing an answer to scepticism about the external world. Objections similar to those we raised against Wittgensteinian attempts to discredit the hypothesis of the demon could be raised against Wittgensteinian attempts to discredit sceptical dreaming-hypotheses via the sorts of arguments discussed in Chapter 1. However, there is one sort of argument against dreaming-scepticism that has no parallel in any of the arguments discussed earlier and thus has in no way yet been discredited. It is proposed by Malcolm in his book *Dreaming*.[2] According to Malcolm, the question 'How do I know whether I am awake or dreaming?' is senseless, because it implies that it is possible for one to judge intelligibly that one is dreaming, whereas such a judgment cannot but be unintelligible. 'I am dreaming' is, according to Malcolm, devoid of sense or meaning, because there are no criteria for telling whether someone understands that sentence or for ascertaining whether it is true. Malcolm's book has been attacked so often and so effectively on just these points that I do not feel I need to give any lengthy arguments of my own here against his views. Malcolm's principal premise is that the existence of thoughts, wishes, experiences, etc. while one is asleep is unverifiable in principle, and so logically impossible.[3] But Hilary Putnam in his 'Dreaming and Depth Grammar',[4] has argued at great length, and to my mind successfully, that scientific evidence for dream thoughts, wishes and experiences (in the ordinary sense of 'dream', 'thought', etc.) not only is definitely possible, but actually exists.

---

[1] For the sake of brevity, I shall sometimes talk of sense and memory experiences rather than, more idiomatically, of sense experiences and memory impressions.

[2] *Ibid.*, p. 109 f.   [3] *Ibid.*, p. 110.

[4] In Butler (ed.), *Analytical Philosophy*, 1st series, Oxford, Blackwell, 1962, pp. 211–35. Cf. H. D. Lewis's *Dreaming and Experience*, Hobhouse Memorial Lecture, London: Athlone Press, 1968.

Malcolm's argument for the view that thought and experience are impossible while one is asleep is totally lacking in force. And, in addition, that view contradicts commonsense opinion about such matters. For most ordinary, fairly well-educated non-philosophers will, when suitably questioned, talk as if they thought various wishes, experiences, images and thoughts occurred in dreams, and thus while people are asleep. It is a perfectly ordinary view, for example, that when we have nightmares, we are sometimes scared of being eaten up by a wild animal. But being scared of being eaten up is not just a feeling in the breast; it involves having certain beliefs as well.[1] One cannot be scared of something's happening (that something will happen) unless one thinks it may well, or may possibly, happen. So if one can be scared of being eaten up—during the course of a dream—one can in a dream also think that one may (well) be eaten up. And as far as I can tell, ordinary people are consistent in this matter. Those who say that fear is possible during dreams are also willing to say that fearful *thoughts* are possible during dreams.

But even if thoughts and experiences are impossible during sleep, Malcolm's line of argument will not give us a clear-cut way to combat dreaming-scepticism. For one can always ask: what reason is there for thinking that I am experiencing and thinking right now, rather than just dreaming that I am doing so? Of course, if Malcolm is right, then, if I am asleep, I cannot ask this question, but only dream that I am asking it. But why shouldn't a question that I am only dreaming that I am asking not be worthy of consideration and of being answered? And, in any case, I may not be dreaming, and so be in a position to ask and think about the above question. And, if Malcolm's argument leaves open the possibility that someone should meaningfully raise, and be in doubt about the correct answer to, the above question, and does not *itself* provide an answer to that question, then he has not, I think, provided a complete answer to the sort of scepticism about dreaming that we wish to overcome. I am inclined, consequently, to think that Malcolm's attempts to undermine dreaming-scepticism fail chiefly because of the implausibility of his claim that thoughts and experiences cannot occur while one is asleep, and of the arguments he gives for this claim; but, even if his arguments in this matter were successful, I do not think that an answer to

---

[1] This sort of point is made about the emotions (and feelings) in general by P. R. Foot in 'Moral Beliefs', *Proc. Arist. Soc.*, 59, 1958–59, *passim*.

D

dreaming-scepticism and to sceptical dreaming-hypotheses would immediately be forthcoming.

In the light of the argument of Chapter 2, it is natural at this point to wonder whether sceptical dreaming-hypotheses can be eliminated as unacceptable on grounds of being inquiry-limiting, the way so many demon-hypotheses can be eliminated. It is commonly assumed, of course, that someone who is asleep may later awake and gain true warranted explanatory beliefs about the causes and mechanisms of his previous dreaming. And I have no desire to question this commonsense belief here. But it still may be true that if someone accepts a certain hypothesis entailing that he is dreaming, and holds the hypothesis in question to be the best and completest then available explanation of his having certain sense experiences and memory impressions (of the sort we all at present have), he thereby is making it impossible for himself to obtain further warranted true explanatory beliefs about the causes of his experiences, for as long as he accepts the hypothesis in the manner indicated. And in that case, sceptical dreaming-hypotheses may, some of them, be inquiry-limiting for us at present as explanations of the kinds of experiences[1] we currently have, and so rationally unacceptable for the same reason that certain demon-hypotheses are. I think it would be possible to give some sort of plausible argument for the inquiry-limitingness of those sceptical dreaming-hypotheses that are not eliminable via principles like B and C. But such an argument would, I think, probably not suffice to show the unacceptability of *all* the sorts of hypotheses that we have to eliminate in order to show the plausibility of various commonly accepted claims about the present and past nature of the external world and that cannot be eliminated via principles like B and C. I should like, then, now to propose and make use of a principle unlike any we have used thus far in order to eliminate various sceptical dreaming-hypotheses, as well as all the other sceptical hypotheses (not eliminable by principles like B and C) that we need to eliminate in the present chapter.

Consider, then, the sort of hypothesis that says that one's present sense experiences and memory impressions are occurring in a dream, are caused by certain specific (physical) factors or events x, y, and z, and are (as) totally non-veridical and illusory

---

[1] I am henceforth assuming that, even if we are dreaming, we may have outer and other experiences, though this is really not essential to our argument.

(as possible, compatible with the first-mentioned conditions).[1] Such an hypothesis says, in effect, that (almost) all the things that it (sensibly) appears to one as if there are do not, in fact, exist; and that (almost) all the events, things, etc. one seems to remember (having experienced) never, in fact, existed. We can, I think, divide hypotheses of this sort into two parts, a part that asserts the non-veridicality and illusoriness of one's experience, and a part that goes on to hypothesize certain causes of that illusory experience. What I should like to suggest is that anyone who is rationally justified in believing the second part of this sort of hypothesis cannot be rationally justified in believing the first part, so that one cannot ever be rationally justified in believing the conjunction of the two parts, i.e. the hypothesis as a whole. For the second part of such an hypothesis makes a claim about the causes of certain phenomena, and one surely cannot be rationally warranted in believing any (fairly specific) causal statement unless one has some sort of inner or outer, direct or indirect, evidence for its truth. But how can one have any sort of evidence or good reason for believing a specific causal claim unless one is not justified in believing that all one's sense and memory experience is illusory? If one *were* justified in believing all one's experience was illusory— and I am not even sure how one *could* be justified in believing such a thing—one surely could not reasonably claim that one saw certain things in the external world that indicated that x, y, and z were the cause of one's experience, for one would not in such a case be justified in believing that the things one seemed to see existed (in anything like the way they appeared). Nor could one in such a situation reasonably argue as follows. The things I seem to see do not exist. But, whenever I have sense experience w, there are always entities x, y, and z in the world causing my experience w. For, if one is justified in believing that one's experience is non-veridical, and thus not justified in believing one's experience to be anything but minimally veridical, how can one be justified in asserting a correlation between w and x, y, and z? Surely not because one is justified in believing one remembers such a correlation from the past. For by hypothesis one is not justified in believing in the veridicalness of any of one's memory impressions.

Thus I should like to put forward the principle, for whose validity we have, in effect, just been arguing, that one who is (even to the slightest degree) rationally justified in believing any

[1] See footnote 2, p. 95.

(fairly specific) causal claim must have evidence which he is rationally justified in trusting or using in order to support that claim, and must, therefore, not be rationally justified in believing that all his sense and memory experiences are illusory (non-veridical). We can call this principle the *Principle of Illusion and Evidence*. It is a principle whose validity seems clear apart from any assumptions about the external world and that seems to be presupposed by scientists in the doing of science. In the first place, scientists demand evidence for causal statements. That is part of what distinguishes science from hunches, intuition, and the like. Scientists also assume that such evidence comes from experience: in the present and as it is remembered to have been. Furthermore, scientists tend to be more wary of making specific causal claims the more they are convinced that their experience is non-veridical. An astronomer, who realizes that he has been drinking heavily or has just taken an hallucinogen and in looking through his telescope seems to see a star in a place where none has previously been known to exist, will be more hesitant in thinking that he has made a discovery (or thus in thinking that a star in a new place in the heavens has *caused* his experience) than he would have been in the absence of taking drink or an hallucinogen—at least if the drinking or the hallucinogen has not made him entirely irrational. And that is because a rational scientist who thinks he may well be hallucinating and having non-veridical experiences will be reluctant to put forward any new specific causal explanations of things. For similar reasons, if an anthropologist on a field trip reasonably believes that he has taken an hallucinogen, he will not trust the evidence of his senses. For example, if he all of a sudden starts to see monsters leaping about in huge thunderclouds, he will not conclude that there are such clouds and that the clouds will bring rain (even though thunderclouds, unlike monsters, are things he sometimes believes to exist)—at least if the hallucinogen is not affecting his reasoning powers or his memory. For the more scientifically-minded or rational people are convinced that their experience is hallucinatory and illusory, the less they are willing to rely on it for evidence of what is going on 'beyond' or independently of that experience, and of causal relations in particular.

Thus the Principle of Illusion and Evidence (henceforth, for brevity, the PIE) generalizes the methodological practices that are implicit in the doing of science, and is thus, I think, a scientifically reasonable assumption, as well as an epistemically reasonable one. And we can use that assumption—without actually presupposing that there is an external world with scientific activities going on within it—to show what is wrong with the sort of dreaming-hypothesis mentioned above. For, if the PIE is valid, any hypothesis to the effect that we are dreaming, that our sense (outer) experiences and memory impressions are illusory, and that those experiences and impressions have certain physical causes x, y, and z will of necessity be completely rationally unjustified for anyone who believes it.[1] And so we are justified in totally rejecting any such sceptical dreaming-explanation of our current experience.

There are also, of course, sceptical dreaming-hypotheses that contravene Principles B and C, or principles similar to them. For example, there is the hypothesis that my experience is dream-experience that is illusory and caused by physical factors x, y, and z in such a way that my illusions will soon end and my (dream) experience become veridical.[2] Such an hypothesis does not contravene B or C or C' in any obvious way. But it does seem to be unacceptable for much the same reason that hypotheses conflicting with those principles are unacceptable. The hypothesis at hand says in effect that certain factors are now causing my experience to be out of line with the way things are, but will not do so in the future; in other words they are currently creating a 'mismatch', i.e. a relation of illusoriness, between my experience

---

[1] I am not here assuming that when one believes one is dreaming, one is committed to believing that one shouldn't believe anything, or that when one believes one is dreaming, one cannot reasonably believe anything (even perhaps that one is dreaming). Descartes in the *Meditations* holds that even if one thinks one is dreaming, one can reasonably believe certain mathematical truths, etc., and reasonably trust in the soundness of a mathematical or other proof one (dreams one) is producing. And I cannot see that he is mistaken about this. But if he is, and if one cannot have rational beliefs while believing one is asleep and dreaming, then it is obvious why any dreaming-explanation of our experience is scientifically and rationally unacceptable.

[2] R. Yost and D. Kalish (in 'Miss MacDonald on Sleeping and Waking', *Phil. Quarterly*, 5, 1955, p. 120 f.) point out that it is only a contingent fact that our dreams and hallucinations are generally non-veridical and illusory. For an experience is hallucinatory in virtue of the way it is caused. But there is a natural sense of 'veridical' or 'non-illusory' in which a certain sense experience is veridical or non-illusory just in case it (sensibly) appears to the person who has it as if certain things are the case and those things *are* (for the most part) in fact the case. And so one could have a (waking or dream) hallucination of a red box at a time when there was in fact a red box in an appropriate position in front of one, so that one's experience was veridical and non-illusory to a great extent.

and reality, but will not do so in the future. But then the hypothesis contravenes the following Principle B″ that reads: it is unreasonable to hypothesize that a certain thing or group of things *either* acts one way to some entity at one time but differently with respect to it at another time *or* creates a situation between two entities at one time that is unlike the situation it creates between them at another time, unless one has a definite reason that justifies doing so. This principle is valid, I think, if B, C, and C′ are valid. If, for example, we know that John is now being hospitable to Joe, then it is unreasonable also to believe that he will later be inhospitable to Joe, unless one has a definite reason that justifies belief in such a difference of treatment on John's part. Since the above sceptical dreaming hypothesis clearly contravenes this new and valid Principle B″, we have every reason to reject it. Note further that the hypothesis in question *also* contravenes the PIE: it assumes total present illusion and yet makes causal claims of a specific nature. And so it is doubly unacceptable.

Consider next the hypothesis that my present sense and memory experiences are occurring in a dream and are caused by factors x, y, and z in such a way that the left half of my visual field is illusory, whereas the right half is not. This hypothesis does not obviously contravene Principles B, B″, C, or C′. Nor does it run counter to the PIE, since it does not posit (almost) total illusion. However, it does clearly contravene the following Principle C″ that closely resembles the just-introduced Principle B″. C″ says: it is unreasonable to hypothesize that a certain thing or group of things *either* acts one way with respect to one entity and differently with respect to another, *or* creates between two entities (e.g. the left half of my visual field and those things in the world that are to my left) a situation dissimilar to that which it creates between two others (the right half of my visual field and those things that are to my right), unless one has a definite reason that justifies doing so. This principle is valid, I think, if B, B″, etc. are valid. If, for example, we know that John is hospitable to Joe, it is unreasonable also to think that he is inhospitable to Jim, in the absence of definite good reasons for thinking so. Similarly, with regard to the dreaming-hypothesis in question, we have no reason that justifies thinking that x, y and z are operating differently on the right and left halves of our visual fields, or are creating situations (of mismatch) between the left halves of our visual fields and the objects to our left that are unlike the situations (of matching) they are creating between the right halves of our visual fields and the objects to our right. So, via C″, that hypothesis is one we cannot reasonably accept.

For similar reasons the hypothesis that our sense and memory experiences are being caused by factors x, y, and z that cause our sense experiences to be veridical and our memory experiences (impressions) to be illusory (or vice versa) can also be handled by Principle C″.[1]

We have not, however, introduced any principles capable of eliminating the very unspecific sceptical dreaming-hypothesis that our experience is illusory and caused by *some* physical entity or entities. Such an hypothesis does not fall foul of the PIE, because it is so unspecific about the causation of our experiences of sense and memory. (Someone might wonder why we limited the PIE to causal hypotheses that are not totally unspecific. The reason is this. Someone who holds the above unspecific explanation of his experience to be true is not committed by believing the part of it that claims his experience is illusory to believing that he has no right to believe the other part of it, which says that his experience has a physical cause. For why can he not rationally hold that his experience is totally illusory but that, because of the PUI and Principles A, B, C, and D of Chapter 2, he is justified in rejecting the hypothesis of chance and of the demon as explanations of his experience, and so justified in believing that his experience is physically caused, even if non-veridical? Whether one believes one's experiences to be illusory or not, one may be able to justify rejecting the demon and chance, and accepting the external world as the cause of one's experience, and do so without making any assumptions about the veridicalness of any of one's experiences.)

How, then, is this weakly explanatory sort of sceptical dreaming-hypothesis to be eliminated? Notice that any attempt to change this hypothesis by making it explanatorily richer will yield an hypothesis eliminable via the PIE, an hypothesis that is totally preposterous and unacceptable. But consider the hypothesis that our experience is not illusory and is being caused by objects of the sort our experience seems to be 'of' (in the appropriate intentional

---

[1] It is worth adding that even though Principles like B, B″, C, etc. seem intuitively reasonable, Nelson Goodman's New Riddle of Induction raises some interesting questions about how such principles are to be understood and applied, and about how, if at all, they can be justified. More on this in ch. 5, which will in large part be devoted to Goodman's Riddle.

sense of 'of'). This hypothesis (that we generally accept about our experience) is one of several explanatorily richer versions of the hypothesis that our experience is not illusory and is caused by something physical. (Other richer versions of this hypothesis include, e.g. the hypothesis that our experience is veridical experience created by scientists with delicate wires and electrodes.) Now, if one has reason to think that a given explanation f of a phenomenon p is such that every explanatorily richer version of it is totally unacceptable, and if another explanation g of p that is inconsistent with f but just as explanatorily rich as f, is such that one has, after rational examination, found nothing unacceptable or preposterous about one or more explanatorily richer versions of g, then one has reason to favour g over f. The just-stated principle —call it Principle E—is, I think, a valid principle of scientific inquiry and of rational thought in general. Thus, if a Negro leader has been killed, and if one is trying to decide whether a white man or a Negro killed him, then, if for all motives or reasons m to suppose that a Negro killed the leader for or out of m is to suppose something clearly preposterous, and if for some motive n it is not preposterous to suppose that a white man killed the leader for or out of n, one should, other things being equal, favour the hypothesis that a white man is responsible for the killing. It might, for example, be the case that all Negroes at least liked the leader and that he was not rich enough for someone to want to rob him, etc. And it might also be the case that the leader had inspired anger and resentment among some whites. If so, the hypothesis that a white man did the killing can be enriched explanatorily to become the hypothesis that a white man did the killing out of race-resentment, without becoming preposterous or totally unacceptable. And by hypothesis this cannot be done with respect to the hypothesis that a Negro did it. Such being the case, therefore, it is more reasonable, *ceteris paribus*, to (tend to) believe that a white man did the killing than to (tend to) believe that a Negro did it.

The case just used illustrates the validity of Principle E. And this very principle can be used to show that the hypothesis that our experience is veridical and physically caused is scientifically preferable to the hypothesis that our experience is physically caused but non-veridical. For we have shown via the PIE that every explanatorily richer version of the latter is totally unacceptable. But the hypothesis that objects of the kind that it appears to us as if there are and have been, are responsible for our present, veridical, experiences of sense and memory—which is the hypothesis of common sense—cannot be shown to be totally unacceptable, or so at least it seems after rational consideration of the matter. Since this is an explanatorily richer version of the hypothesis that our experience is veridical and caused by something physical, this latter hypothesis is superior to the hypothesis that our experience is illusory and physically caused. And so we can eliminate all sceptical dreaming-hypotheses—even the most unspecific of them—via principles of scientific thought and methodology.

Indeed, our principles can also be used to show the unacceptability of sceptical non-dreaming hallucinatory hypotheses, and even of sceptical hypotheses that admit that we perceive and remember things in the external world, but claim that our perceptions and memories of things are so distorted that they are as illusory as possible consistent with their being perceptions and memories, i.e. claim that we perceive and remember the world as through a glass darkly. For nothing about the argument we have given to eliminate sceptical dreaming-hypotheses relies in any way on the fact that those hypotheses are sceptical *dreaming*-hypotheses, but only on the fact that those hypotheses are *sceptical*, i.e. posit the illusoriness of our experience(s).

Thus it seems that the principles used here and in the preceding chapter are sufficient to eliminate as unacceptable all alternatives to the commonsense view or claim that our current sense and memory experiences are veridical ones caused by physical entities (past and present).[1] Furthermore, rational scrutiny of this view or claim gives us no particularly good reasons, I believe, for thinking that there is anything definitely wrong with it or implausible about it.

One sort of argument, for example, that might be used to fault the claim that our experiences are veridical and physically caused would be an argument for the illusoriness of all secondary qualities,

---

[1] We have not yet considered any of the various *disjunctive* sceptical explanations of our experience that might be put forward as alternatives to the claim that our experiences are physically caused and veridical. There is, for example, the hypothesis that our experiences are either caused by a demon of type *t* or by physical factors that create illusions in us (while we are asleep). If the reader bothers to examine strange hypotheses like this one, however, I think he will see that they can be shown to be unacceptable via principles of scientific and rational thinking of the sort proposed here.

i.e. for the claim that no physical objects really are red, etc., even though they appear to be. If such an argument worked, it would show that our experience is in large part not veridical. Nor could I counter such an argument by saying that it relies on facts of physics and physiology that one who is arguing against scepticism cannot and need not assume. For I in no way wish to deny, in the course of attempting to overcome scepticism, any assumption that common sense or science makes. (On this, see the Introduction, *passim*.) If there really were presented a sound argument based on common sense, or commonly accepted scientific assumptions, for the illusoriness of redness, sweetness, etc., then we would have reason to think there was something wrong with the claim we are arguing for here, which says that our experience is non-illusory. And then we could not say we were justified in believing that claim because there was nothing wrong with it, but something wrong with all its alternatives.

As far as I can tell, however, there are no really strong or conclusive arguments that show that nothing physical is really coloured, etc. Furthermore, even if there are, we can restate the hypothesis we want to support to make it read: our experiences are veridical at least with respect to primary qualities like length, motion, etc., and are physically caused. This would be enough to enable us to argue in Chapter 4 below for other minds, and is all we really need here.

Another possible argument against the hypothesis we are seeking to defend derives from the fact that many philosophers have attempted to *reduce* physical objects to micro-objects or to abstract entities like classes, and have then gone on to claim that physical objects can be *eliminated* in favour of the latter sorts of entities.[1] If such philosophers are correct, then, again, the claim that our experience is physically caused and non-illusory (even just with respect to primary qualities) can be faulted. As far as I can see, however, the step from reduction to elimination is just not warranted (by Ockham's razor or any other principle). If physics can do its explaining and predicting without mentioning macro-objects, that just shows that there are some entities physics can safely ignore, just as there are some physical entities posited in physics that sociologists can safely ignore. And if we can create an analogue of theories about the physical world without referring

---

[1] Cf. G. Harman's 'Quine on Meaning and Existence II', *Review of Metaphysics*, 21, 1967, pp. 363 ff.

to anything but (classes of) real numbers, that only shows that the world of physical things can be rationally ordered in terms of numbers, is fully comprehensible numerically, not that there is nothing physical.

One might also attempt to fault the hypothesis that our experience is veridical (and physically caused) by claiming that we sometimes have distorted or somewhat non-veridical experiences of things, and that we may well be having such experience now. It is true that people, oneself included, sometimes have (partly) illusory experiences, e.g. under the influence of drugs or bad lighting conditions or brainwashing. But if the reader is having the sorts of sense experiences and memory impressions I am having at present, he will see that he has no particular reason to think he is under the influence of drugs. Those who have some memory impression of having recently taken drugs or who are having blurred or hazy experiences may have reason to think they are having non-veridical experiences, but someone in our position presumably does not. All he has is the fact that even people who have no particular (in some sense of 'particular') reason to be suspicious of the veridicality of their experience sometimes, rarely, have non-veridical experience. If there is, say, a one-in-a-million chance that our experience is in some substantial way illusory, then there is at least a one-in-a-million chance that the hypothesis we are trying to support is mistaken. But this is not just a fault of *that* hypothesis. Every alternative to it presumably suffers from the same failing: fallibility. For any alternative to that hypothesis, one would, I think, have to admit that there was at least some minute chance of its being wrong. Are we not as rational beings in everyday life prepared to admit that there is always some minute chance that any given specific explanation of certain data may be wrong? This line of thought, then, provides no significant objection to the hypothesis we are attempting to support.

And so, since we cannot fault that hypothesis, but can fault the alternatives to it, we have reason to accept the claim that our experience is veridical and physically caused, at least on a tentative basis, as (part of) the explanation of data (namely, our experiences of sense and memory) in whose existence we have every reason to believe.[1]

---

[1] The principles of the present chapter, including all the various versions of B and C, are, I think, sufficient to overcome the sceptical hypotheses of the

Note that we have *not* attempted to show the reasonableness of tentatively believing that we *perceive* and *remember* the world as it is and was. To do this, we would have to overcome certain hypotheses that say our experience is veridical but claim that it is caused not by the objects the experience is phenomenologically of, but by other physical entities. In this class belong the hypothesis that scientists with electrodes and fine wires are giving us veridical experiences, the hypothesis that physical factors are giving us veridical dream-experiences, etc. Inasmuch as we have not *yet* proposed any means of showing there to be something wrong with hypotheses of these sorts, I cannot *yet* show the reasonableness of believing that we perceive and remember things accurately and veridically. Thus at present I cannot show that the hypothesis that I am now perceiving my typewriter is a reasonable one (for us tentatively to accept), and cannot, in general, justify our various commonsense perceptual and memory claims. But that does not mean we cannot now justify the sorts of beliefs about the past and present nature of the world that most of us take to be justified *because* of what we perceive and remember. For we can justify claims about the present and past nature of the world around us via the argument presented here. One who seems to see a box can, in normal circumstances (where he does not have reason to believe he has just taken a drug, etc.) use the argument of the past two chapters to justify his believing that his experience is veridical and thus that there is a box in front of him. Similarly, one who seems to remember having seen a box some time ago can give a slightly more indirect argument for believing that such a box existed. If he seems to remember a past sense experience that was phenomenologically of a box (i.e. if he seems to remember its having looked to him as if there was a box in front of him), he can argue that it is reasonable tentatively to believe that experience did occur because it is reasonable tentatively to believe his memory impression is veridical. But, then, the best explanation of his having had that sense experience of a box in the past can be shown, via the argument of the present chapter, to involve claiming that that experience of a box was veridical and thus that that box

demon and of chance, without using the complex Principle A, of Chapter 2. Detailed sceptical demon-explanations either contravene some version of B or C, or can be eliminated via the PIE. And the simple hypothesis of a demon causing our experience can be eliminated via Principle E. Chance can be eliminated via Principle D or the PUI without assuming Principle A. The significance of this will be discussed at length in Ch. 5, below, pp. 179 ff.

existed. For, indeed, all alternatives to this claim are eliminable via our principles as unreasonable (e.g. the claim that he had the experience of a box, but there was no box, the claim that there was no box-experience, and even the disjunction of the two).

We have thus made good the promise made in Chapter 2 to provide an inductive argument, i.e. an argument based on scientific methodological principles, for the reasonableness of trusting our memory impressions (as well as our outer, or sense, experiences), even if we have not yet given any justification for thinking that when we have such memory impressions and outer, or sense, experiences we are, respectively, remembering past (sensory or other) events, etc., and perceiving present physical events, etc. And so, in Chapter 4, we will be able to use assumptions about (the reasonableness of believing various claims about) the past and present nature of the physical world around us in order to show the reasonableness of belief in other minds (i.e. justify believing in other minds), and thus to overcome the sort of scepticism that grants one the reasonableness of beliefs about one's own experience and even about the world, but holds that it is unreasonable for anyone to believe in anyone except himself. And the argument we shall present will in effect rest solely on assumptions about cur experience and rational principles of the sort we have been using up to now.

Although we have up to now assumed the reasonableness of believing that we are having various sorts of sense and memory experiences in the (epistemological) present, our argument for various claims about the past and present nature of the world (as well as the argument we shall be giving for other minds, and for objects that we are not observing) can be made to rest on *even weaker* assumptions. For if we assume *just* that it is reasonable to believe that *we think* we are having certain sorts of sense and memory experiences, we can still argue for the conclusions we have attempted to justify in the present chapter (and for the conclusions we shall attempt to justify in Chapter 4). That is because, if we assume that we think that it looks as if there is a box but that it does not in fact look as if there is a box (to us), we are involved in assuming that we are mistaken about the nature of our own experience. And any hypothesis that claims that we are mistaken in general about the nature of our own experience and then also claims that our (mistaken) beliefs about our experience are caused by certain physical or spiritual factors x, y, and z, will be eliminable via the PIE. And the variations on such hypotheses can be eliminated by others of our principles in ways we have already described at length. Thus, if we assume just that we think we have certain impressions of sense and memory, it is more reasonable to think those thoughts (beliefs) are caused in such a way that in fact we are having the experiences we think we are, than to assume the contrary. So we can eliminate all explanations of our thinking that we have certain experiences that do not assume that we have those experiences and that they are veridical, and thereby argue for the tentative reasonableness of believing that there are and were things of the kind (we are reasonable in believing) that *we think* we have sense and memory impressions 'of'. Our whole argument up till now, actually, need only assume certain rational principles and assume the reasonableness[1] of our thinking that we think that we are having certain sorts of memory and outer experiences.[2] (And, if we were intellectually nimble enough, we would need only to assume that it is reasonable for us to think that we think that we think that we think . . . that we are having certain outer and memory experiences, for some large number *n* of iterations of 'we think that'.)

[1] Cf. Chapter 2, p. 84.

[2] Except that we are also assuming in our argument that we have rationally considered our evidence and found nothing wrong with certain hypotheses. Note that those like Geach (see his *Mental Acts*, N.Y.: Humanities Press, 1957, p. 116) who seem willing to allow the possibility of a disembodied spirit that thinks and wills, but not of a disembodied spirit that has sense experiences, cannot easily claim or argue that our premises beg the question of the external world. For we are assuming only that we think (or can reasonably claim that we think) that we have sense and memory experience. And it is not clear that *such* premises entail our having a body, *even if* having sense experiences *does* entail having a body.

CHAPTER 4

INDUCTION, OTHER MINDS AND UNOBSERVED OBJECTS

In Chapter 3 we argued that various of our naïve commonsense assumptions about the present and past nature of the physical world can be justified as (rationally) belief-worthy. In the present chapter, I shall assume the *truth* of many such assumptions in order to argue for the existence of other minds and for the existence of objects, events, etc., that exist or take place when one is not perceiving them. (Later, in Chapter 5, I shall try to show that our argument for (the reasonableness of belief in) other minds and unobserved objects can be based on premises solely about the *reasonableness* of certain beliefs about the nature of the world; and, in that case, our argument for other minds and unobserved objects is just a continuation of the argument of Chapters 2 and 3, and requires only claims about experience and certain rational scientific principles as its premises.) In order to argue for the (reasonableness of belief in the) existence of other minds and unobserved objects, I shall employ a new version of the traditional Argument from Analogy that rests on a principle of enumerative induction that we have not yet made use of in this work.

It might be wondered at this point why I do not attempt to use principles we have already introduced in order to show the reasonableness of belief in other minds. For consider the alternatives to the claim that there are other minds 'animating' the humanoid bodies we see around us. One might hypothesize that the seemingly intelligent and skilled behaviour of the human (and animal) bodies around us was being manipulated by some sort of machine that operated by remote control from some far 'corner' of the universe. Couldn't one perhaps eliminate such hypotheses as inquiry-limiting, and certain variations on those hypotheses via Principles B, B'', C, etc.? For one might claim that, if we accept certain such hypotheses, we make it impossible to get warranted explanations about certain things (in particular, about the device or machine that manipulates the movements of other bodies than our own). I am not at all sure, however, that this claim is at all a reasonable one; but even if it is, there is another hypothesis that is sceptical about (the existence of) other minds that is pretty clearly *not* inquiry-limiting. This is the hypothesis that other humanoid bodies behave intelligently and skilfully as a result of the same physiological factors that operate in our own bodies to produce intelligent and skilful activities, but that there is no consciousness (i.e. no thoughts, feelings, pains, etc.) in those bodies as there is in our own. This hypothesis does not posit any special entities inaccessible to common human scientific observation, and so does not seem in any way to be inquiry-limiting.

Of course, the above hypothesis does seem to contradict the tenets of Logical Behaviourism, which defines the possession of consciousness, feelings, thoughts, etc. in terms of behaviour and dispositions to behave. But, in recent years, Logical Behaviourism has undergone severe attacks from philosophers of various different persuasions. And at least some of those attacks seem to me to succeed in showing the implausibility and inadequacy of definitions of consciousness in terms of behaviour.[1]

In recent years there has been a large number of attempts on the part of philosophers influenced by Wittgenstein to overcome scepticism about other minds. Some of these attempts rely on forms of argument we have already criticized in Chapter 1. Others provide interesting new lines of argument against scepticism about other minds, and would deserve our serious attention here, if they had not already been exhaustively examined in Plantinga's *God and Other Minds*. In Chapter 9 of his book Plantinga gives what seems to me to be a thorough examination and a philosophically adequate refutation of the recent arguments of Malcolm,[2] Strawson,[3] and Shoemaker[4] for the existence of other minds. And so I shall assume that Wittgenstein-type arguments will not serve to show what is wrong with sceptical hypotheses about other minds.

I think it is possible to justify belief in other minds on the basis of (at least) one version of the Argument from Analogy.[5] Of course, there has been a great deal of criticism of the very idea of

---

[1] See, e.g., H. Putnam's 'Brains and Behaviour', in Butler (ed.), *Analytical Philosophy*, vol. II, Oxford: Blackwell, 1965, pp. 1–19.

[2] 'Knowledge of Other Minds', in his *Knowledge and Certainty*, Englewood Cliffs: Prentice-Hall, 1963, pp. 130–40.

[3] *Individuals*, London: Methuen, 1959.

[4] *Self-Knowledge and Self-Identity*, Ithaca: Cornell, 1963.

[5] I do not wish to claim as a fact about human experience that we first come to believe in other persons via an Argument from Analogy.

such an Argument from Analogy for other minds, on the part of philosophers in the Wittgensteinian tradition. But, in Chapter 8 of *God and Other Minds*, I think Plantinga has shown that such criticisms of the Analogical Argument fall short of the mark. On the other hand, some readers may think that the Argument from Analogy does not require defence on my part, since others have already succeeded in using one or another version of it to justify belief in other minds. But in the first place, no one, I think, has yet shown how belief in unobserved objects can be justified either by an Analogical Argument, or by any other sort of rational argument. And in the second place, Plantinga, in his 'Induction and Other Minds',[1] has pointed up some very interesting objections to the Argument from Analogy for the existence of other minds. The major burden of the present chapter will be to provide an answer to Plantinga's objections to the Argument from Analogy, as well as to formulate a satisfactory version of the Argument from Analogy that will enable us to justify belief in other minds, as well as belief in the existence of objects that we are not perceiving.

I

In his (original) 'Induction and Other Minds', Plantinga casts the Argument from Analogy in the form of an inductive argument in the following way:

(1) Every case of pain behaviour such that I have determined by observation whether or not it was accompanied by pain in the body displaying the behaviour in question *was* accompanied by pain in that body.

Applying the so-called 'straight rule' of induction, I conclude that:

(2) Probably every case of pain behaviour is accompanied by pain in the body displaying it.

---

[1] *Review of Metaphysics* XIX, 1966, pp. 441–61. This article also forms the major part of Ch. 10 of Plantinga's book. Most of what I shall be saying in the present chapter comes from a reply that I wrote to Plantinga's original article. My reply is also entitled 'Induction and Other Minds' (*Review of Metaphysics* XX, 1966, pp. 341–60'). Plantinga has since then replied to my reply in an article entitled: 'Induction and Other Minds II' (*Review of Metaphysics* XXI, 1968, pp. 524–33). We shall have much to say about this later article of Plantinga's both in the present chapter and in the one to follow.

But, then, on a certain occasion I observe that:

(3) *B* over there (a body other than my own) is displaying pain behaviour.

From (2) it follows that *B* is [probably] pained; since I don't feel a pain there, I conclude that:

(4) [Probably] some other sentient creature has a pain.[1]

Plantinga proceeds to define *a simple inductive argument for someone S* as an argument of the following form:

'Every *A* such that *S* has determined by observation whether or not *A* is *B* is such that *S* has determined by observation that *A* is *B*. Therefore, probably every *A* is *B*.'[2]

Clearly the above inductive version of the Argument from Analogy involves a simple inductive argument; and Plantinga proceeds to make some telling criticisms of it. He points up an oddity in the inference from (1) to (2), namely, that it is logically impossible for a counter-example to (2) to turn up in the sample, which is described in (1), which serves as the basis for the inductive inference to (2). For if, as Plantinga believes, and I am inclined to

---

[1] 'Induction and Other Minds', p. 443 f.

[2] In his original article (esp. p. 448) Plantinga speaks of the 'Analogical Position' as involving the claim that a whole cluster of commonsense beliefs about other minds can be justified by using *simple inductive arguments* based on premises about one's own mind and about physical bodies, etc. I shall here be interested only in justifying belief in the existence of other minds or persons, rather than in justifying some of the other commonsense beliefs Plantinga mentions (e.g. the belief that I am the only person who feels pain in my body). Incidentally, Plantinga's definition of the Analogical Position is too narrow. The argument I shall propose for other minds is not based on a simple inductive argument in Plantinga's restricted sense. But it is clearly an inductive Analogical-type Argument for other minds, none the less.

According to Plantinga, one cannot determine by observation that another is, or is not, in pain, because one cannot see, touch, hear, etc. another's pain. And there is some sense, perhaps a technical sense, of 'observation' in which this would seem to be so. Of course, even if we *can* observe or see another's pain (or that another is in pain), we do not have an automatic answer to scepticism about other minds. One can always wonder whether one sees that another is in pain (so that he in fact does have pain) or only thinks one sees this. (Cf. *God and Other Minds*, pp. 187 ff.) By 'pain behaviour', both Plantinga and I mean a 'recognizable pattern of behaviour' which common sense associates with pain, but from whose existence it does not logically follow that anyone is in pain.

believe, it is logically possible for someone else to feel pain in my body, then even though I can determine by observation that *I* do not feel pain in some body, I cannot determine by observation that *no one* feels pain in that body. Thus it is logically impossible for me to determine by observation that a case of pain behaviour is not accompanied by pain in the body displaying that pain behaviour. Plantinga points out that other, highly dubious arguments resemble the above version of the Analogical Argument, and suggests the following Principle A[1] to rule out such fallacious inductive arguments:

'A simple inductive argument [for some contingent conclusion] is acceptable only if it is logically possible that its sample class contains a counter-instance to its conclusion.'[2]

This principle is, I think, clearly valid. And it rules out the Analogical Argument for other minds proposed by Plantinga because that argument rests on a simple inductive argument (the step from (1) to (2)) which is clearly ruled out by Principle A.[3]

Plantinga then proceeds to produce an inductive argument that does not contravene A but that can be used by any Negro to argue

[1] This Principle A has nothing to do with our Principle A of Chapter 2. In contexts where I am dealing with the problem of other minds, I shall use 'Principle A' to refer to Plantinga's Principle A.

[2] 'Induction and Other Minds', p. 450.

[3] Given what Plantinga means by a 'sample class', this principle is valid with respect to simple inductive arguments, but not with respect to inductive arguments generally, I think. In 'Induction and Other Minds II', Plantinga defines the sample class of an argument as the subset of the reference class of which x is a member, if and only if it has been determined by observation (on the part of the appropriate person or persons) whether or not x has the sample property (p. 529). But consider the argument: all men born before 1850 were mortal; we have no reason to think this class of men constitutes an unfair sample of the class of men in general, with respect to mortality; therefore, it is reasonable to believe that all men are mortal. In this argument, the reference class is the class of all men and the sample property the property of being mortal. And it is logically impossible for the sample class of this argument to contain a counter-instance to the conclusion of the argument, because it is logically impossible to determine by observation of some man that he is immortal. Thus the argument just given for the conclusion that all men are mortal would be ruled out if Principle A applied to all inductive arguments. And since this argument is in no way obviously faulty as an inductive argument, A must be restricted to simple inductive arguments (or at least not extended to all inductive arguments) if it is to be plausible. And this is something Plantinga does not point out or seem to think. Plantinga also states that I do not seem to accept Principle A ('Induction and Other Minds II', p. 529). But in fact I do accept that principle, and would only question generalizing it to all inductive arguments.

that any given white humanoid body lacks a mind, i.e. is not the body of any person. He defines a *croite* as something that is either a crow or a white human body. And he defines *being minded* as being the human body of a human person with a mind, pointing out that any Negro can argue as follows:

(20)[1] Every *croite* such that I have determined by observation whether or not it was either black or non-minded, *was* black or non-minded.

So probably

(21) Every *croite* is either black or non-minded.

But

(22) Jim Clarke over there is a *croite* and Jim Clarke is not black.

So probably

(23) Jim Clarke is non-minded.[2]

A similar argument in terms of *swanegs* (things that are either Negroid bodies or swans) can be given by any white man to prove the probable non-existence of Negroes (with minds).[3] Now neither of these clever arguments is an inductively acceptable one; yet neither is ruled out by Principle A. So Plantinga suggests a Principle A' that he claims will rule out these and other unacceptable arguments. Plantinga first defines the notion of a property's being *part of* another property. P is part of P' just in case P is the same property as P' or is a disjunct or conjunct or antecedent or consequent of P' or of a part of P'. And he assumes that being black is a disjunct of being black or non-minded, but not, say, of being dark-coloured. He then states A' as:

'Where α, β is a [simple] inductive argument for [person] S, β is of the form *All A's have B*, and C is any part of B, α, β is acceptable for S only if the propositions *S has examined an A and*

---

[1] I am using Plantinga's numbering for premises and conclusions in arguments for the convenience of those who wish to check on his original articles.
[2] Plantinga's 'Induction and Other Minds', p. 452.
[3] *Ibid.*, p. 451 f.

determined by observation that it lacks C and *S has examined an
A and determined by observation that it has C* are both logically
possible.'

This principle is clearly capable of ruling out the objectionable
croite and *swaneg* arguments. And it will also rule out any inductive argument for other minds based in any way on a simple
inductive argument.[1] (Thus it, like A, rules out the argument
from (1) to (4) above.) But it does not rule out the possibility of
some sort of analogical-inductive argument for other minds, based
solely on the sorts of premises about one's own experience and
about physical entities that the Analogical Arguer is supposed to
rely on. Of course, one might generalize A' so as to make it
applicable to inductive arguments that are not simple in Plantinga's sense; and that more general principle would rule out any
analogical-inductive argument for other minds as unacceptable,
since any such argument will have some psychological property as
its sample property, and it seems to be logically impossible, with
respect to any such property, that both its presence and its absence
be discoverable by observation. However, there seems to be not
the slightest reason to think a generalized version of A' would be a
valid inductive principle. Nor does Plantinga wish to claim that
such a generalized version would be valid.[2] Thus we shall accept
Principles A and A', which enable us to rule out the dubious
arguments we would like to see ruled out, but not the generalization of either one to include every sort of inductive argument. It is
time now to provide a sound analogical-inductive argument for
(the reasonableness of belief in) other minds that does not fall foul
of A or A' or any other rational principles.

II

Consider the following argument for other minds, based solely on
assumptions about one's own experience and about material
objects and their motions, that in no way involves a *simple* inductive argument of the kind used in the argument from (1) to (4)
above:

---

[1] For an interesting example of such an argument see Plantinga's 'Induction
and Other Minds', p. 451.

[2] 'Induction and Other Minds II', p. 527. See also my 'Induction and Other
Minds', p. 346 f. A generalized version of A' would entail the sort of generalized
version of A that we have argued (in footnote 3, p. 115) is invalid.

(a) Every case of (full-blown) pain behaviour on the part of this (i.e. my) (human) body (that I have a memory impression of having had) has been accompanied by pain or the pretence of pain (namely, on my part).

So

(b) (It is reasonable for me to believe that) every case of (full-blown) pain behaviour (on the part of any human body) is accompanied by pain or the pretence of pain.

But

(c) That (human) body over there is displaying (full-blown) pain behaviour.

So

(d) (It is reasonable for me to believe that) someone is feeling pain, or else pretending to be in pain.

But

(e) I am not feeling pain, nor pretending to be in pain.

So

(f) (It is reasonable for me to believe that) someone else (or something else) is either feeling pain or pretending to be in pain, and so there is at least one other mind.

This argument involves no *simple* inductive argument, in Plantinga's sense, so that it does not offend against A or A'. But the argument, and any similar inductive argument for other minds, is open to at least one traditional objection, the objection, namely, that it is an argument 'from one case alone'. In the above argument one is generalizing from a correlation of pain behaviour with pain or pretence of pain that exists in the case of one's own body to such a correlation in the case of other bodies. It should be clear, however, that there is some sort of ambiguity here in the notion of one case, for the argument from (a) to (b) above refers to many cases of pain behaviour, not just one. That argument is based on one case alone only in the sense that the cases of pain behaviour mentioned in (a) are all cases of the behaviour of one and the same body or person. But, even if there is a definite sense in which the basic premise (a) of the above argument is based on many cases, and not just one, a problem still arises from the fact that the cases described in (a) involve only the single body of a single person, the problem, namely, of how one knows that what is true of oneself in many cases will be true in general of others. This problem is basically just the problem of how one can know that cases of a certain body's (i.e. one's own body's) pain behaviour are a fair or unbiased sample of all cases of pain behaviour, as far as the property of being accompanied by pain or the pretence of pain is concerned. And one cannot get around this problem, as has been suggested by A. J. Ayer,[1] by absorbing the difference between oneself and others into the differences between one's own situation and characteristics and those of others. For, if one's body is unique, i.e. if it has a scar or fingerprint or general look h that no other body has, one still is left with the problem of knowing that cases of pain behaviour involving a body with h are a fair or unbiased sample of all cases of pain behaviour. And how can one ever know with any certainty that having h does not make a difference with respect to the property of being accompanied by pain or pretence of pain, in such a way that pain behaviour of a body with h *is* thus accompanied, while pain behaviour of a body lacking h is *not*?

My answer to these problems—and it is by no means an unfamiliar answer to these problems—is that it is not necessary to have definite *knowledge* that one's sample of x's that are f is a fair or representative or unbiased sample of all x's as far as f-ness is concerned, in order to be justified in believing that all x's are f. In order for it to be reasonable to believe in such generalizations it is usually only necessary that one should have found, after thorough, careful and rational scrutiny of the relevant empirical information available to one, no reason to believe that one's sample is biased, unfair or unrepresentative. I wish to suggest, therefore, that the following Strong Principle of Induction is a valid one, in accordance with which it is reasonable to make inductive inferences:

[1] *The Problem of Knowledge*, p. 220 f.

'If one has examined a certain class C of x's and found all the x's in C to be f (and there are numerous x's in C), and if one has, after careful, rational, thorough examination of one's evidence, discovered no reason to think that C constitutes an unfair or biased sample of the x's in general as far as f-ness is concerned, then it is reasonable to think that all x's are f.'[1]

If this principle is valid, then our above argument for other minds will provide us with a justification for belief in other minds, if we but supplement it with what seems to be a perfectly reasonable assumption, (a'), to the effect that I have, after careful, thorough, and rational examination of the relevant evidence available to me, discovered no reason for believing that cases of this (i.e. my body's) pain behaviour are a biased or unfair sample of all cases of pain behaviour on the part of human(oid) bodies, as far as the property of being accompanied by pain or the pretence of pain is concerned. Indeed, we need assume only a weaker version of the above Strong Principle of Induction to make our argument for the reasonableness of belief in other minds go through. We need assume only that: if one has examined a certain class C of x's . . . as far as f-ness is concerned, then it is reasonable to believe of any given x that it is f. We then can argue from (a) and (a') to a weakened version of (b), (b'), which states that it is reasonable for me to believe of any given case of pain behaviour that it is accompanied by pain or its pretence; and from (b') to (f).

But why believe in the validity of the Strong Principle or of the weaker version of it just proposed? The answer I propose to this question is that, if enumerative inductive generalization represents a valid form of inference at all, something like the Strong Principle is valid too, because fundamentally presupposed in such inference. For, typically, when we generalize from what is true of observed x's to what is true of the whole class of x's, we do not *know* that the unobserved and observed x's resemble each other in the appropriate respect, do not *know* that our sample is fair and unbiased. Usually we have at best only the knowledge that we

---

[1] C needn't contain all the x's one has examined. If there are any x's not in C that one has found not to be f, one will have reason to think C is an unfair or biased sample of the x's with respect to f-ness, in which case the above principle will not apply. If there are x's outside of C that one has examined *without* learning whether or not they are f, the above principle can be applied to argue for the reasonableness of thinking *those* x's are f. And there is no reason why this should not be possible.

have not, even after much careful scrutiny, been able to find any reason to believe in such bias. If, for example, I discover an urn in the desert and the first twenty things I pull out of it at random are red balls and I conclude that there is (probably) nothing but red balls in the urn, my basis for this claim is nothing more than the fact that all the things I have taken out of the urn so far are red balls, plus the fact that I can discover no reason to think my sample of the contents of the urn is biased or unfair. I have no mysterious knowledge of the unobserved contents of the urn obtained through any special or occult psychic power.[1] So, if this sort of enumerative induction is valid, which it seems, intuitively, to be, then either our Strong Principle, or something closely resembling it, must also be valid.

There are many sorts of commonsense beliefs that can be justified in terms of our Strong Principle of Induction (or the weaker version of it). This principle can, for example, be used in arguing inductively from past to future, from the fact that all past men have been mortal to the conclusion that all future men will be mortal. For there is no reason to think that past men (say, men born before 1850) are a biased or unfair sample of future men, as far as mortality is concerned. It is interesting that the Strong Principle can be used not only to answer the problem of the reasonableness of belief in other minds, but also to provide a solution to the venerable problem of the reasonableness of belief in the continued existence and law-abiding behaviour of objects and processes when they are no longer being perceived (by us). In his famous 'Refutation of Realism',[2] Professor Stace has argued that no deductive or inductive argument can show the reasonableness of the view that objects, etc. continue to exist and operate in the same way when one is not perceiving them as when one is perceiving them, a view he considers to be a major, if not the major, tenet of Epistemological Realism.[3] And so Stace concludes that even if Realism is true, we have no reason to think that it is.

[1] Cf. Goodman's *Fact, Fiction, and Forecast*, 2nd edition, N.Y.: Bobbs-Merrill, 1965, p. 62.

[2] *Mind* 43, 1934, pp. 145–55.

[3] Actually Stace seems to take Epistemological Realism to entail that there are sometimes objects that *no one* is observing. But then Realism is incompatible with the existence of an omnipercipient Deity. And most Realists, perhaps even Stace himself, have not *intended* to build into Realism such a strong anti-religious view; and so I am here using 'Realism' in such a way that someone who believes in the (occasional) existence of objects he is not perceiving, but who also believes God always perceives everything, can count as a Realist.

According to Stace, no inductive argument for (the reasonableness of belief in) the existence of physical objects that one is not observing is possible, because one cannot argue, for example, from the fact that all fires one has observed have kept burning when one was no longer observing them, to the conclusion that all fires do, without begging the question at issue. For the premise of that argument assumes knowledge of objects when one is not perceiving them, assumes that objects sometimes behave the same way when one is not perceiving them as they do when one is perceiving them. And this, of course, is just what has to be proved. So this sort of inductive argument cannot be used to show the reasonableness of Epistemological Realism. It is surprising, however, that Stace did not see the possibility of another sort of inductive argument, based solely on premises about the nature of objects *when they are being observed*, for the reasonableness of believing in (a major part of) Realism. Indeed, in a reply to Stace's article, R. E. Stedman and H. B. Acton suggest that very possibility, but then do nothing themselves about providing such an argument.[1] But consider the following argument, based on an inductive inference that accords with the Strong Principle of Induction:

(*g*) All roaring fires watched (by me) continuously, until they burned out, have obeyed certain laws, and have continued to burn for a long time unless they were directly interfered with by some physical thing.

(*h*) I have, after careful, rational, and thorough examination of the relevant evidence available to me, discovered no reason to believe that roaring fires that have been watched until they burned out constitute an unfair or biased sample of all roaring fires, as far as obeying certain laws and continuing to burn unless interfered with.

So

(*i*) (It is reasonable for me to think that) all roaring fires obey certain laws, etc.

---

[1] 'Mr Stace's "Refutation of Realism" ', *Mind*, 43, 1934, pp. 349–53.

But

(*j*) I just stopped watching and left a roaring fire, and have seen nothing interfere with it.

So

(*k*) (It is reasonable for me to think that) the fire I just left is obeying certain laws and continuing to burn and will continue to burn for a long time after the time when I left it, unless some physical thing directly interferes with it after that time.

So

(*l*) (It is reasonable for me to think that) at least one thing is obeying or has obeyed certain laws, even though it is (was) not being observed by me.

And

(*m*) (It is reasonable for me to think that) either the fire I left continued to burn thereafter or some physical thing that I didn't see interfered with its burning.

So

(*n*) (It is reasonable for me to think that) some physical thing or other has existed unobserved by me.[1]

This argument can be used to show the reasonableness of a major part of Realism, as Professor Stace and others have construed it. And, of course, similar arguments could be employed to show the reasonableness of belief in the existence of just about any of the sorts of objects, processes, etc., in whose (temporarily) unobserved (by us) existence we all believe.

The fact that the Strong Principle of Induction (or its weaker version) is involved in (what seems to be sound) enumerative

---

[1] Like the above argument for other minds, this argument could be altered in such a way as to make use only of the weaker version of the Strong Principle of Induction.

inductive reasoning in many areas gives that principle much plausibility in general and helps to justify its implicit use in the argument from (*a*) to (*f*) given above for the reasonableness of believing in other minds. Quite recently, however, it has been claimed by G. Harman that our belief in other minds *cannot* be justified by enumerative induction, but *can* be justified by showing that such belief provides the *best explanation* of the behaviour of other human bodies.[1] And Harman indicates that he thinks that it is in terms of such scientific standards of the acceptability of hypotheses as simplicity, plausibility and 'non-*ad-hoc*-ness' that the hypothesis of other minds can be shown to be the best explanation of the behaviour of human bodies other than our own. In a similar vein, P. Ziff has suggested that our belief in other minds can be justified as the most complete, simple, and coherent explanation of certain facts about other bodies.[2] However, in a reply to Ziff's paper, Plantinga has cogently argued that it is far from clear that Ziff, Harman, or anyone else, has provided adequate reasons for believing that the hypothesis of other minds is a simpler, more coherent, or more complete explanation of the behaviour of other bodies than, e.g. the sceptical hypothesis of a demon who for certain motives (e.g. malice) and by certain means causes human bodies other than our own to behave as if they were 'minded'.[3] Thus, as far as I can see, no one has ever *given* us good reason to think that commonsense beliefs about other minds can be justified on anything but an enumerative inductive basis, i.e. via something like our Strong Principle or its weaker version. There may be reasons of coherence, simplicity, etc., for preferring the hypothesis of other minds to its sceptical alternatives, but as far as I know, no one has ever succeeded in spelling them out explicitly.[4] More importantly, the argument we have given from (*a*) to (*f*) for other minds is based on enumerative induction and seems to be perfectly acceptable. And, if it is, Harman is mistaken in his claim that we cannot justify belief in other minds via enumerative induction.

As I said earlier, in order to have a complete argument for other minds, the argument from (*a*) to (*f*) must be supplemented by a premise (*a'*) to the effect that one has, after careful, etc., ex-

[1] 'The Inference to the Best Explanation', *Phil. Review*, 74, 1965, pp. 88–95.
[2] 'The Simplicity of Other Minds', *J. Phil.*, 62, 1965, pp. 575–84.
[3] 'Comments', *J. Phil.*, 62, 1965, p. 585 f.
[4] However, see Ch. 5, sections 2–4 below.

amination of the relevant available evidence, found no reason to think that cases of pain behaviour on the part of one's body are an unfair sample of the class of all cases of pain behaviour on the part of any human body. Then the argument to (*b*) and thence to (*f*) will go through making implicit use of the Strong Principle of Induction. Clearly *we* are justified in normal circumstances in which we are viewing pain behaviour on the part of a human body other than our own in believing (*a'*). But note that if the *croite* argument given above were an acceptable one, a Negro could use it to show that every *croite* was black or non-minded and so that every white *croite*, every white human body—even those displaying pain behaviour—was probably non-minded. And this would imply that we did have a reason to think our own cases of pain behaviour were a biased or unfair sample of all cases of pain behaviour as far as being accompanied by pain or the pretence of pain was concerned, in which case (*a'*) would be false and our argument for other minds would not go through. Fortunately Plantinga's A' rules out the *croite* and *swaneg* argument, so that one cannot use it to show that we have reason to think the sample described in (*a*) is biased, or thus to vitiate our argument for other minds. It is also worth noting that arguments that offend against A or A' will *not* be arguments whose validity is guaranteed by the validity of the Strong Principle of Induction. For example, arguments that fall foul of A are arguments of the form: all *f g*'s are *h* therefore, all *g*'s are *h* (or this *g* is *h*), where it is logically impossible for there to be an *f g* that is not *h*, even though it *is* possible for there to be a *g* that is not *h*. And, clearly, any such argument is based on a biased or unfair sample.[1] (To argue in a way that contravenes A is like arguing that all fish must be bigger than two inches long, because all the fish one has caught in one's net, which has two-inch spaces between its strands, are longer than two inches.) Thus arguments contravening A will not be guaranteed by the Strong Principle (or its weaker version), which only certifies arguments based on samples we have no reason to think unfair or biased. And similarly for arguments contravening A'. There is no incompatibility, then, involved in accepting Principles A and A' and the Strong Principle (and its weaker version) all at the same time, as in fact I do.

---

[1] Note that the argument for 'all men are mortal' in footnote 3, p. 115, is not open to these criticisms. A generalized version of A is not very plausible, it seems.

III

In his more recent 'Induction and Other Minds II', however, Plantinga claims to have found a way to undermine any attempt to justify belief in other minds by an analogical-inductive argument. He presents an argument that challenges an essential premise in the argument for other minds I have given above, namely, premise (*b*) of that argument. The argument Plantinga presents goes as follows:

(8) Every case of pain behaviour on the part of my body that has been accompanied by pain or the pretence of pain, has been accompanied by pain or the pretence of pain on my part.

Hence

(9) Probably every case of pain behaviour (on the part of any human body) is accompanied by pain or the pretence of pain on my part.

My total evidence, however, will contain the information that

(10) There are many cases of full-blown pain behaviour that are not accompanied by pain or the pretence of pain on my part.

Hence probably

(11) There are many cases of full-blown pain behaviour that are not accompanied by pain or the pretence of pain.[1]

Premise (or sub-conclusion) (b) of my argument above reads:

'(It is reasonable for me to believe that) every case of (full-blown) pain behaviour (on the part of any human body) is accompanied by pain or the pretence of pain.'

And surely Plantinga is correct in suggesting that, if the argument from (8) to (11) is valid, I cannot use (*b*), (or (*a'*)), or thus bring off my analogical-inductive argument for other minds. Plantinga then suggests that this argument contravenes his Principle A, but that it does not contravene any of the principles I

[1] 'Induction and Other Minds II', p. 532.

proposed in my 'Induction and Other Minds' or any principle that he has proposed and that I have accepted.[1] (He thinks, mistakenly, that I do not want to accept his Principle A.) But this argument clearly does *not* contravene Principle A, as Plantinga thinks it does, because it is *not* based on a *simple* inductive argument, as Plantinga defines such arguments, and because Plantinga states A in such a way that it applies *only* to simple inductive arguments. (There is some evidence in this passage that Plantinga thinks A should apply to *all* inductive arguments; and we saw the implausibility of such a general version of A in footnote 3, p. 115.)

Furthermore, it is not necessary to bring in any special principles to see that the argument from (8) to (11) is a complete *non sequitur*. For if one looks closely at that argument, the step from (8) to (9) is comprehensible, but everything else about the argument is totally perplexing. As far as I can see, the conjunction of premise (9) with the assumption that premise (10) is (probable as) part of our total evidence (as arguers from analogy for other minds) involves a self-contradiction. Furthermore, the conclusion (11) seems in no way to follow either from (9) or from (10) or from their conjunction, except in so far as that conjunction is self-contradictory. For (11) speaks of pain behaviour that is not accompanied by pain or its pretence, whereas both (9) and (10) speak only of pain behaviour that is or is not accompanied by pain or its pretence *on my part*. As stated, then, Plantinga's argument seems to me to be incoherent, and its conclusion a total *non sequitur*. 'Induction and Other Minds II' does not, then, undermine the argument we have given for the reasonableness of belief in other minds (or in objects that we are not observing).

However, Plantinga has written me that in his 'Induction and Other Minds II', the argument from (8) to (11) is misstated and, in particular, that premise (9) should have read:

(9) Probably every case of pain behaviour that is accompanied by pain or the pretence of pain is accompanied by pain or the pretence of pain on my part.

The argument can then be completed as Plantinga completed it, or in the following slightly more perspicuous (from the standpoint of our own exposition) way:

[1] 'Induction and Other Minds II', p. 532.

So

(12) It is reasonable to believe that every case of pain behaviour that is not accompanied by pain or its pretence on my part is not accompanied by pain or its pretence on the part of anyone (by contraposition of (9)).

But

(13) It is reasonable to believe that that (human) body over there is exhibiting full-blown pain behaviour that is not accompanied by pain or its pretence on my part.

So

(14) It is reasonable to believe that that (particular) case of full-blown pain behaviour is not accompanied by pain or its pretence on the part of anyone.

If *this* argument works, premise (or sub-conclusion) (b) of my argument from (a) to (f) for other minds (as well as premise (a'), which is used to reach (b)) can be effectively countered; in that case, sub-conclusion (d) of my argument for other minds, which claims that someone is feeling pain or else pretending to feel pain can also be effectively countered. And, since (d) is crucial to the argument for other minds that I have given, we shall then have to look elsewhere for an acceptable Analogical Argument for other minds, or for unobserved objects, as well.

Now the problems raised by the above argument from (8) and (9) to (14) are similar to certain very general problems about induction raised by R. Sleigh in his unpublished doctoral dissertation, *An Examination of Thomas Reid's Account of our Knowledge of the External World and Other Minds* (Brown Univ., 1963). So I should first like to consider the problems that Sleigh raises in his dissertation, and then relate them to the problem of the validity of the above argument from (8) and (9) to (14), which presents a very definite challenge to our argument for other minds (and to our argument for unperceived objects—because of the possibility of constructing an argument, similar to that from (8) and (9) to (14), which calls into question premises (h) and (i) of our argument for unperceived objects, processes, etc.).

Sleigh brings up the following perplexing example: Imagine that one has before one a crow that has a characteristic one has never before seen in an animal (say, a broken claw). Furthermore, every crow one has previously examined carefully enough to determine whether or not it caws has in fact cawed, and one has never seen any other cawing animals. In this situation, before I have determined whether the crow in front of me will caw, I can surely present a reasonable argument for thinking it will caw. For every crow previously examined has cawed. Unfortunately, as Sleigh points out, the matter is not so simple. For every cawing animal I have examined so far has *lacked* a broken claw. So why can I not argue that (probably) every cawing animal lacks a broken claw; argue thence by contraposition that (probably) every animal *with* a broken claw does *not* caw; and conclude, finally, that the animal in front of me (probably) does *not* caw?

As Sleigh is the first to point out, there is surely something wrong with the latter argument. In the situation described, there is good reason to conclude that the crow in front of one will caw. Or at least there is more reason to think it will caw than to think that it will not. So the argument for the conclusion that it (probably) will not caw is either fallacious and unacceptable, or else *very* weak. The source of difficulty with that argument lies, I think, in the fact that it is in effect an argument for the conclusion that a certain non-C is a non-B that is put forward in a situation where one knows of many B C's, but where it is *not* part of the evidence from which one is arguing that certain non-C's are non-B's.[1] In other words, in the situation described by Sleigh, one is not making, or is not allowed to make, the assumption that certain things with broken claws have been found (either by examination or otherwise) to be things that do not caw. And that, I think, affects the soundness of arguing that the broken-clawed thing in front of one does not caw. In the situation described by Sleigh, one *is*, on the other hand, making and permitted to make the *assumption* that certain crows have been found to caw. And this, I think, makes it possible to give a reasonable argument for the conclusion that the crow in front of me caws. The following Principle Y, therefore, suggests itself as a way of stating what is

[1] With respect to the argument under examination, the B's are cawing things and the C's are things with claws intact. It is clear, incidentally, that the whole inductive situation described by Sleigh (and by me here) is very simple, and perhaps very artificial. This has been done in order to facilitate bringing out the crucial inductive issues that arise with respect to that situation.

E

wrong with arguments like that put forward in the situation described by Sleigh for the conclusion that a certain broken-clawed thing is not a thing that caws: if, in a given situation, there are available two arguments M and N that make use of enumerative induction to support opposing conclusions, and if the conclusion of M (or M's premises and principles of inference taken jointly)[1] entail that (one knows or has reason to believe that) a certain non-C is a non-B (for some appropriate values of 'B' and 'C') and M's premises taken singly do not entail that (one knows or has reason to believe that) various other non-C's are non-B's, but this is not true of N, then, other things being equal, N is superior to M and M is unacceptable.

In the situation described by Sleigh the inductive issues have been made so simple, I think, that other things are equal; and so, in that situation, the argument for the conclusion that the thing in front of me is a broken-clawed non-cawer is inferior to the argument for the conclusion that the thing in front of one is a crow that caws, and is unacceptable *per se*, despite the fact that one has already examined many cawing things and found them all to lack broken claws.[2] If so, then it seems possible, in that situation, to

[1] This qualification is in order, because one might naturally argue: every cawing animal examined has lacked broken claws; so probably all broken-clawed animals do not caw; but this animal has a broken claw; therefore, this animal probably does not caw—instead of concluding (more elaborately): therefore, this broken-clawed animal probably does not caw. And in the former case, it is not the conclusion of one's argument *per se* that entails that a certain non-C is a non-B (even though one's premises taken singly do not), but only one's premises and principles of inference taken jointly that do. But such an argument is still unacceptable because it *entitles* one to conclude that a certain non-C is a non-B, even if its conclusion does not actually *say* that a certain non-C is a non-B, in the absence of premises which, taken singly, entail that various other non-C's are non-B's.

[2] It is natural to imagine, at this point, that what is wrong with the argument for the conclusion that the broken-clawed thing in front of me does not caw is that it involves an illicit contraposition from the (in that situation) inductively justified claim that all cawing things have claws intact to the claim that all things with claws broken are non-cawers, and thence to the conclusion that the broken-clawed thing in front of me is a non-cawer. But this is not the heart of the matter. For one can in Sleigh's situation argue for the same conclusion without explicitly using contraposition, as follows: all things one has examined have been (found to be) things that were either non-cawers or lacking broken claws; so probably all things are either non-cawers or lack broken claws; so this thing probably is either a non-cawer or lacks broken claws. But this thing definitely is broken-clawed, so probably this thing is a non-cawer. In the light of this argument, it should be clear that it is not illicit contraposition *per se*, but the contravening of Principle Y, that makes arguing for the conclusion that the thing before one does not caw unreasonable in the situation Sleigh proposes.

give an acceptable argument, via the Strong Principle of Induction, for the conclusion that the crow in front of one probably is, or can reasonably be believed to be, a cawer. For one has evidence that many previously examined crows have been cawers, so that one's argument need not contravene Principle Y. And no one can claim that one's sample of crows is biased by arguing that since all cawing things have been found to have claws intact, the broken-clawed crow in front of me probably does not caw, since in the circumstances such an argument contravenes Y.

Of course, Principle Y assumes that knowledge of B C's is less inductively relevant to the claim that a given non-C is a non-B than is knowledge of non-C non-B's. But this seems quite reasonable on the face of it, and accords with our intuitions about particular inductive cases (like that presented by Sleigh). Nor does Principle Y in any way contradict Hempel's view that both B C's and non-C non-B's are positive or confirming instances of 'All B's are C's' and 'All non-C's are non-B's'.[1] In the situation Sleigh described, the cawing things with claws intact that one has examined confirm the claim that 'All things with broken claws do not caw', but it does not follow from this that one can reasonably argue that a particular thing with broken claws (probably) does not caw. For one thing, Hempel's notion of a positive or confirming instance of an hypothesis is much weaker than the notion of a well-supported or acceptable or probable hypothesis; and for another thing, a generalization of the form 'All non-C's are non-B's' may be acceptable when one has no reason to believe there are any non-C's, but not when one has reason to believe there are non-C's. In the situation described by Sleigh, one knows of a non-C (of a broken-clawed thing), so that it may not be reasonable to believe that all broken-clawed things are non-cawers, even if it *was* reasonable to believe that generalization before one knew there were any non-C's (and when one knew of many cawers that lacked broken claws, so that it was, perhaps, reasonable to believe that all cawers lack ˉbroken claws). It should be clear, then, that Principle Y and the rest of what I am saying here is perfectly compatible with what Hempel says about confirmation.

[1] Of course, strictly speaking only *sentences* of the form 'a is a broken-clawed thing and a doesn't caw' confirm a general *sentence* like 'all broken-clawed things do not caw', according to Hempel. But if this is understood, I think there is no harm in speaking of certain *things* (*animals*) as confirming certain *generalizations*. Hempel's classic study of confirmation, 'A Purely Syntactical Definition of Confirmation', appeared in the *Journal of Symbolic Logic*, VIII, 1943, pp. 122–43.

Returning now to the argument from (8) and (9) to (14) above, we can see that it too is ruled out by Principle Y. For its premises and/or principles of inference (when supplemented by an appropriate premise (8') to the effect that my sample of pain behaviour is unbiased) entail that (it is reasonable to believe that) a certain case of non-pain on my part is a case of non-pain on anyone's part, even though none of its premises entails that (it is reasonable to believe that) there are any other cases of non-pain on my part that are also cases of non-pain on the part of anyone. And if we let the B's be cases of pain on anyone's part and the C's be cases of pain on my part, we can see that the argument from (8) and (9) to (14) contravenes Principle Y. In the situation where one is giving our argument from (a) to (f) for other minds, the conclusion (14) of the argument from (8) and (9) to (14) is supposed to oppose sub-conclusions (b) and (d) of the argument from (a) to (f). And the argument from (a) to (b) and (d) in no way involves arguing (for any choice of 'B' and 'C') that a certain non-C is a non-B on the basis of premises that do not involve the claim that there are any other non-C non-B's. If so, the argument from (8) and (9) to (14) falls foul of Principle Y. Given the validity of Principle Y, therefore, that argument is unacceptable, and so cannot be used against premise (a') of our argument for other minds (which says that we have no reason to think cases of our own pain behaviour are a biased or unfair sample of cases of pain behaviour in general with respect to accompaniment by pain or its pretence) or thus against either sub-conclusion (b) of that argument (which says that it is reasonable to believe that all cases of pain behaviour are accompanied by pain or its pretence), or sub-conclusion (d) of that argument (which says, in effect, that a certain case of pain behaviour is accompanied by pain or its pretence). And, in that event, we have still been given no reason to believe that there is anything wrong with our argument for the reasonableness of belief in other minds.

The argument from (8) and (9) to (14) constituted a genuine challenge to our argument for other minds, a challenge, which, I hope, we have met. But challenges to our argument also arise from other quarters. Most significantly we have not yet said anything about Nelson Goodman's New Riddle of Induction,[1] and the sceptical challenge it presents to any inductive argument one claims to be valid and acceptable. For, whenever one argues inductively to a conclusion of the form 'All A's are B', there is a

[1] See Goodman's *Fact, Fiction, and Forecast*, ch. 3.

'queer' Goodmanian predicate (like '*grue*') waiting in the wings
that can be brought in as the means to forming an inductive argument to the conclusion that all A's (not yet examined) are non-B.
And, as we shall see later when we consider the matter more
closely, there is no difficulty in doing this with respect to (b) of
our Analogical Argument for other minds (or with respect to (i)
of our argument for unperceived objects). So again there is a way
of challenging premise (a') and subconclusion (b) of our above
argument for other minds. Of course, one thing we might do is
just claim that the argument used to challenge (a') and (b) is clearly
unacceptable, and claim that it is (scientifically) rational to think
so. For surely scientists reject arguments using '*grue*' out of hand
and feel justified in so doing. And one could repeat this for any
particular argument based on any Goodmanian predicate 'p' that
was used to challenge (a') or (b), by employing a completely
specific rule saying that any argument based on (Goodmanian)
predicate 'p' was unacceptable. One could then claim that one
could find no (good) reason to think the sample mentioned in
premise (a) was biased or unfair, i.e. accept (a'), and argue
thence to (b) and, ultimately, to the reasonableness of belief in
other minds.

I do not see why this would not be a perfectly (scientifically)
acceptable way of defending our argument for other minds, or
indeed any inductive argument, from sceptical challenges on the
part of arguments that use Goodmanian predicates. After all,
Goodman himself agrees that it is perfectly clear that arguments
based on '*grue*' are unacceptable from the standpoint of science
and rational thought in general.[1] So, for our present purposes, we
do not have to try to resolve Goodman's Riddle, in order to be
able reasonably to claim that our arguments for other minds and
for objects that one is not perceiving are acceptable, even if
arguments based on Goodmanian predicates can be constructed
against them. (Indeed, if this were not the case, then no one,
presumably, would be reasonable in accepting inductive arguments until he had reason to believe he had solved Goodman's
Riddle or knew its solution.) Given our purpose, in the present
work, of justifying belief in the external world and in other minds,
etc. on the basis of scientifically reasonable and acceptable
principles, we could, I think, quite reasonably just claim that
particular challenges to our argument for other minds based on

[1] See Goodman's *Fact, Fiction and Forecast*, p. 79.

predicates like '*grue*' were without validity, and thereby claim to have justified belief in other minds on the basis of scientifically reasonable and acceptable principles.

But, of course, even if we can for our purposes here meet the challenge of arguments with predicates like '*grue*', it would be gratifying to know what is wrong with or unacceptable about such arguments. For one thing, if we could find a characteristic or set of characteristics that characterized '*grue*-type' arguments, but not the arguments we intuitively feel are valid, we would not have to rely on a different specific principle (mentioning a specific predicate '*p*') every time there was a challenge to an inductive argument we wanted to espouse. Secondly, we might by answering Goodman's Riddle be able to explain various other troublesome or merely unexplained aspects of the rationality of scientific inquiry. (In particular, I hope that what we shall have to say about Goodman's Riddle will illuminate and perhaps further justify our Principle Y and the Principles B, B'', C, etc., used in Chapters 2 and 3.) And finally, Goodman's Riddle lies at the very heart of (enumerative) induction; and if we have something to say about it, we may be able to say some worthwhile things about the nature of (enumerative) induction *in general*. And so in Chapter 5 we shall deal with Goodman's New Riddle of Induction, attempt to give some sort of answer to it, and use that answer in an attempt to gain a clearer understanding both of principles we have used thus far and of (enumerative) induction in general.

In the present chapter we have presented an argument for the reasonableness of belief in other minds, and another, similar argument for the reasonableness of belief in objects, processes, etc., that one is not perceiving or observing. And we have attempted to meet various sceptical challenges to those arguments. Since I am aware of no other sorts of objections to the crucial premises (a') and (h) of those arguments, those premises are true for me now, assuming that I have been rational, careful and thorough in considering whether my evidence gives me any reason to be hesitant in generalizing from (a) to (b) or from (g) to (i). But, of course, someone might in the future come up with objections to premises (a') and (h), and thus to both the argument for other minds and that for unperceived objects, objections that cannot be handled via any principles we have proposed up till now. Such new sceptical challenges can be met only when and if they arise; we have no way of answering them in advance. And hopefully, such challenges, if and when they occur, will be able to be countered by principles *like* Principle Y, or by highly specific but clearly reasonable principles that eliminate only individual arguments (or individual inductive predicates), or, perhaps, by the sorts of highly general principles we shall be introducing in the next chapter.

CHAPTER 5

THE NEW RIDDLE OF INDUCTION
AND THE EXTERNAL WORLD

I

In *Fact, Fiction, and Forecast*, Nelson Goodman not only proposes the New Riddle of Induction, but seeks to present a thoroughgoing solution to his Riddle. He suggests that the fact that the predicate 'green' is projectible (validly projected or generalized), whereas his specially introduced predicate '*grue*' is not, is intimately connected with the fact that 'green' is an 'entrenched predicate' whereas '*grue*' is not.[1] 'Green', that is, 'as a veteran of earlier and many more projections than "*grue*", has the more impressive biography'.[2]

Now I think there are two possible ways in which one might interpret Goodman's attempt to understand the superior projectibility of 'green' (i.e. the reasonableness of believing that all emeralds, e.g., are green and that they are not all *grue*) in terms of the greater entrenchment of 'green' (as opposed to '*grue*'). He may be saying that the superior entrenchment of a predicate like 'green' *makes* it reasonable to project that predicate rather than its less well-entrenched alternatives. Or he may just be saying that the fact that a certain predicate is better entrenched than certain (appropriate) others indicates, or gives us a (conclusive) reason to think, that it is more reasonable (or valid) to project the former. And there is evidence in the text for each of these interpretations of what Goodman means to assert about the relation between entrenchment and projectibility. For example, on one and the same page of *Fact, Fiction and Forecast* he says: '. . . the superior entrenchment of the predicate projected is . . . a *sufficient* even if not a necessary *indication* of projectibility. . . .' And he also says: 'The reason why only the right predicates happen so luckily to have become well entrenched is just that the well entrenched predicates have *thereby* become the right ones [to project].' (Italics mine.)[3]

---

[1] '*Grue*' is introduced (or defined) as applying to things examined before (some present or future time) *t* if and only if they are green but to other things if and only if they are blue. See *Fact, Fiction, and Forecast*, p. 74.

[2] *Fact, Fiction and Forecast*, p. 94. [3] *Ibid.*, p. 98. See also pp. 64 ff., 96 f.

Now there are important differences between these two ways of interpreting Goodman's views about the relation between projectibility and entrenchment. As Paul Ziff has pointed out in a quite different context, there is an important distinction to be made between 'reasons why' something x has property p and 'reasons to suppose' that x has p. Thus, according to Ziff, if all the critics like a given painting, that may give me a reason to suppose it to be a good painting; but it hardly follows that their universal approval is what *makes* the painting good. There is a difference between signs or indicators or concomitants of goodness and things that contribute to or create goodness (in a painting).[1] And if this is so, there surely is a similar valid distinction between things that indicate (or give one reason to think) that an hypothesis is projectible and things that make an hypothesis projectible (things such that an hypothesis becomes or is projectible by having them). Goodman may want to hold that greater entrenchment makes a predicate more projectible. But if he does, he will be committed to a view that is no more plausible, on the face of it, than is the view that critical approval is what makes a painting a good one. Many philosophers have been dissatisfied with Goodman's solution to his own Riddle, I think, because they have thought he meant to claim that entrenchment creates projectibility. For if it does, then presumably if *'grue'* and other Goodmanian predicates had been projected more frequently than 'green' and other 'normal' predicates over the centuries, so that they had become better entrenched than those predicates, it would thereby have become reasonable to project *'grue'*, etc., rather than 'green', etc. And such a conclusion seems highly implausible to many philosophers. Such philosophers feel, instead, that if, for example, we were to stop projecting predicates like 'green' and to start projecting predicates like *'grue'*, that would show only that we had somehow become irrational, or for some reason deliberately perverse or uncaring about being rational; and they do not think that, if such a change were to occur in our habits of projection, that would eventually make it reasonable to project *'grue'* and unreasonable to project 'green'. And I cannot help but think that such philosophers are right on this score. I can see no reason to think that frequency of generalization can make for or contribute to the validity of generalization. Such a view seems to me to be closely related to

[1] See his 'Reasons in Art Criticism', in *Philosophic Turnings*, Ithaca: Cornell, 1966, p. 53.

the Coherence Theory's claim that what is consistently believed is *ipso facto* belief-worthy or reasonable for one to believe, and to suffer from similar objections and criticisms.[1] I can only conclude, then, that Goodman cannot justify his claim that entrenched predicates are projectible by claiming that entrenchment creates or contributes to projectibility.[2]

Of course, Goodman may simply want to claim that entrenchment is a concomitant or a (conclusive) indication of projectibility, that if we know that one of two competing predicates is better entrenched than the other, we have (conclusive) reason to suppose that the former predicate is one with which we can make (more) valid projections, or is one that it is more reasonable to project. And such a claim may well be true, just as it may well be true that knowing that all the critics admire a work of art gives us good reason to think that that work is a good one. But in art criticism we are also interested in knowing what *makes* a certain work of art a good one, in knowing *why* it is good; and the same is true in Epistemology (or the Philosophy of Science). For we are interested in explaining *why* a given predicate is one that we can reasonably project, in saying what it is about that predicate that *makes* it projectible, not merely in finding reasons (even conclusive reasons) for supposing that that predicate is reasonably projected. And the claim that entrenchment gives us reason to think a predicate projectible does not explain *why* those predicates that are projectible *are* projectible. So, if Goodman is only talking about what is a sign of projectibility, or about what characteristics are present in and only in projectible hypotheses, and does not intend to make any claims about what *makes* a predicate projectible, then his solution to his own Riddle does not go as deep, from an epistemological standpoint, as one would like to go.

It is worth noting, furthermore, that, even if the entrenchment of a predicate is always a reason for supposing a predicate to be projectible, that fact will not help us to provide a general justification for projecting the predicates we do, for making enumerative

---

[1] See the Introduction, p. 22 f.

[2] Goodman could support the claim that entrenchment makes for projectibility by saying, as in fact he does say (*op. cit.*, p. 65 n.), that inductions that 'are normally accepted as valid' are *by definition* valid inductions. But then it would be self-contradictory to say that (for some reason) everyone was irrational in the use of inductive arguments, and I think it is highly implausible to hold that saying this sort of thing involves an outright contradiction. Thus I think there is no reason to think that entrenchment makes for projectibility.

inductions of the sort we are in fact generally inclined to make. For, when we argue from the fact that a given predicate is entrenched and the fact that entrenchment is a good indication of projectibility to the conclusion that it is reasonable to project the predicate in question, we are already assuming the acceptability of certain sorts of inductive arguments and the projectibility of certain sorts of predicates. If, for example, I claim that 'green' is better entrenched than '*grue*' (as part of an attempt to show the superior projectibility of the former), I am already involved in a generalization from the fact that, within my own usage and the usage of those with whose usage I am directly acquainted, 'green' is preferred to '*grue*' in projections, to the conclusion that *in general* 'green' is thus preferred. And such a generalization is itself susceptible to challenge via contrary generalization making use of a 'queer' Goodmanian predicate. One who argues that 'green' is better entrenched than '*grue*' assumes that (most) occasions, when one of 'green' and '*grue*' is projected, are occasions when 'green' is projected. But one can define '*goccasions*' as 'occasions when "green" is projected within my own immediate ken or occasions when "*grue*" is projected outside my immediate ken'. And then one could use this Goodmanian predicate to challenge the superior entrenchment of 'green' by arguing that, since all occasions in my immediate ken in which one of 'green' and '*grue*' has been projected have been *goccasions*, it is reasonable to believe that all occasions in which one of 'green' and '*grue*' is projected are *goccasions*, in which case '*grue*' is always preferred to 'green' in situations outside my ken, and is thus, presumably, better entrenched than 'green'. So, unless one already assumes that 'an occasion when "green" is projected' is projectible and that 'a *goccasion*' is not, one cannot justify projecting 'green' rather than '*grue*' in terms of the superior entrenchment of the former. Thus one cannot use facts about entrenchment and the weak principle that entrenchment is (reasonably taken to be) a sign of projectibility to give a *general* justification for projecting the predicates we typically project and consider projectible. And this is yet another weakness of Goodman's entrenchment approach to the problem of valid projection. For, from an epistemological standpoint, we very much want to be able to justify (show the acceptability of) making the projections we do in a general sort of way.

In the light of the above, therefore, it would seem that Goodman's attempt to solve the New Riddle of Induction by using the notion of entrenchment either involves implausible assumptions or is epistemologically incomplete and unsatisfying. And the same, I think, can be said for all the various attempts to solve the New Riddle of Induction that have been put forward since Goodman first proposed it. Many such attempts, for example, single out characteristics that differentiate Goodmanian from normal predicates, but leave it far from obvious how those differentiating characteristics contribute to or detract from projectibility. But in order to solve Goodman's Riddle in an epistemologically satisfying way, it is not enough to find characteristics that Goodmanian predicates lack and that normal predicates have, that indicate the absence or presence of projectibility; those characteristics must also make for (contribute to) projectibility. On the other hand, many attempts to solve Goodman's Riddle deal with characteristics that seem to make for projectibility but differentiate only between *certain* normal predicates (usually observational predicates) and their Goodmanian competitors. And such attempts, even if they serve to show why, for example, it is reasonable to project normal observational predicates but not predicates derived from those predicates in the way *'grue'* is derived from 'green', do not provide us with a general solution to Goodman's Riddle; do not, for example, help us in explaining the projectibility of such non-observational predicates as 'soluble', 'vain', and 'conducts electricity'. In the present chapter, therefore, I shall attempt to provide a general solution to Goodman's Riddle of an epistemologically satisfying kind, i.e. of such a kind as to explain why (and justify the claim that) the sorts of predicates we generally project *are* projectible (reasonably projected) in appropriate situations. I shall then make use of this (attempted) solution to Goodman's Riddle to clarify certain questions whose treatment we have been postponing till the present chapter.

II

Consider the notion of a *differential property* or *characteristic*. The characteristic of being (an) *f* is differential if and only if, given that anything *x* is (an) *f* and anything *y* is not (an) *f*, it follows logically (it is logically impossible for it not to be the case) that *x* and *y* are not exactly (or entirely) alike (or similar, or resembling one another). Thus, being green (greenness) is a differential property, since it follows logically from the fact that one thing is green and another thing not green that the two things are not entirely alike. Such properties as being hard, being round, being soluble, being vain, etc., are clearly also differential. But not so the property of being surrounded by a red ring. This property is not differential in the sense defined above, because there might (logically) be a penny surrounded by a red ring that was exactly like another penny that was not surrounded by a red ring. Two such pennies might be entirely alike, even if their relations to other objects were different.[1] Such other properties as being a father, being near the Moon, and being indigenous to Australia are also non-differential. Furthermore, it is logically possible for there to be a green emerald examined before *t* that is exactly like a green emerald that will in fact never be examined, or that will be examined only after *t*. And, on Goodman's definition of '*grue*' the first of these emeralds will be *grue* and the second not *grue*. Of course, we might never be able to *know* that such a pair of emeralds existed; but it is still logically possible for them to exist; and so it is logically possible for one thing that is *grue* to be entirely like another thing that is not. *Grueness* is a non-differential property.

The distinction I am making between differential and non-differential properties might be questioned on the grounds that the notion of a differential property is defined in terms of the notion of logical possibility, which is one of a whole cluster of inter-related notions that Quine and others have criticized at length in recent years. The concept of a differential property also depends on the concept of two things being exactly alike or similar; and it might be claimed that this latter concept, and thus the concept of a differential property, is a somewhat vague one. But if we are willing—as I, in the present work, have been—to accept and make use of the notions of logical possibility and impossibility, then the fact that the concept of two things being exactly alike is (to some degree) vague should no more prevent us from distinguishing between differential and non-differential properties in most run-

[1] As Moore points out in 'The Conception of Intrinsic Value', *Philosophical Studies*, Paterson, N.J.: Littlefield, Adams, 1959, p. 271. Moore's distinction between properties that depend solely on the intrinsic nature of the things that possess them and properties that do not is pretty much the same as my distinction between differential and non-differential properties. Note that the notion of a non-differential may *not* be the same as that of a relational property. The property of having existed only a finite amount of time is non-differential, but not, I think, relational.

of-the-mill cases than the fact that the concept of baldness is vague should prevent us from saying that some things (e.g. heads) have the logical possibility of being bald, while other things (e.g. tickles) do not.[1] The property of being surrounded by a red ring is non-differential because the concept of two things being exactly alike, somewhat vague though it may be, is clearly used in such a way that things differing with respect to the having of this property need not (logically) fail to be exactly alike or similar or resembling one another. And a *grue* emerald and a non-*grue* emerald need (logically) only differ in that the former, but not the latter, possesses the property of having been observed before *t*. But this difference of property need not create an unlikeness between those two objects.[2]

[1] However, in a paper called ' "Grue" ' (*Analysis* 28, 1968, p. 128), R. G. Swinburne has claimed that the notion of 'two things being exactly alike' is 'hopelessly vague', and concluded that my attempt to deal with Goodman's Riddle (in an article entitled 'Some Thoughts on Goodman's Riddle' that appeared in *Analysis* 27, 1967) in terms of differential properties is doomed to fail. Swinburne's reason for saying this is that 'all objects are exactly alike in some respects and no objects are exactly alike in all respects'. Why this should render the notion of exact alikeness hopelessly vague I find hard to understand. Swinburne may think that the fact that every possible two objects are alike in some respects shows that the notion of being exactly alike in some respects is vacuous and hence, in some sense, meaningless or vague. But even so, how would it follow that the notion of being exactly alike *simpliciter* was hopelessly vague or in any other way faulty? There is as great a difference between the concept of exactly like or similar objects and the concept of objects that are exactly alike *in some respects*, as there is between the concept of equally good fathers and the concept of fathers who are equally good *in some respects*. The burden of proof is surely on Swinburne to show the relevance of the vacuity of 'exactly alike in some respects' to the vacuity, or hopeless vagueness, of 'exactly alike'. And this he has not attempted to do. Of course, Swinburne also points out that no two things are *in fact* exactly alike. But, again, I cannot understand why he should think that this makes for the hopeless vagueness or meaningless-ness of the notion of exact alikeness. There are no unicorns or perfect circles, but does that mean that 'perfect circle' or 'unicorn' is either hopelessly vague or meaningless?

[2] In his 'Differential Properties and Goodman's Riddle' (*Analysis* 28, 1967, p. 59) John O'Connor has argued (in reply to my 'Some Thoughts on Good-man's Riddle') that my attempt to deal with Goodman's Riddle in terms of the notion of a differential property can succeed only if I can show that 'green' and 'blue' are not legitimately definable in terms of '*grue*', '*bleen*', and a temporal term, and only if I can *demonstrate* 'that greenness is a differential property while *grueness* is not'. But I would never wish to deny the legitimate inter-definability of the pair '*grue*'-'*bleen*' and the pair 'green'-'blue', and the argu-ment of the present chapter (and of my earlier paper) in no way depends on denying it. For granting such interdefinability, and even granting that I cannot 'demonstrate' that greenness is and *grueness* is not differential, it does not follow that one can justifiably claim (as O'Connor thinks one can) that if *x* is

It is my belief that the notion of two things being exactly alike or similar as it is used in ordinary language is not the same as the notion of two things having all their properties in common (where the *properties* of a thing are thought of as being as numerous as the things that can be said truly about it). The latter notion, in fact, may well be a self-contradictory or incoherent one. For it is logically necessary (and perhaps analytically true) that, if there are *two* things *a* and *b*, *a* will have the property of being identical with *a*, whereas *b* will lack that property, so that the two things will not have all of their properties in common. But things that do not have all their properties in common may still (logically) be exactly or entirely alike or similar. Thus, if two things have had different past histories and have thus been unalike in the past, they may still be exactly like one another at the present time, even though their past unlikeness means that at present they do not share all their properties (e.g. the property of having had a past of such and such a sort). But when we say that two things *are* exactly alike (at present) we exclude the relevance of their *past* histories. That is, I think, how the notion of exact likeness is used by ordinary educated speakers of English. Things exactly alike at present may have dissimilar histories; and things with exactly similar past histories may (logically) become dissimilar in the future.[1] Likewise a thing *x* may be nearer the Moon than a thing *y*, but they may still be exactly like one another. For the notion of exact alikeness is used in common parlance in such a way that one can distinguish between things that are exactly alike (in themselves) but that bear dissimilar *relations* to different things and things that

---

grue and *y* is not, they are necessarily unalike. That is because, given *our concept of alikeness*, it is clear that a green thing examined before *t* (and therefore *grue*) and a green thing not examined before *t* (and therefore not *grue*) could (logically) be exactly alike. Similarly, it is indeed true (as O'Connor says) that a green thing *v* and a non-green thing *w* may (logically) be alike in all (other) respects save that the former has been observed and the latter has not. They may both be *grue*, both be non-*bleen*, etc. But one cannot thereby conclude (as O'Connor thinks one can) that greenness is not differential; for from the mere fact that *v* is green and *w* is not green it immediately follows logically that they are not exactly alike, and anyone who understands the concepts involved will, I claim, see this. Of course, this is not a 'demonstration' in any strict sense that greenness is and *grueness* is not differential. But there is no reason why one cannot be *justified* in believing in this difference between *grueness* and greenness on the basis of one's *understanding* of the concepts involved in claiming that that difference obtains between them.

[1] Cf. C. B. Martin's 'Identity and Exact Similarity' (*Analysis* 18, 1958, p. 85 f.).

are *not* (even) exactly alike (in themselves). And if that is so, there seems to be no reason why a green object that has been examined before *t* (and that is therefore *grue*) and a green object not examined before *t* (and that is therefore not *grue*) should not be exactly alike (at some time), in which case greenness *is* and *grueness is not* differential in the sense defined above.

But why should the difference between *grueness* and greenness with respect to the property of being differential have anything to do with the projectibility of '*grue*' and 'green'? For even if the differential property of greenness allows for valid projection, this is also the case with many non-differential properties (even if not with *grueness*). The property of having been (originally) formed in limestone is a good example of a non-differential property that is also *projectible*. For, if we can in some way validly generalize from the fact that all emeralds observed so far are green to the conclusion that all emeralds are green, surely we can in a similar manner validly generalize from the fact that all observed emeralds have been found to have been formed in limestone to the conclusion that all emeralds are and have been thus formed. And the property of having been formed in limestone is surely as good an example of a non-differential property as one could want. But, even if the distinction between differential and non-differential properties does not mark the distinction between projectible and non-projectible properties, it has a great deal to do with that distinction, as I shall try to make clear in what follows.

Consider the hypothesis or claim that all emeralds (tenselessly) are *grue* and that some emeralds (tenselessly) are and some (tenselessly) are not examined before *t*. If such an hypothesis or claim is true, then some emeralds are (at least to some degree) unlike other emeralds. For some emeralds will be blue, while others (the ones already examined) are green.[1] No such unlike-

---

[1] The hypothesis that all emeralds are *grue*, however, does not alone entail such unlikenesses, since it is compatible with claiming that there are no emeralds not examined before *t*. However, Goodman is interested only in the case where it is assumed that there are emeralds not examined before *t*, and where, in consequence, it is assumed that it cannot be true both that all emeralds are *grue* and that all emeralds are green. (Indeed, for Goodman, a predicate is 'projected' only when the hypothesis in which it appears has some undetermined cases, i.e. only when there are things as yet unexamined that are relevant to the truth of the hypothesis. *Ibid.*, p. 90 f.) In our present discussion, therefore, we are attempting to show the superiority of the hypothesis that all emeralds are green, on the assumption that some emeralds have not been examined before *t*, to the hypothesis that all emeralds are *grue*, on that same assumption. Goodman,

nesses are entailed by the hypothesis that all emeralds are green
and that some emeralds are and some are not examined before *t*.
Now, science is fundamentally opposed to the positing of unlikenesses or dissimilarities between things or classes of things, except
when there are overriding reasons for doing so. In particular,
science and scientists are loath to postulate unlikenesses between
what has been observed (of some object or class of objects) and
what has not yet been observed (of that object or class of objects).
One of the most basic patterns of scientific thinking is, rather, to
claim that what has not yet been observed (and may not even yet
exist) is (probably) like, that is (probably) resembles, what has
already been observed (and may no longer exist). Science and
scientists, that is, constantly assume that the observed gives us a
good indication of what the (as yet) unobserved is *like*.

Now, of course, the hypothesis that all emeralds are green and
that some emeralds are and some are not examined before *t does*
posit differences of property between emeralds examined before *t*
and emeralds not examined before *t*, namely, that the former are
examined before *t*, and are *grue*, while the latter are *not* examined
before *t* and are *not grue*. But, since these properties are not
differential, the hypothesis that all emeralds are green and that
there are both emeralds examined and emeralds not examined
before *t* commits itself to no unlikenesses (or dissimilarities or
non-resemblances). On the other hand, the hypothesis that all
emeralds are *grue* and that some emeralds are and some emeralds
are not examined before *t* is committed not only to differences of
property between emeralds examined before *t* and emeralds not
examined before *t*, but to certain unlikenesses between emeralds
examined before *t* and emeralds not examined before *t*. But for a
scientist, an hypothesis that posits differences of (mere) property
and no unlikenesses is, other things being equal, to be preferred
to an hypothesis that posits differences of (mere) property as well
as *unlikenesses*. From a scientific standpoint, I think, positing
unlikenesses is far more unacceptable than merely positing
differences of property. And so it would seem to be preferable to
project 'green' rather than '*grue*' with respect to the reference class
of emeralds, i.e. to hold that unexamined (before *t*) emeralds are

however, never explains why it is reasonable to assume that there are (or will be)
more emeralds than one has already examined. And surely such an assumption
is a reasonable one for us, given our knowledge of the world. I shall attempt myself to provide a justification of this sort of assumption later on in this chapter.

green, rather than *grue* (blue). And thus we have given some explanation of why 'green' is projectible and '*grue*' is not projectible, in general.[1]

But we need not stop here in our explanation of the superior projectibility of 'green' over '*grue*' with respect to normal reference classes like the class of emeralds. For, although no one has ever given a totally adequate definition of simplicity, it seems clearly to be a part of our notion of simplicity (and/or a valid methodological principle concerning the notion of simplicity) that an hypothesis that posits both (mere) differences of property *and* unlikenesses (between observed and unobserved phenomena, or in any other way) is, other things being equal, less simple than an hypothesis that only posits (mere) differences of property.[2] Furthermore, there is no other factor that distinguishes the hypothesis that all emeralds are green and that some emeralds are and some are not examined before *t* from the hypothesis that all emeralds are *grue* and that some emeralds are and some emeralds are not examined before *t*, with respect to simplicity, or, at least, no other factor tending to render the '*grue*' hypothesis simpler than the 'green' hypothesis. So we can safely conclude that the 'green' hypothesis in question is simpler than the '*grue*' hypothesis in question. But, from a scientific standpoint, a simpler hypothesis is to be preferred to a less simple, or more complex, one, in the absence of any independent good reason to prefer the less simple hypothesis. Therefore, hypothesizing that future or unexamined emeralds are green is more reasonable from a scientific standpoint than hypo-

---

[1] By 'in general', I mean 'with respect to most reference classes scientists are interested in'. With respect to the class of emeralds, we have seen, 'green' is preferable to '*grue*' and the latter is not projectible, whereas the former is. Quite recently, however, Donald Davidson has argued that even predicates like '*grue*' may be projectible with respect to certain queer sorts of reference classes. (See, e.g., his 'Emeroses by Other Names', *J. Phil.* 63, 1966, pp. 778 ff.) If Davidson is correct here, and I am inclined to think he is, then it is unwise to emphasize the projectibility of predicates taken individually, the way Goodman does in *Fact, Fiction and Forecast*. '*Grue*' may not be unprojectible *per se*, but only with respect to certain 'normal' reference classes, like the class of emeralds or of ravens, etc. In consequence, I shall, in the present chapter, be placing greater emphasis on the comparative merits of *certain hypotheses* involving Goodmanian and normal predicates than on the comparative merits of those predicates themselves.

[2] The view that it is possible to talk meaningfully about simplicity without being able to define it has been propounded and discussed, e.g. by S. Barker in 'On Simplicity in Empirical Hypotheses' in M. H. Foster and M. L. Martin (eds.), *Probability, Confirmation, and Simplicity*, N.Y.: Odyssey Press, 1966, p. 249.

thesizing that future or unexamined emeralds are *grue* (and also blue), at least in circumstances like ours where we have seen green, and no blue, emeralds and where we have no special reason to favour the projection of '*grue*'.[1]

Note that our argument for the superior projectibility of 'green' over '*grue*' in no way depends on the fact that 'green' is an observational predicate, whereas '*grue*' is not, that is on the fact that greenness can be detected by immediate observation, whereas *grueness* can be detected only by observation *and* knowledge of what time (or date) it is. For, even if we could properly distinguish these two predicates along these lines, we would still have no way of distinguishing such non-observational predicates as 'soluble', 'vain', 'radioactive', 'conducts electricity', and numerous other scientifically important predicates from predicates derived from them in the way that '*grue*' is derived from 'green'.[2] The solution presently being offered to Goodman's Riddle, however, can be used to show the unacceptability of any unacceptable hypothesis based on Goodmanian predicates, whether those predicates are derived from observational predicates or not.

With one significant class of exceptions. Let us define a predicate '*formous*' as applying to all things examined before *t*, if and only if they were formed in limestone, but to other things, if and only if they were not formed in limestone. Then, given circumstances in which all observed emeralds have been found to have been formed in limestone, we cannot *by methods used above* show that the generalization that all emeralds are formed in limestone (and that not all emeralds are examined before *t*) is any simpler, or more acceptable, than the clearly unacceptable generalization that all emeralds are *formous* (and that not all emeralds are examined before *t*). That is because the hypothesis that all emeralds are *formous* and that there are emeralds not examined before *t*, as well as emeralds examined before *t*, posits no unlikenesses *between emeralds*, which, in turn, is due to the fact

---

[1] Surely there *could* be circumstances where it would be reasonable to think that there are unexamined emeralds and that all of them are *grue* (blue), even though one had seen only green emeralds. E.g. if one had a magic wand which one had every reason to think worked and wished on it that all emeralds one had not examined turn to blue and that all future emeralds be blue. In such a situation, simplicity considerations would presumably dictate that one favour the '*grue*' hypothesis over the 'green' hypothesis with respect to unexamined (and thus all) emeralds.

[2] As Goodman himself points out in a reply to critics (*J. Phil.*, 63, 1966, p. 330).

that the property of having been formed in limestone is itself non-differential. In other words, the sort of argument given above will only serve to show the superiority of hypotheses generalizing *differential* properties over hypotheses generalizing Goodmanian properties defined in terms of those differential properties.

But when we say that there are emeralds examined and emeralds not examined before *t* and that all of them are *formous*—and do so on the basis of a sample of emeralds all of which have been found to have been formed in limestone—we may not be positing unlikenesses between emeralds, but we *are* positing unlikenesses between those parts of the earth where emeralds we have examined were formed and those parts of the earth where emeralds unexamined before *t* were formed. For being (composed of) limestone is a differential property, so that any part of the earth or universe where limestone surrounds an emerald is unlike any part of the earth or universe where something other than limestone surrounds an emerald. To say, then, that emerald *x* was formed in limestone and that emerald *y* was not is to posit an unlikeness between that part of the earth (or universe) that immediately surrounded *x* when *x* was formed, as it was when *x* was formed, and that part of the earth (or universe) that immediately surrounded *y* when *y* was formed, as it was when *y* was formed.[1] Thus the hypothesis that there are emeralds examined and emeralds not examined before *t* and that they are all *formous* posits unlikenesses, though not unlikenesses between emeralds, that the corresponding 'formed in limestone' hypothesis does not, so that the latter hypothesis seems, in terms of principles offered in the present chapter, to be simpler and more acceptable scientifically than the former hypothesis. So it would seem that in our circumstances projection of 'formed in limestone' is more reasonable than projection of '*formous*', at least with respect to the reference class of emeralds. We are thus, I think, in a position to show the superiority of various hypotheses involving non-differential properties to hypotheses involving Goodmanian properties that are derived from those non-differential properties in the way that '*grue*' is derived from '*green*'. And so our solution to Goodman's Riddle seems to work both for differential

[1] Assuming that *y* was formed at all. But if it wasn't and has existed from eternity, then *x* and *y* have *dissimilar* histories. What has happened to *x* is *unlike* what has happened to *y*. So whether *y* is thought to have been formed or not, one is committed to unlikenesses when one says that *x* was formed in limestone and that *y* was not.

and for non-differential properties, and thus to be an entirely
general solution to that Riddle.

Certain qualifications, however, must be made before the above
argument will go through. For, if one looks carefully enough, one
will notice that even an hypothesis like 'there are emeralds examined and emeralds not examined before t and all of them are
formed in limestone' (logically) commits itself to certain unlikenesses. After all, emeralds are not and could not be exactly like
hunks of limestone in chemical structure, colour, etc. And the
above hypothesis posits the existence of both emeralds and limestone. Since the principles used above talk only of the superiority
of hypotheses that posit *no* unlikenesses, they obviously cannot
handle the case at hand, cannot be used to show the superiority of
'formed in limestone' over *'formous'* with respect to projection
over the class of emeralds. (And the same problem may even exist
for our above attempt to show the superiority of 'green' over
'grue' with respect to projection over the class of emeralds.)

But notice that, in the case where one claims that emeralds
unexamined before t are formed in limestone, on the basis of a
sample of examined emeralds all of which have been found to have
been formed in limestone, unlikenesses of the type one is positing
between *unexamined* emeralds and certain hunks or deposits of
limestone have already been posited in one's description of the
evidence from which one is generalizing; that is, one is not
committed by one's generalization to the existence of any entity
that is unlike all the other entities one has already posited (before
making one's generalization). But, if one claims, on the basis of
the fact that one has taken a sample of emeralds and has found
them all to have been formed in limestone, that all emeralds
(including some not examined before t) are *formous*, one *is* positing
things that are unlike any of the other things one was committed
to before one claimed that all emeralds are *formous* (and that some
emeralds are not examined before t). For, if one claims that some
emeralds unexamined before t are formed in something other than
limestone, then one is positing a situation where some substance
other than limestone surrounds an emerald. And such a situation,
or the part of the earth where that situation exists, is unlike any
situation where limestone surrounds an emerald, or any part of
the earth where such a situation exists.

Consider, then, the following Principle Z: If one has a sample
of x's all of which have been found by one to be both f and f', and

if saying that the x's in one's sample are f (or that they are f') already involves one in positing certain unlikenesses between things, then it is simpler, and more reasonable, other things being equal, to conclude that all x's (including some not examined before t, for appropriate t) are f than to conclude that all those x's are f', if the two conclusions cannot both be true and if the latter conclusion involves one in positing entities unlike any others one has found to exist in one's sample, but the former conclusion does not (even if the former conclusion commits one to a greater number of unlike things than does the latter); and, in such circumstances, the argument from the fact that all sampled x's have been found to be f' to the conclusion that all x's (including some not examined before t) are f' is unacceptable. (To say that a conclusion involves one in positing entities unlike any others one has found to exist in one's sample is short for saying that, for some predicate 'f', the conclusion in question entails the existence of something f and one's available evidence commits one to holding that anything f is unlike anything else one has already posited in one's sample.) Furthermore, if one has, in general, to choose between two hypotheses P and Q, and P commits one to the existence of certain entities E unlike any others one has already posited, but Q does not commit one to E, then, other things being equal, Q is more acceptable than P. This complex principle seems to be a valid one, and one that scientists adhere to. For scientists not only consider it unreasonable to posit unlikenesses, unless one has a definite reason to, but also are loath to posit things unlike the things they have already posited, even when they already have posited unlikenesses between things. Thus, consider the case of a person who has observed that certain zebras have black and white stripes and is considering whether a given zebra (so far away that he cannot determine its colours) will turn out to have such stripes when he examines it at close hand. Of course, he has already accepted the existence of certain unlikenesses, has already accepted the belief that some things are unlike others, inasmuch as he already holds that certain parts of the bodies of zebras are white and other parts black. But if he says that the unexamined zebra in the distance has black and white stripes, he will be positing (logically committed to) no entities unlike any others that he has already posited.[1] If, on the other hand, he claims that the distant

---

[1] Of course, the distant zebra may be unlike those already examined in many ways; but it is not reasonable for him to assume that it is unless he has definite

zebra is *not* striped he will avoid positing certain unlikenesses between parts of that zebra's coat, and thus perhaps posit a smaller *number* of unlike things than if he were to hypothesize that the distant zebra had stripes. But on the other hand, he will be positing a thing unlike anything else he has posited before: namely, a uniformly-coloured zebra. And that, I think, makes it less simple and less acceptable for him to say the distant zebra is uniformly coloured than to say that it has black and white stripes. In other words, if one is already assuming that there are zebras with black and white stripes, then it is simpler and more acceptable to assume that a zebra whose coat one has not yet examined has a black and white coat than to assume that it is uniformly coloured. And I think anyone who is rational about his inductions will see that this is so and think accordingly, because I think Principle Z above is a valid principle of scientific thinking and of rational thinking in general. In other words, if one is rationally investigating the nature of some class of objects, one will be even more loath to posit things unlike those other things one has already posited than to posit (greater numbers of) things that are unlike one another, but not necessarily unlike everything else that one has already posited, and one will recognize that doing the former results in a greater loss of simplicity (for one's system of scientific beliefs) than doing the latter.

In the light of the above, seemingly valid, Principle Z, we can, I think, see why it is more reasonable to assume that emeralds examined only after *t*, if at all, will (turn out to) be green, than to assume that they will (turn out to) be *grue*, and hence blue. And we can also see why it is more reasonable to project 'formed in limestone' with respect to emeralds than to project '*formous*' with respect to emeralds. For, as I mentioned above, when one argues from the fact that all emeralds one has examined have been found to have been formed in limestone to the conclusion that there are emeralds not examined before *t* and that all emeralds are *formous*, one posits things unlike any of the things one has posited in the premises (describing the emeralds one has examined) from

reason to do so. Indeed there are various higher-order considerations of simplicity that make it reasonable (for us) to assume that nothing (macroscopic) is exactly like anything else. But these considerations become relevant, I think, only after one has accumulated a whole body of scientific knowledge. And at present I am only interested in relatively elementary and 'pure' inductive situations and the problems that arise with respect to them. And indeed Goodman himself takes this very sort of approach in *Fact, Fiction, and Forecast*.

which one is arguing. And this is not true when one argues to the conclusion that there are emeralds not examined before *t* and that all emeralds are formed in limestone. Thus, in normal circumstances, where other things are equal, it is more reasonable to assume that those emeralds not examined before *t* are formed in limestone, than to assume the contrary, if all the emeralds one has already examined are known to have been formed in limestone.

III

I think we are now in a position to defend arguments via the Strong Principle of Induction (introduced in Chapter 4) against attack from arguments based on Goodmanian predicates. One who argues to the conclusion that all emeralds are formed in limestone, for example, need only assume that he has a sample of emeralds all of which he has found to have been formed in limestone and that he has found no reason (after careful examination of his evidence) to think his sample is biased, in order to use the Strong Principle and get to that conclusion. And any Goodmanian attack on his argument would presumably have to question his assumption that his sample is reasonably thought to be unbiased. Such an attack would run somewhat as follows: all emeralds examined so far have turned out to be *formous*, so probably all emeralds are *formous*; and, since one can assume there are emeralds that have not been examined before *t*, one can reasonably assume that there are emeralds that were not formed in limestone, in which case there is reason to think that one's sample of examined emeralds is a biased one, as far as the property of being formed in limestone is concerned. But this whole attack depends on arguing from the fact that all examined emeralds have been found to be both *formous* and formed in limestone to the conclusion that there are emeralds not examined before *t* and that all emeralds are *formous*, rather than to the conclusion that there are emeralds not examined before *t* and that all emeralds are formed in limestone. But according to Principle Z, it is in such a situation more reasonable to argue to the latter conclusion than to the former (barring other evidential factors, which we have presumably ruled out by making the case a simple and an isolated one). And the inductive argument for the former conclusion is definitely unacceptable and unsound. If so, we can conclude that the above Goodmanian argument fails in its attempt to undermine our argument, via the Strong Principle, for the conclusion that all emeralds are formed in limestone. And the same is true for (sound) arguments via the Strong Principle in general. Such arguments need not fear from arguments attacking the fairness of their samples that make use of Goodmanian predicates. Thus we can not only defend arguments via the Strong Principle via highly specific *ad hoc* (but reasonable) principles that rule out *particular* Goodmanian arguments, but also have discovered a single more general principle in terms of which we can rule out all such arguments.

Principle Z can also be used to defend the argument for other minds (as well as the argument for unobserved objects) which we presented in the last chapter from Goodmanian criticisms. Thus it is possible to construct with respect to the predicate 'accompanied by pain or its pretence' a Goodmanian predicate '*prue*' that applies to cases of my own body's pain behaviour, if and only if they are accompanied by pain or its pretence (somewhere in the universe), and to cases where there is pain behaviour (only) on the part of other bodies, if and only if they are not accompanied by pain or its pretence (somewhere in the universe). Then one can easily construct an argument from the fact that every case of pain behaviour on the part of one's own body has been *prue* to the conclusion that (probably) all cases of pain behaviour are *prue*, so that (probably) cases of pain behaviour on the part of other bodies (only) are not accompanied by pain or its pretence (anywhere). And this argument can then be used to challenge the analogical-inductive argument from (*a*) to (*f*) that was put forward in Chapter 4 (p. 118) as a means of showing the reasonableness of belief in other minds. For the person who gives the argument from (*a*) to (*f*) has to assume that there is a case of pain behaviour on the part of a body other than his own occurring when his own body is not pain-behaving. But if (probably) all cases of pain behaviour are *prue*, then (probably) there is a case of pain behaviour that is not accompanied by pain or the pretence of pain; and in that case (one has reason to think that) the generalization from (*a*) to (*b*), on which the whole argument from (*a*) to (*f*) depends, is based on a biased sample of cases of pain behaviour as far as the property being accompanied by pain or its pretence is concerned, and is thus unacceptable. And, in that case, we will have produced no sound argument for the reasonableness of belief in other minds; and our argument in Chapter 4 for the reasonableness of belief in objects that one is not observing will fail for similar reasons.

The Goodmanian challenge to our argument for other minds depends on projecting '*prue*' rather than 'accompanied by pain or its pretence' with respect to at least one case of pain behaviour that is *not* a case of one's own pain behaviour. But, then, one who puts forward that Goodmanian argument is committed to saying that, even though there has been pain (or its pretence) in the universe in the past at certain times (when he was pain behaving), there is no pain (or its pretence) in the universe at present (since at present there is pain behaviour only on the part of someone else). And, in that case, he is forced to posit a state of the universe (or of some part of it) unlike anything else (in particular, any state of (some part of) the universe) he has had to posit in describing the evidence from which he is arguing, i.e. in assuming that all cases of his own pain behaviour have been accompanied by pain or its pretence, that there is presently a case of pain behaviour on the part of another body and not on his own part, and that he is neither feeling pain nor pretending to be in pain. For he is saying that there is now no pain or pretence of pain in (his part of) the universe (even though there is pain behaviour there); and this state of affairs is unlike any state of affairs where there *is* pain or its pretence in (some part of) the universe. On the other hand, if he claims that all cases of pain behaviour are accompanied by pain or its pretence, he will be committed to no entity or entities unlike those other entities he has to assume before he makes this generalization. And, once one sees this, it should be clear that our argument from (*a*) to (*f*) for other minds can be defended from Goodmanian attack in much the same way that the inductive argument for the conclusion that all emeralds are formed in limestone was defended just above from attack via an argument based on a Goodmanian predicate. And the same goes for our argument in Chapter 4 (p. 122 f.) from (*g*) to (*n*) for the reasonableness of belief in objects that one is not observing.

In Chapter 4, we also mentioned a challenge to our argument for other minds proposed by Alvin Plantinga and based on a technique of argument explored by R. Sleigh in his doctoral dissertation (pp. 126–32). And we attempted to meet that challenge with Principle Y. But that principle can itself, I think, be further justified in terms of the sorts of considerations we have been making use of in the present chapter.

Consider, for example, the case where one has before one a crow that one sees has a broken claw, where all crows one has examined have cawed, and where all cawing and other animals previously examined have been found to lack broken claws. One who in such a situation argues that the thing in front of him is a non-cawing broken-clawed thing will presumably base his argument on the assumptions that all the various cawing things previously examined have turned out to have intact claws and that the claws of the thing in front of him are not intact. And in that case his conclusion commits him to the existence of a *kind* of thing that he is not committed to by any one of the premises on which he bases his argument—where k counts as a kind of thing just in case the members of k are necessarily unlike non-members of k. For none of the premises of his argument entails the existence of non-cawing broked-clawed things, but its conclusion (and its premises taken jointly) do entail the existence of such things (of that kind of thing). On the other hand, anyone who argues from premises to the effect that: all the various crows previously examined have turned out to be cawers and that there is a crow in front of him, to the conclusion that the crow in front of him is a cawer is committed by his conclusion (or by his premises taken jointly) to no kind of thing that none of his premises taken singly commits him to.

At this point, the following Principle Z' suggests itself: if, in a given situation, there are available two arguments M and N that make use of enumerative induction to support opposing conclusions, and if the conclusion of M (or M's premises and principles of inference taken jointly) entail (the existence of) kinds of things different[1] from any entailed by any one of M's

---

[1] Two kinds k and l constitute different (non-identical) kinds if k can (logically) exist without l or l can (logically) exist without k. Thus the kind crow is not identical with the kind, 'cawing crow', because the former kind might continue to exist even though the latter kind did not (became extinct). Two different kinds can be related as genus and species, in other words, and obviously a genus may continue to exist even though certain of its species have become extinct. I am assuming here that biological species and genera, etc. are kinds, and that certain kinds or species (or genera or families or classes, etc.) of things can go out of existence. Some philosophers (e.g. Quine in *Methods of Logic*, N.Y.: Holt, 1959, p. 204 f.) have assumed that species, etc. are abstract entities like the number five. But species, and other kinds, can come into and go out of existence—it is legitimate, e.g., to speak of the 'origin of the species'—whereas the number five, presumably, cannot, if it exists, go out of existence, and never came into existence. Furthermore, biological species occupy certain regions of the earth, and so are spatial in a way that the number five is not. So I think it is a

premises, but this is not true of argument N, then, other things being equal, it is simpler and more acceptable to accept N than to accept M, and M is clearly unacceptable (in that situation). Furthermore, if, in a given situation, there are available two competing hypotheses (or explanations of a phenomenon) P and Q, and P commits one to a kind of thing K to which Q does not commit us, then, other things being equal, Q is simpler and more acceptable than P and P is unacceptable (in that situation). Principle Z', like Principle Z, relies on the existence of a connection between the notion of unlikeness (in terms of which the notion of a kind is defined) and inductive simplicity and acceptability.[1] And it seems to be a principle that encapsulates our intuitions about the acceptability of particular inductive arguments, and also to be a principle that scientists implicitly adhere to. When, for example, a biologist discovers a new species of animal, he tends to be reluctant to posit a new genus (or family, or order, etc.) to which it belongs, and will try, instead, to see if he can fit the new species into already accepted genera, etc. For to posit a new genus (or order, or family, etc.) further complicates his scheme of animal classification, and biologists prefer the simplest classificatory scheme with which they can account for all the data (other things being equal). Thus, if classificatory or categorical simplicity is a valid scientific aim or goal, one should prefer not to posit new kinds, other things being equal. And so one should also prefer an *argument* whose conclusion commits one to no new kinds (kinds to which one was not committed by

mistake to think of species, etc. as abstract entities in any traditional sense of the term, or as being incapable of perishing in the way that the number five has been thought to be incapable of perishing (if it exists).

I am assuming here that the notion of a kind is closely related in ordinary speech to the notion of unlikeness, inasmuch as I am assuming that, if x is and y is not a member of some kind k, then it follows that x and y are not exactly alike. After all, when we say that particular things x and y are *of* different kinds, we mean that they are not (exactly) alike. And to say that x and y are of different kinds is also, presumably, just to say that there is some kind (of entity) to which the one belongs and the other does not. And in that case, something counts as a kind only if its members cannot be exactly like its non-members.

[1] Principle Z' differs from Principle Z, because there is a difference between positing new kinds of things and positing things unlike the things one has already posited. If I claim that there are fish, and then later claim that there are trout, I have posited a new kind of thing at that later time (a species I did not posit earlier); but I am not at that later time committed to the existence of things unlike any I earlier posited, because when I earlier said that there were fish, I never said that those fish were *not* trout. Thus, Principle Z' seems to entail, but not to be entailed by, Principle Z.

any of the premises of the argument) to an *argument* whose conclusion does commit one to new kinds, other things being equal, in which case Principle Z' is clearly valid.

Given the validity of Z', we can see why Principle Y of Chapter 4 is valid. For when one argues inductively for the conclusion that a given non-C is a non-B on the basis of premises, no one of which entails that (one has reason to believe that) certain other things are non-C non-B's, one will as a result of that argument be positing a kind of entity that one has not posited in any of the premises from which one is (enumeratively) inductively arguing. (Unless 'B' or 'C' is a Goodmanian-type predicate of such a sort that saying that x is B (or C) and y is not commits one to no unlikenesses. But in that case, the argument contravening Principle Y will presumably fall foul of the principles presented here that eliminate unacceptable arguments involving Goodmanian predicates.) And such an argument will be unacceptable if there is any argument that opposes it, that does not posit new kinds, and that is otherwise lacking in inductive deficiencies. Thus Principle Z' (and the other principles produced here) vindicate our earlier Principle Y.

Now in Chapter 4, we presented an argument, from (8) and (9) to (14) (p. 126 ff.) to challenge our argument, from (a) to (f) (p. 118), for other minds. But I think we could easily show that the former argument contravenes Principle Z' (just as it contravenes Principle Y), and so does not render our argument for other minds unacceptable. If so, we have, I think, vindicated the use of the Strong Principle of Induction in arguments, like those of Chapter 4 or like those involving emeralds that we have discussed in the present chapter, which can be challenged by sceptical arguments. Whenever one is entitled to use the Strong Principle in the face of such challenges, it is because of the validity of Principles like Z and Z', in terms of which those challenges can be met. In other words, I am saying that whenever enumerative induction is proper and acceptable there are considerations of unlikenesses and simplicity that ensure that propriety and acceptability.[1]

In arguing for the existence of other minds and unobserved objects in Chapter 4, we assumed the *truth* of certain claims about our bodies and the bodies of others, about certain physical

---

[1] Cf. S. Barker (*op. cit.*, p. 246) who claims that inductive reasoning depends on simplicity considerations, rather than the other way around.

objects like fires, and about our experience. But in Chapter 3, we argued only for the *reasonableness* of certain (tentative) assumptions or claims about the nature of the external (physical) world, and only assumed the *reasonableness* of certain assumptions about our experience. We must, then, do something to tie up the argument of Chapters 2 and 3 with the argument of the past two chapters, if we are to have one continuous train of argument going from assumptions about our present experience via certain general epistemic and scientific principles to conclusions not only about the reasonableness of belief in external objects of various kinds, but also about the reasonableness of belief in other minds and unobserved objects. This can be done, I think, by slightly altering the first premises of the arguments for unobserved objects and for other minds of the last chapter, and by making one change in the Strong Principle of Induction (or in its weaker version). Instead of saying that all cases of pain behaviour on the part of one's own body have been accompanied by pain or its pretence, we can say: it is reasonable to believe tentatively that all cases of pain behaviour. . . . And instead of saying that all roaring fires watched continuously . . . we can say that it is reasonable to believe tentatively that all roaring fires watched continuously. . . . Then we can alter the Strong Principle of Induction (or its weaker version) to read: If it is reasonable to believe (at least tentatively) that one has examined a certain class C of x's and that all the x's in C are f (and that there are numerous x's in C), and if one has, after careful, rational, thorough examination of one's evidence, discovered no reason to think that C constitutes an unfair or biased sample of the x's in general as far as f-ness is concerned, then it is reasonable to believe (at least tentatively) that all x's are f, or at least reasonable to believe (at least tentatively) of any given x (that one has reason to believe exists, but that might not exist) that it is f. The Principle thus altered is still, I think, valid, especially in its weaker version. And, using that principle and assumptions about the reasonableness of tentative belief in various sorts of objects and present and past experiences, we can justify the generalization that all cases of pain behaviour are accompanied by pain or its pretence, that is, show the reasonableness of our tentatively accepting that generalization. But Chapters 2 and 3 also provide us with arguments for the reasonableness of tentatively believing that another body is displaying pain behaviour (when it looks as if there is another body displaying pain behaviour), and we are entitled in the present work to assume (although we can also show)[1] the reasonableness of assuming we are not in pain or pretending pain (when we think that we are not in pain and not pretending pain). So presumably we can argue that it is reasonable for us to believe (perhaps only quite tentatively) that someone or something else is in pain or pretending pain, at least in circumstances where there appears to be another body pain-behaving and where we have the sorts of other sense and memory impressions we normally do. Thus we can graft our argument for other minds on to our argument for the reasonableness of various claims about the external world, and, presumably, we can do the same for our argument for unobserved objects. We can argue for other minds and unobserved objects, therefore, solely on the basis of assumptions about immediate experience and valid principles of rational (scientific) thinking, and we have made good our promise to provide a single train of argument to overcome scepticism about the external world, scepticism about the nature of the external world, and scepticism about other minds and unobserved objects.

It is worth pointing out, however, that someone might want to challenge our argument for other minds, while accepting the validity of our argument for unobserved objects, on the grounds that he can in principle never observe another's pain or pretence of pain, although he can in principle observe an object that is at some one time unobserved (by him). Such a person might wish to restrict or revise the Strong Principle in such a way that it can be used only to argue for the reasonableness of believing in things that can in principle be observed by the person arguing. But why think that the Strong Principle must be restricted in this way? Both our argument for other minds and our argument for objects unobserved by the person arguing can be justified in terms of principles, relating unlikeness and simplicity and inductive acceptability, that are pervasive of scientific practice and theory. Furthermore, when a person is at a given time t not observing an object o, why should the fact that he can or cannot *at some later time* observe o affect the reasonableness *at t* of believing that o exists? Surely, for example, if he knows as an empirical fact that he will die before he gets to see a certain object, he is not less reasonable in believing in the existence of that object than he would be if he (knew that he) were capable of eventually

[1] See Chapter 3, p. 109 f., above.

seeing the object in question. And if the empirical impossibility of seeing or observing a given object after t need not affect the reasonableness at t of believing in the existence of that object, why should the impossibility in principle of such observation affect it?

The assumption of the falsity of the Strong Principle as applied to entities unobservable in principle is implausible for yet another reason, namely, that it implies the unreasonableness of inductive practice in physics. For there are certain subatomic particles that cannot, according to physicists, in principle be observed; and yet physicists make inferences to their existence under certain experimental or other conditions, and make generalizations about how such particles will behave under similar conditions. So, unless one wants to deny the validity of certain inductive practices in physics, one cannot deny the validity of the Strong Principle as applied to arguments for the existence of entities that are unobservable in principle for one who is using the Strong Principle, e.g., other minds. Thus I do not think there is any reason to think that the Strong Principle needs to be changed or restricted or that it cannot be used to justify belief in other minds. (Cf. p. 181 f., below.)

(Incidentally, we have talked about 'other minds' because of traditional philosophic usage. Actually we have at best only shown the reasonableness of tentative belief in the existence of some other conscious being. Many philosophers tend to confuse conscious beings with their minds. But a conscious being is not his mind. His mind is, I think, just his ability to think, and this is, I think, true by virtue of the very meaning of the word 'mind'. This is a far cry from the way most modern philosophers (e.g. Russell in the *Analysis of Mind*; Wisdom in *Problems of Mind and Matter*; and Descartes in the *Third Meditation*) have used the term 'mind', but I think it is part of the ordinary meaning of that term, none the less. Indeed, Aristotle in *De Anima* comes very close to defining 'mind' in this way. If I am right, then, one is not one's mind because one could go on existing without retaining one's ability to think ('become a vegetable'). Thus, if one gives one's mind the proper name 'Mindo' and one's own name is 'Slote', the claim that Mindo and Slote go out of existence at different times is not necessarily false. If, in consequence, one is not one's mind, then we have really not argued for the existence of other minds, since we have only argued for the existence of pain *or* its pretence on the part of another conscious being, and the existence of pain does not entail the existence of the ability to think. But that is not, of course, to say that we *could* not use the Strong Principle to argue for the existence of other minds, for the existence of other beings with the ability to think.)

IV

In the present chapter we have relied on the notion of unlikeness (and the closely related notion of a *kind* of thing), as well as on the notion of simplicity, to show the acceptability of some arguments and hypotheses and the unacceptability of others. But we were really already using those notions in an implicit way in Chapters 2 and 3 when we made use of Principles B, C, B'', etc. Principle B, for example, says that it is unreasonable to hypothesize that something has acted or operated one way in the past, but will act or operate in a different way in the future, unless one has a definite reason that justifies thinking so. But acting in different ways at different times is not acting *f*-ly at one time and non-*f*-ly at another, for any value of the adverbial variable '*f*-ly'. We can, for example, define an adverb '*tempily*' that applies to a man who is sitting, if and only if it is earlier than some time *t*, and to a man who is not sitting if and only if it is after *t*; then a man would be acting or behaving *tempily* before *t* and non-*tempily* after *t*, if he just sat in a chair before and after *t*. But he is surely not necessarily acting in a different manner or way before and after *t* if he does this. That is because to act in two different *ways* or *manners* is to act in ways or manners that are *unlike*. A man who sits from before *t* to after *t* may (logically) be such that the way he acts before *t* is in no way unlike or dissimilar to the way he acts after *t*.

Whenever one claims that something acts in one way at one time and in a different way at another, therefore, one is positing unlikenesses. And Principle B (and C, and B'' and the rest) are valid just because any hypothesis that posits an unlikeness has a strike against it, is unacceptable unless there is a definite reason that justifies positing that unlikeness. Indeed, the following Principle Z'' seems to be an absolutely fundamental and pervasive principle of rational scientific and other thinking: if a certain hypothesis or explanation of certain evidence posits certain

F

unlikenesses (or kinds of things) that an alternative hypothesis or explanation of that evidence does not, and if the other unlikenesses (or kinds of things) they posit balance each other out and all other factors are equal, then the latter hypothesis or explanation is simpler than and to be preferred to the former, and the former is unacceptable. If Z and Z' are valid, surely Z″ is also valid; and Principles B and C, etc., all follow from (and thus derive plausibility from) this single general Principle Z″. Furthermore, if anyone were to challenge the validity of Principles B and C, etc., by attempting to produce hypotheses involving 'queer' Goodmanian adverbs that seem to be ruled out by B, etc., even though they also seem perfectly acceptable, we could meet that challenge by use of the distinction between acting in different ways and acting f-ly and non-f-ly. Someone who claims that if I see a man sitting just before t, it is totally unreasonable for me to believe he will be sitting just after t, in the absence of other information, because that involves assuming that he acts *tempily* before t and non-*tempily* afterwards, can be answered by pointing out that such an assumption does not contravene Principle B or Principle Z″. A man may act *tempily* at one time and non-*tempily* at another without there being any dissimilarity or difference between the *way* he acts at the one time and the *way* he acts at the other. It is only when one assumes that a man has acted or will act *tempily* both before and after t, without having a reason for such an assumption, that one is involved in positing unlikenesses without justification, and thus, according to B and Z″, thinking in an unnecessarily complex and unreasonable way.

The notions of unlikeness and of a kind are, I think, fundamental and inescapable in assessing the validity of enumerative inductive arguments and general hypotheses. Indeed, I think it is not an exaggeration to say that differences with respect to unlikenesses and kinds of things posited are the most important sort of differences between acceptable and unacceptable enumerative inductive hypotheses and inferences. We have already illustrated the usefulness of the notion of unlikeness in explaining why some arguments, etc. are sound while others are not. But there is a whole range of other inductive arguments and generalizations that have perplexed philosophers, whose acceptability or unacceptability can be explained via the notions we have been making use of here.

Consider the following arguments: (1) All crows I have examined have been in America (and I know of no other investigations of crows), so probably all crows are in America. (2) All emeralds examined thus far have been identical with emerald *a* or with emerald *b*, etc., so probably all emeralds are identical with *a* or *b*, etc., in which case there are probably no emeralds that have not been examined.[1] Or (3) All sunrises examined by us preceded the birth of my first child, so probably the sun will not rise again *after* my first child is born.

What is wrong with all these inductive arguments, I think, is that their conclusions posit unlikenesses that can be avoided by accepting contrary conclusions for which one can also give inductive arguments. To say that all crows are in America is to posit a faunal unlikeness between America and other large parts of the world, whereas to claim that other large parts of the world are inhabited by crows is precisely not to posit such an unlikeness. Thus one can argue via the Strong Principle of Induction that since all large (enough) areas of America contain at least some crows, it is reasonable to believe that all large (enough) areas of the world contain some crows. (Assuming, for simplicity's sake, that one does not know, for example, that certain huge desert areas exist outside this country and that there are no crows or similar forms of life in these areas.) And this argument cannot be successfully challenged by argument (1) above, since (the conclusion of) (1) can be ruled out by Principle Z″.

Similarly, one can give an argument via the Strong Principle from the fact that, in all sufficiently large areas of the earth's crust where we have looked for emeralds, we have found emeralds to the conclusion that in all sufficiently large areas of the earth's crust (including those we have examined without bothering to look for or find emeralds in them) there are emeralds, and thence to the claim that there are emeralds that have not yet been examined (by us). (This argument depends on our ability to know that there are parts of the earth's surface we have examined but are not now examining. But this sort of assumption can be justified by the sort of argument given in Chapter 4 for unobserved objects.) Argument (2) above constitutes a challenge to our argument for the existence of as yet unexamined (by us) emeralds. But accepting its conclusion involves one in claiming that certain large parts of the earth's crust are unlike one another in mineral content, because it involves one in claiming that all parts of the

[2] Cf. I. Scheffler's *The Anatomy of Inquiry*, N.Y.: Knopf, 1963, p. 308 f.

earth where one has not found emeralds lack emeralds. On the other hand, the conclusion that all sufficiently large areas of the earth's crust contain emeralds is involved in no such unlikenesses; so, given the data or evidence that one has found emeralds a, b, etc., it is, other things being equal, more reasonable to assume that there are emeralds one has not yet examined than to assume the contrary, if Principle Z'' is valid. Argument (2) would seem, then, to yield an unacceptable conclusion, and so is itself unacceptable, and there is no reason to think that one cannot use the Strong Principle (or its weaker version) to justify the claim that there are emeralds one has not yet examined.

I think we could also easily use principles developed here to undermine argument (3) above. What seems to be wrong with arguments like (1), (2), and (3) is that they involve *particular times* or *places* or *entities* in such a way that their conclusions involve one in accepting unlikenesses that certain alternative conclusions are not committed to. The reason why one who says that there are emeralds other than a or b, etc., or crows outside America is not committed to unlikenesses is just that one who says that certain particular things have a certain property need not be positing any new unlikenesses or kinds of entities when he says that other particular things have that property. To posit those other particular things may be to posit a greater number of unlike things; but even then it may not involve positing any new kind of thing or anything unlike all the other things one has already posited. That is because the identity of a non-abstract particular is never a differential property of it (at least, where identity is attributed via a phrase of the form 'is identical with a' and 'a' is a proper name or a logical constant). A and b are never unlike just because a is identical with a, and b is not identical with a. Since the positing of a greater number of unlike things is, as we have said, less significant inductively than the positing of things unlike any one has already posited or than the positing of new kinds of things, arguments like (1), (2) and (3) above must be held to be unacceptable and unsound from an inductive (scientific) standpoint. And, inasmuch as the principles developed here in the present chapter are capable of explaining the unacceptability of such arguments as those with which we have just been dealing, the pervasiveness and importance of those principles in inductive thinking is still further illustrated, and it becomes even more plausible to think that those principles, and the notion of unlikeness which they enshrine, provide the key to the inductive unacceptability of arguments involving Goodmanian predicates (or contravening Principle Y) and to the acceptability of our arguments via the Strong Principle of Induction for other minds and for unobserved objects.

We have been assuming all along in the present chapter that rational science accepts simplicity as a standard for judging the acceptability of hypotheses and that unlikenesses are relevant in certain important ways to simplicity. But actually we need never have brought the notion of simplicity into the discussion of the present chapter. We could simply have claimed that various sorts of hypotheses and arguments are unacceptable because they posit unlikenesses or new kinds of things in various ways. We could, in other words, have directly related unlikenesses and kinds to inductive acceptability, without bringing in simplicity at all. Nor is the relation between the positing of new entities unlike any which one has previously posited, or the positing of new kinds of entities, and inductive acceptability (other things equal) merely a matter of contingent empirical fact. Arguments positing unnecessary unlikenesses are, *ceteris paribus*, unacceptable, but not because accepting such arguments has got us into trouble in the past or because of certain contingent features of the world (and our means of getting information in it). Even if one were possessed of absolutely no other relevant empirical information except the fact that all the balls one had found in an urn so far had been the same shade of red, it would be more unreasonable to assume that the next ball taken out of the urn would be green than to assume that the next ball would be red. Of course, I cannot *prove* that this is so, but I think that anyone who examines the matter carefully and with an open mind will have the same intuition that I do on this matter, will see clearly that it is more reasonable to think the next ball picked will be red than to think it will be green. And that is because he implicitly accepts principles like Z, Z', and Z" as regulative of scientific inquiry independently of particular information or particular facts about the nature of the world.

Of course, one might question the relevance even of the notions of *likeness* and of *kind* to the acceptability of inductive arguments, etc. One might, for example, create two predicates '*gounlike*' and '*different gokinds*' that bore the same relation to the predicates 'unlike' and 'different kinds' that '*grue*' bears to 'green'. And one might then question whether one should not use *gounlikeness* and being different *gokinds*, rather than unlikeness and being different kinds, as one's basic standards for evaluating enumerative inductive arguments, etc. But that is just because one can question any inductive standard in a sceptical manner, however plausible that standard may seem intuitively, upon reflection, and in practice. And as Hume showed us, there can be no proper inductive or deductive argument that justifies all one's inductive standards and practices. Given, then, that one wants to claim that the avoidance of unnecessary unlikenesses and kinds of entities is a fundamental standard of the acceptability of scientific hypotheses and (enumerative) inductions, the sceptic who asks for a justification of that standard is really bringing up Hume's Riddle or Problem, and that, I think, is a problem that it really is impossible to solve, and that I am in no way attempting to solve here.[1]

On the other hand, I think we really *have* provided a solution of a general sort to Goodman's New Riddle of Induction. I think the principles proposed in the present chapter not only provide us with general traits that (allow us to) *differentiate* good inductive arguments from fallacious or unsound inductive arguments based on Goodmanian predicates, but also provide us with explanations of why (what makes) certain inductive arguments are acceptable and others not. For I think that the fact that a certain hypothesis posits unnecessary unlikenesses (or kinds of entities) *makes* that hypothesis unacceptable or *contributes* to its being unacceptable, other things being equal. And just the opposite, of course, for those hypotheses that are acceptable. On the other hand, even if Goodman's attempt to deal with his own Riddle is successful on its own terms, that is, finds predicates that distinguish acceptable from unacceptable predicates and/or arguments, it does not explain why 'grue' arguments are (typically) unacceptable or why 'green' arguments (typically) are acceptable.[2] Furthermore, inasmuch as the claim that an hypothesis (or the conclusion

---

[1] Goodman seems to think that he can solve Hume's Riddle since he thinks that the inductions that 'are normally accepted as valid' are *by definition* 'valid inductions' (*ibid.*, p. 65 n.). (Note how close Goodman's view here is to that of proponents of the Paradigm Case Argument.) But such a definition seems totally implausible to me, so that I cannot agree that he has solved Hume's Riddle, or 'dissolved' that Riddle.

[2] Of course, there have also been objections to Goodman's solution to his own Riddle on its own terms, e.g. by Davidson, *op. cit.*, and by J. Wallace (*J. Phil.*, 63, 1966, p. 780 f.).

of an argument) posits unnecessary unlikenesses is one that does not presuppose the validity of any inductive arguments, the notion of unlikeness provides a standard in terms of which any and all particular enumerative inductive arguments of the sort that scientists are inclined to make can be justified. Goodman's notion of entrenchment, on the other hand, cannot provide such a means of generally justifying the sorts of projections we are generally inclined to make, just because, as we saw earlier (p. 138 f.), the claim that a certain predicate is entrenched presupposes the validity of certain inductive arguments (projectibility of certain predicates) and the invalidity of other inductive arguments (unprojectibility of other predicates). And so I think Goodman's solution to his own Riddle is not as epistemologically deep or satisfying as the one offered here.[1]

Of course, one objection Goodman might make to our use of the notion of unlikeness to deal with his Riddle would be that we in fact have no independent notion of alikeness, that statements about alikeness and unlikeness are nothing but (reduce to) statements about what is or is not inductively acceptable. When, for example, one says that x and y are not alike, one is just saying that a (normally) projectible predicate applies to x but not to y, or vice versa. And to say that an hypothesis posits unnecessary unlikenesses is just to say it is unacceptable—but not for reasons of lack of explanatory power, lack of fertility, or lack of any other factor of this sort. If talk about unlikenesses uniformly reduces to talk about inductive acceptability and the notion of unlikeness cannot be understood as independent of the notion of inductive acceptability, then our attempt to explain greater acceptability in terms of the avoiding of unnecessary unlikenesses (and other things being equal) will be circular and mistaken in principle. But is this in fact the case?

Earlier we pointed out that the distinction between differential and non-differential properties does not correspond to the distinction between inductively acceptable and unacceptable properties. We argued that, given our notion of unlikeness, it is logically impossible for there to be an x and y such that x is green, y not green, and x exactly like y, but logically possible for there to be

---

[1] Goodman would presumably be unhappy with my use of the notions of analyticity and of logical possibility in dealing with his Riddle. But we may, at least, have reduced the New Riddle of Induction to the problem of justifying the use of notions like analyticity and logical possibility.

an x and y such that x was formed in limestone, y was not formed in limestone, and y is exactly like x, even though greenness and the property of having been formed in limestone are both inductively acceptable properties. But, then, it would seem that claims about differentialness (which are claims involving the notions of likeness and of logical possibility) cannot be translated into claims about inductive acceptability. Furthermore, the claim that two things are exactly alike does not seem to be eliminable in favour of any claim about inductive acceptability, since two things may, as we have argued, be exactly alike and yet one of them have and the other lack some inductively acceptable property (like having been formed in limestone). Thus the fact that some non-differential properties are inductively in order seems to indicate that talk about alikeness or unlikeness cannot be reduced to talk about inductive acceptability. (What also tends to show that the notion of likeness is an independent one is the fact that statements like 'Red is more like violet than like green' seem to be true, and yet to involve no claims about what is more or less inductively acceptable. For, as I shall argue in the next section of this chapter (p. 172 f.), the sheer size of the unlikenesses posited by an hypothesis does not affect its inductive acceptability.)

Another objection to our proposed solution to Goodman's Riddle that Goodman might want to make (and which, in fact, is suggested by what Goodman says in the final two pages of *Fact, Fiction, and Forecast*) would be that it is more appropriate to explain the fact that x posits unlikenesses that y does not in terms of the fact that x is less acceptable than y (and other things are equal), than to explain in the opposite direction, as we have done here. Now in the present case 'other things are equal' presumably means that x and y are equally acceptable with respect to the totality of all those factors (aside from the positing of unlikenesses) that make for inductive acceptability: explanatory power, fertility, non-inquiry-limitingness, etc. But surely we would never say that we can explain why y is more fertile than x in terms of the fact that y is more acceptable than x. For this would obviously be to put the cart before the horse. And given the existence of an independent notion of unlikeness, the same seems to be true about explaining positing unlikenesses in terms of inductive acceptability.

Consider a parallel. There are many ingredients that go to

make a fine person: honesty, generosity, friendliness, etc. And it is true that, if man *a* is more honest than man *b*, but they are equal in the other factors that make for fine personhood, then *a* is a finer person than *b*, but also true that, if these other things are equal, *a* will be more honest than *b*, if *a* is a finer person than *b*. However, it would surely be wrongheaded to suggest that what makes *a* more honest than *b*, under the circumstances, is his being a finer person than *b*. Surely, it is the other way round; as Hare would put it: fine personhood is supervenient upon honesty and the like, rather than honesty being supervenient on fine personhood and generosity, etc.

Similarly, in the field of induction, there are many factors that tend to contribute to the acceptability of an hypothesis or its superiority over another hypothesis: explanatory power, avoiding unlikenesses, etc. Avoiding the positing of unlikenesses is an ingredient in inductive acceptability, rather than the reverse. That is, the latter is supervenient upon the former, but not vice versa, just as fine personhood supervenes upon honesty, but not vice versa. And so, just as it seems to be a mistake to explain greater honesty in terms of being a finer person, it seems to be a mistake to explain the positing of fewer unlikenesses in terms of greater inductive acceptability. Fine personhood is an overarching category or mixture in which there are many factors or ingredients; inasmuch as inductive acceptability seems to be a similar sort of overarching category or mixture of various factors or ingredients, within the realm of science though rather than ethics, there seems to be no more reason to explain unlikeness-positing in terms of greater acceptability than to explain greater honesty in terms of being a finer person.

Of course, someone might, finally, object that the notion of unlikeness, on which our whole solution to Goodman's Riddle depends, is no clearer or easier to apply correctly than the notion of projectibility itself (or the notion of inductive acceptability). But no one (including Goodman) has ever claimed that the problem with 'projectible' or with 'acceptable' was that those predicates were unclear or difficult to apply.[1] It is easy enough to tell what arguments are acceptable or what predicates projectible (with respect to 'normal' reference classes); the problem is to find (other) features in terms of which we can distinguish projectible from non-projectible predicates and acceptable from

[1] See *Fact, Fiction, and Forecast*, p. 79.

non-acceptable inductive arguments, and in terms of which we can explain what it is about good arguments and predicates that makes them good, and what it is about bad arguments and predicates that renders them bad. As long as the notion of unlikeness is no worse off in clarity, or ease of correct application, than the notion of projectibility or of acceptability, we can use that notion to explain why certain things are projectible or acceptable and why others are not; just as one can explain smoke in terms of fire, even though the latter notion is no clearer than the former and can no more easily be defined than the former. Thus even though the notion of unlikeness (or of a kind of thing) is not *perfectly* clear and cannot (currently) be defined (by us), we can still use that notion to explain, with respect to a large class of inductive arguments, why some of those arguments are acceptable and others are not, and thus to provide a general and epistemologically satisfying solution to Goodman's New Riddle of Induction.

V

We are now, I think, in a position to use the sorts of principles and arguments we have been making use of in dealing with problems concerning the justification and nature of various forms of enumerative induction, in order to present an argument, independent of the argument presented in Chapters 2 and 3, for the reasonableness of a large number of our commonsense assumptions about the nature of the external world. For our experience is such that it looks, sounds, etc. to us exactly as if there are tables, books, rivers, etc., around our bodies in the external world. Given such experience, the way the universe[1] appears to be is: made up of tables, books, chairs, and other objects, undergoing various changes and/or processes and standing in various changing relations to one another. That is, the universe appears to be the following: a universe made up of (or composed of) real tables and chairs, etc., standing in various relations and undergoing various changes, etc. Now scepticism of the sort that denies an external physical world altogether or of the sort that claims that things, processes, etc., of the sort there appear to be, do not

---

[1] In saying that the universe appears to be a certain way, I am not assuming that there is anything physical, because there is a universe of some sort even if only I and my sense impressions exist.

in fact exist is committed to saying that the way the universe is, in fact, is: not made up of tables, etc. Such scepticism says that the universe is in reality the following: a universe devoid of tables, etc. On the other hand, common sense holds that the way the universe is, in fact, is: made up of tables, etc. And so scepticism posits an unlikeness between the way things appear to be and the way things in fact are, between Appearance and Reality, in a way that the commonsense view of things does not. And for that reason I think we can use Principle Z″ to eliminate sceptical hypotheses that claim that our experiences of sense are caused by certain factors in such a way as to be illusory, for such hypotheses posit an unlikeness between the way the universe appears to be and the way the universe in fact is,[1] whereas the commonsense assumption that our experience is generally veridical does

---

[1] In his 'The Way the World Is' (*Review of Metaphysics* 14, 1960, pp. 48–56), Nelson Goodman has argued that there is no such thing as the way the world (or anything *x*) is, because there are many ways the world (or anything *x*) is at any given time. Indeed, if 'the way the world is' meant something like 'the only way the world is', Goodman might well be correct in saying that there is no such thing as the way the world is. But, in fact, I think there is no such emphasis on uniqueness in the ordinary usage of 'the way the world (or *x*) is (at some time *t*)'. Rather, what is ordinarily meant by 'the way the world is at *t*' is just: that way the world is at *t* that includes (or involves or contains) all (the) other ways the world is at *t*; in other words, that one way the world is at *t* such that any true description of any other way the world is at *t* is also a true description of it. (Compare 'the thing I have in my hand is worth a million dollars', said when one has in one's hand a ring consisting of a gold band and two diamonds. Surely such a statement is not false just because there are *at least* two things one can with truth say are in one's hand: the whole ring (worth a million dollars), each of the diamonds in the ring, etc. Presumably 'the thing in my hand' does not mean 'the only thing in my hand', but rather 'that thing in my hand of which everything else in my hand is a part'.) I think, then, that Goodman has given us no reason to think there can be no such thing as the way the world (or anything *x*) is at *t*, at least as that phrase is ordinarily understood.

Of course, another reason Goodman may have for thinking that there cannot be such a thing as the way the world is may be that whenever we try to describe the way the world is, we can say only some of the things that are true about the way the world is. But surely we also cannot completely describe material objects, and there are such things just the same.

By way of addendum it should be noted that in his latest book, *Languages of Art* (Indianapolis: Bobbs-Merrill, 1968, p. 6 n.), Goodman claims that ways the world is are all descriptions or pictures. In this sense of 'the way the world is' there clearly cannot be such a thing as the way the world is; for there is no unique description or picture of the world and none that contains or includes all others. But, given this usage of 'the way the world is' in which only symbolic entities are ways the world is, one wonders how some of Goodman's claims in his earlier, 'The Way the World Is', are to be understood. For, in that article (p. 55) he says that every true description tells us a way the world is; but how can a true description tell us a true description? Goodman's usage of 'the way the world is'

not. Of course, the hypothesis of common sense posits tables and chairs, etc., and these things are unlike one another in various ways. But sceptical hypotheses posit similar unlikenesses. The hypothesis of the demon, for example, has to posit unlikenesses between the demon's desire to and ability to create the appearance of tables, on the one hand, and his desire to and ability to create the appearance of chairs, on the other,[1] as well as unlikenesses among the various causal means he uses to create these differing appearances. So the unlikenesses between tables and chairs posited by common sense seem to be balanced out by parallel unlikenesses in any full-blown demon or other hypothesis that is sceptical about the nature of the external world.

One might, however, argue that those unlikenesses posited by the hypothesis of the demon, between the demon's ability to create sensations of tables and his ability to create sensations of chairs, count for less than the unlikenesses posited by common sense between tables and chairs, because positing the latter unlikenesses commits one to physical realities, whereas positing the former unlikenesses does not, and because the unlikeness between physical and mental entities is so great compared with any unlikenesses between strictly mental entities.[2] But, even if the unlikeness between a chair and a sensation of a chair is greater than that between a demon and a sensation of a chair, or between certain mental abilities and certain experiences, this will not necessarily mean that the unlikeness between Appearance and Reality posited by sceptical hypotheses like that of the demon is so counterbalanced by the fact that such hypotheses do not commit themselves to physical entities (in addition to mental or psychical ones), that the hypothesis of some sort of demon is no worse off than the commonsense assumption of some sort of

differs from ordinary usage, clearly, for on the ordinary usage of that expression, there can conceivably be ways the world is at various times, even if there never are any descriptions or pictures. There can be ways the world is in a universe without symbols just as there can be objects in a universe where there never are any symbols. Thus, even if there can be or is no such thing as the way the world is, given Goodman's usage of 'the way the world is', there is, I think, no reason to think that there is no such thing as the way the world is at t in the ordinary sense of that expression.

[1] One ability (or desire) can also be unlike another ability (or desire), inasmuch as one who has the first but lacks the second is necessarily unlike someone who has the second and lacks the first.

[2] Cf. D. C. Williams' 'The Inductive Argument for Subjectivism', *The Monist* 44, 1934, p. 101 f., where this suggestion is made and then discarded.

external world that is much as it appears to be. For, in general, I think, the size or greatness of the unlikeness posited by an hypothesis has no significant effect on its acceptability. If, for example, one has seen a tree when it was a sapling, it is not, other things being equal, any more reasonable to assume that that sapling has become only somewhat larger, than to assume that it is now a great deal larger, even though the former assumption commits one to a smaller unlikeness (or change) than does the latter. So I think, in the end, that the unlikenesses (other than those between Appearance and Reality) posited by demon hypotheses are not particularly outweighed by those posited by the hypothesis that our experience is not illusory, so that via Principle Z'' the latter really is more acceptable than the former.

Of course, the hypothesis of chance or accident does not posit any of the sorts of unlikenesses we have just been discussing, even though it does posit an unlikeness between Appearance and Reality; but that hypothesis can be eliminated via Principle D of Chapter 2, which is a clearly reasonable principle of rational scientific inquiry. And so Principles Z'' and D enable us to show that belief in the general concurrence between the way things look and the way things are is more reasonable scientifically (and thus epistemically) than belief to the contrary, in which case it is reasonable at least tentatively to believe in the existence of tables and chairs, etc., of the kind we seem to see and hear, etc.[1]

The argument just produced is distinct from the argument produced in Chapters 2 and 3 for the reasonableness of believing that there is an external world and that that world is much as it appears to us to be. And it also has at least one very important advantage over that earlier line of argument. For it is one thing to use an argument to show the hypothesis of an external world containing things of the sort there appear to be to be superior to all its alternatives as an explanation of one's experiences, and thus acceptable from a scientific and a rational standpoint. And it is quite another thing to show that ordinary people who are unaware of any complicated philosophical arguments for their common-

---

[1] Of course, it is sometimes reasonable to believe one's experience is illusory, but this is only when one has some definite reason—like the knowledge that the lighting is deceptive or that one has taken an hallucinogen—to think so. Unless such reasons exist with respect to a given experience, it is reasonable to believe it to be veridical, for the reasons we have been adumbrating.

sense beliefs are rationally justified *already* in believing most of the things they do about the world.[1] To do the former is to enable people to have justified beliefs about the world, etc., if they did not have them before. It is to produce grounds for certain hypotheses of such a sort that if someone learns of those grounds he will be reasonable in believing those hypotheses. But it in no way shows that people were, or were not, justified in believing certain things about the world, other minds, etc., independently of any knowledge of philosophy or of philosophical arguments against scepticism. Now, we all commonly assume that ordinary non-philosophers are rationally justified or reasonable in believing various things that scepticism, unbeknownst to them, calls into question. And I think we can justify this commonsense belief—assuming ourselves the standpoint of common sense and using the kinds of premises that philosophers generally make use of in arguments when they are *not* attempting to overcome scepticism—and do so via the sort of argument for the external world we have just introduced in the present section.[2]

A man can be justified in believing q on the basis of believing p if he is justified in believing p and if he is *implicitly* adhering to some valid principle(s) of inference in going from p to q. Explicit awareness of such valid principles is clearly not necessary. For a man who argues that the next crow he sees will probably be black, because all crows he has seen have been black, presumably cannot formulate any principle as complex or sophisticated as (the weaker version of) the Strong Principle of Induction. At least, an unlettered intelligent man cannot, typically, do this, and yet we commonly believe that such a man is justified in believing that the next crow he sees will be black if he has seen and heard of nothing but black crows, etc. At best, such a person is only implicitly adhering to our Strong Principle, which means something like: acting as if he had some dim awareness of that principle, and being capable of seeing that that principle is valid and

---

[1] It was S. Kripke who first made me aware of the significance of this distinction, and who pointed out to me that Hume in the *Inquiry Concerning Human Understanding* (section 4, part 2) was also well aware of its significance.

[2] I think the task of showing that the ordinary man is already justified in his commonsense beliefs is an important and difficult one even for the philosopher who *assumes* common sense and makes use of his ordinary philosophical assumptions, so I feel justified in taking that point of view in undertaking this task. This task is separate from the task of overcoming scepticism about the external world, and either can, I think, be undertaken separately.

that his reasoning conforms to it, if he is made explicitly aware of the principle (by someone else). Of course, more work needs to be done on the notion of implicit acceptance of and reasoning in accordance with a principle. But at least this much, I think, is fairly clear: one who believes the next crow will be black is typically justified in so believing, even if he lacks intellectual sophistication, because he is implicitly relying on *something like* our Strong Principle (or its weaker version).

Now the argument for commonsense claims about the nature of the external world that we put forward in Chapters 2 and 3 cannot help us in showing that the ordinary non-philosopher is (already) rationally justified in believing in an external world that is much as it appears to be, because that earlier argument rests on the Principle of Unlimited Inquiry, in accordance with which, I think, no ordinary man ever even implicitly reasons. And it would be absurd, furthermore, to attribute to the common man, even on an implicit level, anything like the sort of complex and philosophically intricate argument used in Chapters 2 and 3 for the purpose of justifying claims about the external world. But the argument of the present section may be of use to us in attempting to show that ordinary non-philosophers are (already) justified in various commonsense claims about the external world (and other minds). For ordinary people do seem often to be aware in an implicit way of the relation between positing unlikenesses and the simplicity and/or acceptability of hypotheses, and so implicitly to follow principles like Z″ in judging the (comparative) acceptability of hypotheses. In the case of enumerative inductive inferences about crows, for example, I think ordinary people will be reluctant to posit white or grey crows after seeing and hearing of only black crows, because they are reluctant to posit unlikenesses where they can avoid doing so (by suspending belief or believing that the next crow will be black). And so they seem to adhere implicitly to Z″. Or consider the case where it looks to an ordinary person as if he is seeing a table. Such a person will, other things being equal, be reluctant to say there is no table there; and that seems to be because ordinary people are reluctant to posit an unlikeness between the way things appear and the way things are in a situation. Of course, an ordinary person could always say that the fact that it looks to him as if there is a table (near his body) is inexplicable, a matter of chance or accident. But, again, I think ordinary people are usually reluctant to attribute things to chance, to say that there is no explanation for a given phenomenon, and so I think ordinary people often implicitly accept Principle D of Chapter 2. And if D is valid, which I think it is, they are justified in discarding chance as the null-explanation of their experience 'of' a table. Thus I think that when ordinary people come to believe that there is a table around, on the basis of its looking to them as if there is a table around, they typically are implicitly relying on valid principles like Z" and D, and so are justified in their belief in the table.[1] And the same is true for most of the other sorts of beliefs about the nature of things around them that ordinary people have on the basis of their sense experiences.[2] So I think we have successfully shown that ordinary men are generally (rationally) justified in a large number of their commonsense beliefs about the nature of the world around them.[3]

Ours is not, of course, the only attempt that has been made by philosophers to show that (or explain how) ordinary people, who know no subtle arguments against scepticism, can be justified in believing in various sorts of external objects. One might, for example, argue quite briefly that whenever it looks as if there is a real table, one is justified in believing there is such a table,

---

[1] I am also assuming that people are dimly aware that the alternatives to belief in a table (e.g. the assumption that one's experience 'of' a table is due to hallucinatory drugs) posit unlikenesses that balance out those posited by the assumption of a table (between the legs and the top of the table, etc.).

[2] Ordinary people can also be shown to be justified in believing in the existence of various objects in the past. For they implicitly see the unreasonableness of positing an unlikeness between the way the world appears to have been (in memory) and the way the world in fact was. Ordinary people may also often implicitly use the Strong Principle when they come to believe of certain bodies that they are the bodies of conscious beings. If so, we can show that ordinary people are typically justified in some beliefs about other minds. Similarly, for claims about unobserved objects.

[3] For the ordinary man to make implicit use of the sort of argument we have discussed he must have the concepts of 'is' and 'appears' and 'not', as well as various material object concepts. Ordinary people with those concepts can, we have shown, have justified beliefs about the world. I am somewhat inclined to believe, in addition, that, *unless* one has the concepts of 'is' and 'appears' and 'not', one cannot be *justified* in having *beliefs* about the external world (even though one may *have* such *beliefs*, perhaps, *before* having those concepts)—at least if one has only normal human means of cognition and normal human experience. Thus I am inclined to think that humans who cannot implicitly argue in the way just described for objects in the external world may not have reasonable beliefs about objects in the external world—and in particular that babies and idiots may be totally lacking in warranted or justified beliefs of that sort.

so that, since it often looks to non-philosophers as if there is a table in their presence, such non-philosophers are often justified in believing in such things as tables.[1] Now, everything in this argument may, when suitably qualified, be true and reasonable. But from an epistemological standpoint it would be nice to be able to *show* that when ordinary people have experiences 'of' tables, they are justified in believing they are confronted with tables, rather than in believing that their experience is illusory (or that they have no right to conclude either that there is or that there is not a table in front of them), and not just to *assume* that this is the case, the way the argument just mentioned does. The argument we presented above, therefore, has an advantage over the one just introduced, inasmuch as it provides a *justification* for the claim that experience 'of' a table justifies ordinary people in believing in the existence of a table rather than in the illusoriness of their experience, etc.

Chisholm offers a slightly different argument (from the one just criticized) concerning the rational justification of the beliefs of ordinary men about the external world. According to him,[2] if someone believes that he perceives something to have a property F, then he is reasonable in believing that he perceives (and that there is) a real thing that has F.[3] Since ordinary people often believe that they perceive objects of various kinds, Chisholm holds that ordinary people are often reasonable in believing in the existence of real objects of various kinds. But this again does not *show*, but rather only *assumes*, that someone with experience 'of' a table is *justified* in believing in such a table if he, in fact, (already) *believes* in such a table. In addition, it does not show that ordinary men are justified in *coming to believe* that they perceive tables (or that there are tables) on the basis of having

---

[1] This would probably have been accepted by Carneades. Cf. Chisholm's *Theory of Knowledge*, p. 41. Presumably an 'other things being equal' clause should be built into Carneades' argument; we are surely not justified in believing there is a table *whenever* it looks as if there is.

[2] *Ibid.*, p. 45. Chisholm and Carneades present arguments for the claim that we are sometimes, without benefit of philosophical argument, justified in believing that we remember certain past things and that those things existed in the past, which are similar to their arguments about perception and open to the same criticisms as the latter.

[3] This argument too is badly in need of supplementation by an 'other thing being equal' type of qualification. This point is also made in H. Heidelberger's (as yet) unpublished 'Chisholm's Epistemic Principles', where Chisholm's views are given an interesting examination and criticism.

appropriate sense experiences. And this latter is clearly something that we would like to be able to show, since people commonly assume not only that their (already existent) beliefs in various sorts of objects around them are justified, but also that they were justified in coming to have those beliefs in the first place. Chisholm's argument does not show this, but the kind of argument we have proposed clearly can, since it does not assume already existent beliefs, but only the sense experiences on which such beliefs are often based.[1]

VI

The problem of justifying the belief or claim or hypothesis that there is an external world containing the sorts of things we commonly assume it to contain is perhaps historically the most important and influential of all the problems of the Theory of Knowledge (Epistemology). Descartes, Locke, Berkeley, Hume, Kant, and innumerable others both before and during the present century have all made major efforts to cope with this problem and considered it to be central for a large number of other issues in the Theory of Knowledge. Many philosophers have held that in order to justify claims about the external world, scientific methodology (of the sort followed in the special sciences) is insufficient and inadequate. H. H. Price, for example, has held that one cannot justify beliefs about the nature of the external world via the 'Method of Hypothesis', i.e. by means of an argument based on strictly scientific considerations that shows that external objects of various kinds provide the best causal explanation of the facts of our sense experiences. According to him, scientific method and valid principles of scientific thinking are insufficient even for showing the superiority of the hypothesis of the external world over the hypothesis of Berkeley's God (as the cause of our experiences).[2] Price thinks that in order to justify claims about the external world, one must assume special principles of inference that are not commonly assumed or required by scientists in making inferences, in the special sciences, and it is for that reason that he introduces his special Principle of

---

[1] Cf. R. Firth's 'Ultimate Evidence', Swartz (ed.), *op. cit.*, p. 493 f.
[2] *Perception*, pp. 74, 89 ff.

Confirmability in order to argue for (the reasonableness of) various beliefs about the external world.[1]

Now, in Chapters 2 and 3, we provided an argument for the reasonableness of various beliefs or claims about the nature of the external world. But that argument rested on the PUI, and consequently, on Principle A, and Principle A is not a principle that scientists rely on in the doing of science. It is, rather, the very sort of special epistemic principle that philosophers like Price and Chisholm have held to be necessary to any plausible demonstration of the reasonableness of belief in the external world.[2] But in Chapter 3, I also pointed out (in footnote on p. 107 f.) that the Principle of Illusion and Evidence (the PIE)— which is a principle implicitly presupposed in scientific thought and inquiry—can be used independently of Principle A and the PUI to undermine sceptical hypotheses. And in the present chapter, furthermore, we have produced another scientific methodological principle, Principle Z″, which we can also use to undermine scepticism about the nature of the external world. Thus it turns out that we can justify the hypothesis of an external world containing many of the objects we commonly think it contains on the basis of purely scientific (and logical) principles, without assuming special non-scientific epistemic principles like Principle A.

But this still leaves us with a problem. For the PIE does not allow one to infer anything about the particular nature of the cause or causes of one's experiences of sense and memory. At the beginning of Chapter 3, we had already justified the assumption that something physical was causing our experiences (via Principle A and the PUI, as well as Principles, B, C, etc.), so we could use the Principle of Illusion and Evidence to show the reasonableness of the hypothesis that our experiences are veridical and caused

[1] Similarly, Chisholm (in ' "Appear", "Take", and "Evident" ' in Swartz (ed.), *Perceiving, Sensing, and Knowing*, Garden City: Anchor, 1965, pp. 473–85) claims that the hypothesis of the external world is *not* more probable than not on the basis of statements about sense experience; and in his *Theory of Knowledge* he presents special epistemic principles not assumed in the special sciences as providing the best means of justifying claims about the external world. Price introduces the Principle of Confirmability on page 185 of his book.

[2] However, inasmuch as Principle A and the PUI do not just assume the unreasonableness of the hypothesis of the demon as an explanation of our experiences, whereas Price's and Chisholm's special principles do, the attempt in Chapter 2 to overcome external-world scepticism goes much further than their attempts to overcome scepticism.

by something physical. But, without assuming the PUI and Principle A, we cannot, merely by using the PIE, show that our experiences have a physical causal origin. So, by dropping Principle A, we may avoid the assumption of non-scientific methodological principles without losing our ability to show the reasonableness of various beliefs about the *nature* of the external world, but we are still left with the task of showing the reasonableness of believing that our experiences are *caused* by something physical, that is, of showing the reasonableness of believing in Causal Realism. And the argument (based on Principle Z") for the reasonableness of various claims about the external world that we introduced in the previous section of the present chapter cannot help us out of our predicament, because it (like the argument based on the PIE) only justifies assumptions about the existence of various sorts of objects, and not about whether such (physical) objects are *causally responsible* for our experiences. So far, then, we have only provided a way of showing that *something* (whether a demon-spirit or something physical) has caused in us veridical experiences of sense and memory. (Principle D allows us to assume that our experiences are not causeless and inexplicable.)

However, considerations of the sort mentioned in previous sections of this chapter can help us to establish (the reasonableness of) Causal Realism. For, given that something is causing our experiences, we need only show the unreasonableness of believing that that cause is some sort of demon (or some mysterious unconscious part of our own minds) in order to show the reasonableness of (at least tentative) belief in Causal Realism. But given that we can use either the PIE or Principle Z" to show the reasonableness of believing that there are all kinds of material objects in the external world, we can then use Principle Z" to show the unreasonableness of believing that a demon (or processes in the unconscious part of our minds) has caused our experiences. For, if we hypothesize instead that objects of the kind it appears to us as if there are are causing our experiences of sense and memory, we can avoid positing a kind of thing (namely, a demon or a mysterious unconscious mental process) that is not identical with any kind of thing that we have already posited and that we can use the PIE and/or Principle Z" to show that we have reason to posit. So on Principle Z" it would seem to be preferable to hold that something physical was the cause of our

experiences rather than to hold that a demon or special unconscious processes in the mind were the cause of those experiences. And so we have shown the reasonableness of tentative
belief in Causal Realism, have given a justification for Causal
Realism of the very sort that Price claims to be impossible,
namely via general scientific methodological principles without
supplementation by any special epistemic principles that the
special sciences can do without.

Of course, someone might object to any argument of the sort
we have just given on the grounds that it involves positing an
unobserved cause of our experiences that it is in no way possible
for us to observe directly. For it might be claimed that whenever
it is reasonable to posit an unobserved thing of kind K as the
cause of an observed thing of kind K', it is only because one has
observed things of kind K *conjoined* with things of kind K' in the
past and because one is capable in principle of observing any
given thing of kind K. Indeed, in most cases where one posits
something of a certain kind to account for something one has
witnessed, these conditions are met. When, for example, I see
smoke and posit fire that I do not see as its cause, it is always in
principle possible for me to see the fire for myself, and I have
already seen fire and smoke conjoined on many occasions.

But it hardly follows that our argument for the external world
is unsound. For one thing, it is not clear to me that in positing
the external world as the best causal explanation of my experiences
I am committed to holding that I cannot directly observe objects
in the external world or observe objects in the world conjoined
with certain sorts of experiences (on my own part). But much
more importantly, the claim that one can reasonably only posit
entities that one (believes one) is in principle able to observe as
the unobserved causal *explanantia* of certain observed phenomena
seems totally implausible because it implies the unreasonableness
of physicists who posit certain unobservable (in principle) subatomic particles (like neutrinos) in order to explain (and as
causally responsible for) various observable phenomena that
occur both inside and outside the laboratory. Now, some philosophers have questioned the reasonableness of what physicists
assume about subatomic particles, or have tried to interpret
statements about subatomic particles phenomenalistically, so that
they are no longer really about unobservables. A. J. Ayer, for
example, at one time held that positing unobservables was ille-

gitimate even in physics, and claimed that Phenomenalism about subatomic particles was reasonable (so that physicists were not positing subatomic particles illegitimately).[1] But Ayer has since changed his views on both these matters. He has more recently claimed that he thinks statements about subatomic particles are not susceptible of a Phenomenalistic analysis, and is no longer adamant about the unreasonableness of positing unobservables.[2] I can myself see no reason to think that Phenomenalism about subatomic particles is any more plausible than Phenomenalism about material objects; nor do I think physicists unreasonable in positing such entities to explain experimental and other data. And so I am inclined to conclude that the sort of objection to our argument for Causal Realism that has just been examined is lacking in force or validity. If the argument of the present work shows anything, it shows that one can use the very same standards that stand behind and justify *enumerative inductive* inferences, to justify *the hypothetico-deductive positing* of certain entities (in this case, an external world of a certain sort) as the best explanation of certain phenomena (in this case, our own experience). Both enumerative inductions and the positing of entities to explain one's data can often be justified as being necessary to avoid positing certain unlikenesses, i.e. via principles like Z, Z', and Z''. I think, then, that it is reasonable for physicists who assume various things about the nature of the external world to posit unobservable subatomic particles; and I also think that even if the external world is not (directly) observable, there are good scientific grounds, of the sort pointed out here, for believing in such a world.[3]

Indeed, every scientific hypothesis accepted in the special sciences that I know of presupposes or entails the existence of an external world with various specific sorts of entities in it,[4] so if it were not scientifically reasonable to believe in an external world, and to believe in the occasional veridicalness of our experience, there would be no scientific justification for believing

---

[1] *The Foundations of Empirical Knowledge*, London: Macmillan, 1940, p. 220 f.

[2] See his 'Perception' in *British Philosophy in the Mid-Century*, 2nd edition, London: Allen and Unwin, 1966, p. 226. For a devastating attack on Phenomenalism about subatomic particles see J. J. C. Smart's *Philosophy and Scientific Realism*, London: Routledge and Kegan Paul, 1963, ch. 2.

[3] Cf. Quine's *Word and Object*, p. 22.

[4] Cf. Max Planck's *The Philosophy of Physics*, N.Y.: W. W. Norton, 1963, p. 28.

any of the things scientists tell us about the world. If so, the argument we have given from Chapter 2 onward can be used to *show*, perhaps for the first time, that the conclusions science and scientists come to can be justified on the basis of scientific method, are scientifically plausible.

Even if we have shown the scientific (and thereby, presumably, the epistemic) reasonableness of a large number of our ordinary assumptions about the external world (via two separate arguments) and have shown the reasonableness of assuming the truth of Causal Realism, we have still not shown that we *perceive* or *remember* objects of the sort it appears to us as if there are or have been. Even if Causal Realism is true, and my experience 'of' a table is caused by something physical, for example, it does not follow that my experience is caused by (and that I perceive) the (ostensible) table it looks to me as if I am seeing, even assuming (as our arguments thus far allow us to do) that our experience is veridical. In fact, it does not even follow that we perceive *anything* physical. And the same holds for memory of past objects. For scientists with wires, chemicals and electrodes might be manipulating our brains in such a way that we hallucinated objects of the very kind there in fact were (or had been) in front of us, so that our experience had a physical origin, was veridical, but was totally hallucinatory. However, I think hypotheses that posit scientists manipulating our consciousness by physical means can be eliminated via Principle Z″, since they posit beings who are disposed to act in such a way as to manipulate our experiences (and various kinds of actions on the part of such beings). For to posit such beings (or such actions) is to posit a kind of entity we do not have to posit if we just assume the commonsense hypothesis that our experiences are caused by objects of the sort they are phenomenologically 'of' (plus commonsense assumptions about the conscious beings around us). Thus the latter commonsense sort of hypothesis is superior (if we assume other things to be equal) to the hypothesis of scientists delicately manipulating our brains.

Furthermore, the hypothesis that we are brains in vats is clearly already ruled out by the assumption, which we justified earlier, that our experience is veridical. After all, we do not appear to be in vats. We need to eliminate certain other hypotheses, however, in order to show that we perceive and remember things in the world pretty much the way they are and have been, but this, perhaps, can be done more briefly. Consider the hypothesis that there is a red box, but that it causes sensations in someone else and that that other person's having sensations causes me to have the experience of a red box. This hypothesis contravenes Principle C″ of Chapter 3, since for no reason at all it posits a difference between the way a certain box affects (or acts on) me and the way it affects (or acts on) someone else. There is also the hypothesis that our experience 'of' a red box is caused by a red box, but not by the one we seem to see. But this hypothesis, if it is to be at all plausible, must assume that for *all* things that we seem to see there are objects just like them causing our experiences. And this involves positing some sort of causal connection between the red box in front of us and the red box that causes our experience of a red box, for we cannot, on Principle D, just say that it is an accident that whenever there is a red box, or green chair, etc., in front of us, another red box, or green chair, etc., causes in us an experience. . . . And so the hypothesis under consideration involves causal connections and activity between the causes of our experiences and certain other objects in addition to the causal connections every causal explanation of our experiences has to posit between our experiences and their causes. And, for that reason, that hypothesis is more complex than that of common sense, which posits only one (present) red object, when we seem to see only one red object—aside from those behind our backs, etc.

We are left, then, with the sort of hypothesis that says that our present sense and/or memory experience, say, of a red box is caused by the very red box that it appears as if there is and/or was. Of course, such a hypothesis attributes a causal property to a red box that we have already posited (in saying that our experience is veridical), and, inasmuch as it does so, it is committed to a new kind of object, namely, red boxes with the power to . . . But this does not cause the hypothesis in question to fall foul of Principle Z″—which says that the positing of new kinds of entities should be avoided, if possible. For every other possible hypothesis about the causes of our experiences or (memory) impressions has to attribute such causal properties to something or other. And so the hypothesis in question seems to be one that we are reasonable (at least, henceforth) in tentatively accepting.

It seems, however, that the sort of hypothesis we are tentatively accepting as the explanation of our experiences of sense and memory is compatible with the assumption that we are dreaming. For surely it is possible to dream of the red box in one's room and possible for that dream to have been caused by that very red box. But this does not, I think, mean that we cannot show that we in some way perceive (and remember) things in the external world. For why should all dreaming have to be hallucinatory? Could one not remember something while dreaming, e.g. that one has been to Dublin, if one's memory impressions have been caused in the right sort of way?[1] And could one not also have non-hallucinatory perceptual experiences while dreaming? If the noise level in a room where one is sleeping rises, and this is reflected in the loudness of one's auditory dream experiences, one may sometimes, I think, properly be said to be indirectly perceiving (or aware of) the rise in the noise level in that room. Thus, even if I do not attempt to show the unreasonableness of believing that one is dreaming (in a veridical way), that need not stand in the way of my showing the reasonableness of believing that we perceive (or remember) the sorts of objects there appear to be (or to have been) around us. For we can show the reasonableness of believing that, when we seem to see (or to have seen) a red box, there is a red box that caused our experience and that is also the red box our experience is phenomenologically 'of'.

Of course, some philosophers claim to have *a priori* grounds for believing that, even if external objects cause our sense experiences in a regular way, this does not constitute perception of the external objects in question, or of any external objects. Some philosophers, for example, take the Argument from Illusion to show that we never perceive physical objects, but only perceive sense data, or our own experiences. Other philosophers, most notably Russell,[2] have used the *empirical* facts of physiology to argue that we never see the objects we seem to see, but always only see some part of our own brains. And similar arguments, of course, have existed with respect to remembering past objects. But I am inclined to think that the most any of those sorts of arguments can show is that we either *don't* perceive, or remember, external objects directly, or only perceive, or remember, objects

[1] Cf. C. Martin and M. Deutscher's 'Remembering', *Phil. Review*, 75, 1966, pp. 161–96.

[2] See *The Philosophy of Bertrand Russell*, ed. by P. Schilpp, N.Y.: Tudor, 1944, p. 704 f.

of the sort we seem to see, or to have seen, *indirectly*.[1] And my only interest here is in showing the reasonableness of believing that we perceive and remember objects *either* directly *or* indirectly.

I have not attempted to show the unreasonableness of non-sceptical dreaming-hypotheses because I do not at present know how to do so. But, because of the possibility of showing that our experience is veridical and caused by objects of the sort it seems to be of, without showing that we are not dreaming, we have still been able to show the reasonableness of Causal Realism, of various assumptions about the nature of the external world, and of the claim that we either perceive (or remember) external objects directly or perceive (or remember) them indirectly. It is only because philosophers have assumed that one had to overcome scepticism about dreaming in order to show that one's experience was veridical or non-hallucinatory that those who have been concerned with overcoming scepticism about the nature of the external world have thought it necessary for their purposes to overcome dreaming-scepticism.[2] But, if the present argument is correct, most of the important forms of scepticism about perception and memory can be dealt with without one's having to deal with dreaming-scepticism.

Some will object that I have granted too much to dreaming-scepticism; for, they will ask, what sense does it make to say that I may be dreaming if I am having veridical experiences caused by external objects? For, if *my* experience is veridical, then I am moving around with my eyes open, and acting in intricate and intelligent ways, and is it possible that I may be dreaming none the less? The question has some force; and, if it can be answered in the negative, we can overcome dreaming-scepticism. But I am inclined to think that it is logically possible to dream with eyes open and while acting intelligently, etc. Sleepwalkers act intelligently while asleep and some people sleep with eyes open. Furthermore, even if I am doing various things intelligently and am having experiences appropriate to the things around me, there

[1] Perceiving *x* indirectly may entail perceiving *x*, or it may not; after all, loving someone in one's fashion does not entail that one loves that person. 'Indirectly' in this context may be an *alienans* adverb. Cf. P. Geach 'Good and Evil', *Analysis*, 17, 1956, p. 334. For a discussion of questions like 'Is perceiving indirectly really perceiving?', see my 'The Theory of Important Criteria', *J. Phil.*, 63, 1966, pp. 211–24.

[2] Cf. Moore's *Philosophical Papers*, London: Allen and Unwin, 1959, pp. 245 ff.

may be other people elsewhere who really are awake, and there may be certain physiological factors operating in them but not in us, such that if we knew of them it would be reasonable for us to say that they were awake and we were asleep. One can even imagine our carrying on scientific investigations while asleep and finding some factor f present when people are asleep with their eyes closed, and thinking that, when f is absent, we are awake, whereas in fact, when f is absent, we are just asleep with our eyes open. Now, all this may be mistaken. It may be that the notions of acting intelligently and of co-ordinating one's physical movements with one's thoughts and experiences (or of such co-ordination appearing to exist) are logically tied up with the notion of being awake. I cannot myself see why this should be so, but if it is, so much the better for the argument of the present work.

CHAPTER 6

RELIGION, SCIENCE
AND THE EXTRAORDINARY

Thus far we have attempted to overcome various forms of scepticism on the basis of certain valid principles of scientific thinking that we have claimed are also valid epistemic principles, i.e. principles governing the intellectually rational acceptance and rejection of claims or hypotheses. And I think it has been made clear how those principles can be used by someone to argue for the reasonableness of accepting a large store of what are, in fact, commonsense beliefs about the (external) world, and the people in it. But we have not yet made any significant mention of scepticism about God, much less attempted to overcome such scepticism. Scepticism about the Deity is, of course, as old and venerable a form of epistemological scepticism as any we have dealt with up till now. From time immemorial, there have been doubters of God's existence, and men who have attempted to assuage such doubts by rational or other arguments.

From the point of view of the philosopher, the most significant attempts to overcome scepticism about the Deity that have taken place over the centuries have centred around various versions of the Ontological Argument, the Cosmological Argument, and the Teleological Argument, for God's existence. There have, of course, been other sorts of arguments given for God's existence, e.g. the Moral Argument. But such arguments, however much they may appeal to religious non-philosophers, are, I think, intellectually much less forceful (or tempting) than the three arguments mentioned above;[1] and I think such arguments simply cannot overcome scepticism about God's existence.

In *God and Other Minds*, furthermore, Plantinga gives what seems to me to be the first successful demonstration of the unsoundness of (certain historically important versions of) the Ontological and Cosmological Arguments for God's existence.[2] What emerges clearly from Plantinga's discussion of various versions of these two arguments is, first, that no one really had succeeded in refuting them before Plantinga, and, second, that

---

[1] Cf. Plantinga's *God and Other Minds*, p. 111. I am indebted to Plantinga on this point.　　　　　　　　　　　　　　　[2] Chapters 1–3.

the burden of proof lies heavily on the shoulders of anyone who wishes to revive one of those two arguments (perhaps in a version that Plantinga does not consider in his book). For the remainder of the present work, I shall *assume* that there is no acceptable version of the Ontological or Cosmological Argument currently available.

Plantinga is not as critical of the Teleological Argument as he is of the Ontological and Cosmological Arguments. Plantinga presents various enumerative inductive versions of the Teleological Argument, and after detailed consideration of them is unwilling to claim that they have 'no force at all'.[1] One example of a version of the Teleological Argument that is presented by Plantinga runs:

(23) Every *contingent* object such that we know whether or not it was the product of intelligent design, *was* the product of intelligent design.

(24) The [physical][2] universe is a contingent object.

(25) So probably the [physical] universe is designed.

And Plantinga considers this argument, and certain others very similar to it, to be weak, but not totally unacceptable. The question arises in my mind, however, whether such arguments cannot be undermined more completely, via principles we have already accepted, than Plantinga attempts to do. For one thing, one who puts forward this argument—and Plantinga does not gainsay him in this—is assuming that we do not *know* that trees for example, are *not* the products of God's intelligent design. For, if we did know this, (23) of the above argument would be unacceptable. The person who gives the argument from (23) to (25), and the other arguments Plantinga gives that resemble it, must hold that, even though we see no one resembling a God constructing or tending trees from 'infancy', the existence of the sorts of trees there are may still be part of a divine plan, or the intended product of things God has done with respect to the universe, etc.; and that no one can know that this is not so. Now, even if we cannot at present know whether trees were not the product of intelligent design, someone might want to say that there are other things, more under human control,

---

[1] *God and Other Minds*, p. 107; see also p. 109.

[2] The universe itself may not be a contingent object, since it exists if anything at all exists and there may be entities (like the number 5) that necessarily exist.

that we can tell are not the products of intelligent design. If, for example, I accidentally spill some water on the floor, the puddle I create on the floor is not the product of design on my part (barring some Freudian explanation of the accident). Might I not claim to know that the puddle was an accident, and that no one, myself included, deliberately brought it about? If I could reasonably claim this, I could not reasonably accept premise (23) of the above argument. One who gives such an argument, therefore, will have to maintain that even in the case of an 'accidental' puddle, what happened cannot be known not to be the result of God's deliberate work, or thus known not to be the product of intelligent design. And Plantinga, who in no way attacks premises like (23) in his book and even attempts to bolster such premises in certain places,[1] pretty clearly agrees that there is no contingent entity whose existence and nature we know *not* to be the product of intelligent design. But, if we do *not* know this of any contingent entity, are there any (logically) possible circumstances in which we *could* know this of a contingent entity? Plantinga, I think, is committed to a negative answer to this latter question. And, if he is, then he will have to agree that the argument from (23) to (25) is of the form: all $f g$'s are h; therefore, this entity, which is a g, is an h; and that it is logically *impossible* for there to be an $f g$ that is not an h, even though it *is* logically possible for there to be a g that is not an h. But as I pointed out in Chapter 4 above,[2] any argument of the kind just described is clearly based on a biased or unfair sample, and is thus unacceptable. (Actually we did not formally name or state a principle that rules out all such arguments; but it would obviously be easy to do so.) I think, then, that if Plantinga wishes to hold to the impossibility of telling (knowing) that something is not the product of intelligent design, he must grant that arguments like that from (23) to (25) are clearly unacceptable. Since those versions of the Teleological Argument that he finds 'not completely negligible'[3] are all like the argument from (23) to (25) in the appropriate way, Plantinga should, I think, hold that the Teleological Argument is in no better shape than the Ontological Argument or the Cosmological Argument for God's existence.

Of course, Plantinga might want to claim that it *is* possible to know that a certain contingent entity is not the product of intelli-

[1] *God and Other Minds*, p. 100.
[2] See p. 125   [3] *God and Other Minds*, p. 109.

gent design. But, if this is so, then judged by Plantinga's own standards, the argument from (23) to (25) is clearly unsuccessful, for it will then be not at all obvious (in the absence of further argumentation) that (23) is true. And Plantinga himself says that the premises of an argument in Natural Theology like the Teleological Argument must be 'obviously true and accepted by nearly every sane man', or else self-evident and/or necessarily true.[1] Thus, if it is possible to know that a certain contingent entity is not the product of intelligent design, (23) is not a necessary or self-evident truth nor an obvious truth accepted by nearly every sane man, in which case the argument from (23) to (25) is definitely unacceptable as a piece of Natural Theology. Of course, one might attempt to buttress the argument from (23) to (25) by means of additional arguments in favour of (23); but I cannot see how or whether this could be done. I shall assume from now on, therefore, that the versions of the Ontological, Cosmological, and Teleological Arguments for God's existence that have thus far been formulated (or, at least, that I know of) cannot be used to overcome scepticism about the existence of some sort of God. In the present chapter, consequently, I shall attempt to confront such scepticism by introducing a type of argument for the existence of some sort of God (or higher being) which, despite its striking simplicity, has never, as far as I can tell, been explicitly promulgated by any philosopher or theologian. I shall claim that this type of argument has *at least some* plausibility and force, due to the fact that it is based on a not-too-implausible general epistemic principle (whose validity seems to be presupposed in a good deal of human thinking both inside and outside the area of religion). This principle, it will be seen, is not specifically a principle of *scientific* thought or methodology, so that if the principle is valid, there may be rational support (epistemic reasons) for belief in some sort of Deity even if there is no *scientific* justification for such belief.[2]

I

The notion of the extraordinary (and also the related notions of the remarkable, the amazing, the wondrous, and the marvellous)

---

[1] *God and Other Minds*, p. 4.

[2] The possibility of rational reasons for claims that are not scientific reasons for those claims was adumbrated in Chapter 2, above, p. 85.

plays, I believe, an important role in the attempts of men to understand the nature of the world. Consider, for example, an idealized primitive man confronted for the first time with the phenomenon of thunder (or thunder-cum-lightning). This phenomenon will be different from anything he experiences in everyday life, and will constitute something amazing and extraordinary for him. I want to suggest that, if the primitive man seeks to explain the thunder (or thunder-cum-lightning) in terms, for example, of a god beating a great drum (or of a god striking huge flints)—which is the sort of explanation often given by primitive people(s) of such phenomena—what he is doing is explaining what strikes him as remarkable or extraordinary in what seems to him the most appropriate sort of way, namely, in terms of something equally extraordinary, that is, in terms of the actions of an extraordinary being[1] with respect to extraordinary objects.[2]

Consider the following epistemic principle that seems to be presupposed in the kind of thinking by which a primitive might, in something like the manner described above, come to believe that thunder was caused by the actions of some higher being:

'If (one reasonably believes tentatively that)[3] x is an extraordinary (or amazing or remarkable) observed or experienced phenomenon, one has some reason to think (and it is, other things being equal, reasonable to think at least tentatively) that x has been brought about by (and is thus to be explained in terms of) something extraordinary (or amazing or remarkable) that is unobserved or that "lies behind" x.'

---

[1] After all, such a god is much larger and more powerful than the conscious beings he (the primitive man) confronts in everyday life.

[2] In his *An Introduction to the History of Religion* (London: Methuen, 1896), F. B. Jevons explains a good deal of primitive religious belief in this way, i.e. as a response to certain awe-inspiring or striking events, like thunder and lightning (pp. 19 ff.). Not all primitive religious explanation, he thinks, involves going from the extraordinary or astonishing, however. A man cut by a rock who says that some rock spirit caused the rock to cut him is thinking animistically, but not in terms of something extraordinary, because it is as natural for him to imagine rock spirits in rocks as to imagine human persons in human bodies (p. 22). Jevons also says that once something extraordinary is used to explain something else that is extraordinary, it may also be used by primitive people to explain many ordinary and unremarkable phenomena (p. 24).

[3] This phrase must be understood if we wish to graft our present attempt to argue for the claim that there is some reason to believe in some sort of Deity, on to the argument of the previous chapters, using premises that we justified (or showed how one could justify) in those earlier chapters.

This principle I call the *Principle of Extraordinary Explanation*.[1] It is not only presupposed in some primitive thought, I believe, but also in the relatively sophisticated thinking of some modern philosophers and scientists, and in religious thought in general, though never in an explicit way. Something like this principle seems, for example, to be behind some of the things Schopenhauer says about music in *The World as Will and Idea*. According to Schopenhauer, everything that the senses perceive is an objectification of the Will achieved by means of ('filtered through') certain Ideas, with the sole exception of music, which is a direct and unmediated objectification of the Will. He says:

'. . . music . . . since it passes over the Ideas, is entirely independent of the phenomenal world, ignores it altogether, could to a certain extent exist if there was [sic] no world at all, which cannot be said of the other arts . . . . Music is thus by no means like the other arts, the copy of the Ideas, but the *copy of the will itself*, whose objectivity the Ideas are. This is why the effect of music is so much more powerful and penetrating than that of the other arts, for they speak only of shadows, but it speaks of the thing itself.'[2]

This passage suggests strongly that Schopenhauer thought that only a major break or discontinuity in his metaphysical system could explain the extraordinary force and beauty of music. (Soon after the above passage, he talks of the 'unutterable depth of all music'.)[3] Only by positing a unique direct objectification of the Will in human experience could the remarkable nature of musical experience, so different, according to Schopenhauer, from any other kind of human experience, be explained and understood. And from the point of view of his system (i.e. if his system is correct), it is indeed extraordinary and remarkable that the Will should reveal itself in such an immediate manner to the human mind in this single case. Thus it seems that Schopenhauer is positing something extraordinary or remarkable to explain something he finds extraordinary in experience, is implicitly

---

[1] This principle can also, I think, be used to explain why primitive people(s) tend to claim that their great heroes are of (partly) divine origin or parentage.

[2] *The Philosophy of Schopenhauer*, ed. I. Edman, N.Y.: Modern Library, 1928, p. 201.

[3] *Ibid.*, p. 209.

G

using or presupposing the Principle of Extraordinary Explanation (henceforth, for the sake of brevity, to be called the PEX).

Perhaps the area where we can most easily and in the greatest variety of instances see the PEX at work, however, is not philosophy, but religion. A great deal of religious conviction can, I think, be plausibly understood as resulting from or receiving sustenance from implicit application of this principle. A dream, for example, can sometimes occur with such force and vivacity as to persuade the dreamer that it was more than just another (crazy) dream. If one has a dream vision of the Lord of Hosts and all his angels, or of the Virgin Mary, there are many possible reactions afterwards. One might wonder whether one had been drugged, or was going mad, for example. One might think one's dream had resulted from mere wish-fulfilment. But some people's lives are transformed by just these sorts of experiences. They come away with a sense of wonder and amazement at the nature of what they have experienced. And they may feel that what they have experienced is so extraordinary and remarkable that it cannot be 'explained away,'[1] as one would tend to do with most dreams, as being due entirely to one's subconscious desires and fears, to drugs, or to the overtime workings of one's imagination or fancy; and they will think that their dream of God or of the Virgin has come from God himself or from the Virgin herself,[2] making use in an implicit way of the PEX,[3] since God and the Virgin are clearly remarkable beings.

People who have not had any special dream experiences also seem to make use of the PEX. Many people, for example, are struck and moved by the immense order and beauty of the world, and this may cause them to believe or reinforce their belief that this order and beauty, this extraordinary network of interlocking intricacies, calls for explanation in terms of some sort of extra-

[1] A man who knows he took an hallucinogen before having a certain dream experience might agree that the hallucinogen had *something* to do with his experience; but he might well want to say that God also had something to do with it.

[2] I have not been able to find any written descriptions of such dream experiences, but an actual occurrence of such an experience has been reported to me by S. Silberblatt, a student at Columbia College. He had a dream about God that he considered more remarkable than anything he had experienced before, and according to him, his current religious faith stems from that dream.

[3] But not just the PEX, which does not permit explanation of something extraordinary in terms of any *particular* extraordinary thing, like God. More on this below.

ordinary being behind nature as a whole. Or, in a slightly different vein, they may feel that the awesome fact that there exists something (contingent), rather than nothing (contingent) at all, in the universe, calls for the same sort of explanation.[1] Others find particular things in the world or facts about the world, rather than the world as a whole, remarkable. For some, it is the extraordinary capacities of the human mind that call for explanation in terms of the PEX.[2] For others, it might be the inexorableness of natural law or the intricacy of a leaf or rock crystal that called for such explanation. But, in any case, whether one is going from the extraordinary character of the world as a whole or of particular facts or things, those who postulate the existence of some extraordinary higher or deeper force or being behind things along these lines seem to be presupposing the validity of something like the PEX.

II

Having talked in a general way about the PEX and the sorts of arguments that can and have been made in accordance with it, it is time to clarify some of the concepts involved in the use of that principle. Later (in section III) we shall consider the all-important question of the validity of the PEX.

The PEX can be used only in cases where one believes something to be amazing, remarkable, or extraordinary.[3] But what is it for something to be amazing, remarkable, or extraordinary? And do we ever have (objectively) good reasons for calling something extraordinary, etc? This latter question arises because there seems to be a greater resemblance between judgments involving extraordinariness, etc. and value judgments involving such qualities as goodness, rudeness, and justice (about which this question has been so persistently asked), than between judgments involving extraordinariness, etc. and judgments involving such

[1] See A. Heschel, *Man is not Alone* (N.Y., 1951), p. 12; also his *God in Search of Man* (N.Y., 1955), p. 45 f.

[2] Heschel, *Man is Not Alone*, p. 14.

[3] And not even in all such cases. According to the PEX, what requires explanation in terms of something extraordinary is an extraordinary *observed or experienced* event or thing. It may be that extraordinary unobserved things call for extraordinary explanation, but I have seen no evidence that this is so, and do not want to be committed here one way or the other on this matter. Thus the PEX, as it stands, is not committed to any infinite regresses of extraordinary *explanantia*.

non-value qualities as redness and solubility. After all, 'extra-ordinary', etc. are all words that express individual feeling and attitude, in a way that value words do, but such words as 'red' and 'soluble' do not. And just as some philosophers have been Emotivists or Subjectivists about value adjectives, so too would it be possible to maintain some sort of Emotivist or Subjectivist position with regard to words like 'extraordinary', 'remarkable', and 'amazing'. In other words, one might claim that to say that something is extraordinary, etc., is just to evince an emotion of awe or wonder or amazement at it, not to describe it or assert about it anything that could conceivably be true or false. Or one might want to maintain about such words as 'extraordinary', etc. the sort of Subjectivism that claims that such words describe (rather than merely evince) the emotions or attitudes of those who use them. However, both Emotivism and Subjectivism about ethical and other value terms are on the wane today, as a result of various logical and epistemological criticisms that have been levelled against these positions. These criticisms are well-known and need not be gone into here. And if they have the sort of cogency I think they have, they will serve equally well to under-mine Emotivism and Subjectivism with regard to such terms as 'extraordinary', 'remarkable', and 'amazing'.

Perhaps the most enlightening and thoroughgoing treatment of terms like these that has been undertaken in recent years occurs in Nowell-Smith's *Ethics*.[1] According to Nowell-Smith, such words as 'extraordinary' and 'amazing' belong to a class of adjectives that he calls 'A-words' which includes words like 'sublime' and 'disgusting' as well. According to Nowell-Smith, although there is an emotive component to A-words, there are, none the less, standards for judging whether something is in fact sublime or amazing or disgusting. Such judgments are, of course, often the subject of serious dispute, but they are still descriptive and statement-making and can be argued about rationally. I find myself agreeing with a large part of what Nowell-Smith is saying here. Statements about what is or is not amazing or remarkable or extraordinary assert something in particular, and we can have good reasons to believe them. Thus, if a man dreams that his wife and children have just been killed in the

---

[1] *Ethics* (London, 1954), pp. 70–91. For an argument for the possibility of (objectively) good reasons for value claims, see my 'Value Judgments and the Theory of Important Criteria', *J. Phil.*, 65, 1968, pp. 94–112.

crash of a plane whose departure was delayed six hours and which contained Bolivian soccer players and was flown by a pilot with two front teeth missing, then, if in fact all these things are true and the man had no way of knowing any of them, his dream is remarkable and amazing, because it involves a remarkable and amazing coincidence. One might dispute that it was a mere coincidence, and claim the man had been secretly informed, but if one grants the facts claimed, there seems no way out of admitting that a remarkable, extraordinary thing occurred.

Of course, what is or is not amazing cannot be so easily ascertained in all cases. Consider someone who thinks that the intricacy, order and beauty of the world are extraordinary and who feels on that basis that there must be something very remarkable and extraordinary that explains all that intricacy, order and beauty. His whole train of thought relies on the assumption that certain facts about and aspects of the world are extraordinary. Now some of us are more impressed or moved by these facts about and aspects of the world than others are, and consequently are readier and quicker to see them as extraordinary or remarkable than those others. Indeed, some of us are simply more apt or disposed in general to feel wonder and awe at things and to find things remarkable, amazing or extraordinary than are others. Thus some people may totally accept the world for what it is and just not feel that the beauty, etc., of the world are so very remarkable, etc. And such people would, of course, not want to use the PEX to argue from the remarkableness of the world to the existence of something remarkable responsible for the world, or for certain aspects of it. Such people, I feel, are also less likely to be religiously fervid, or enthusiastic, or 'intoxicated' than those who find the world or various things in it remarkable and awe-inspiring. If this is so, then perhaps wonderment and the feeling of the extraordinary are central to and fundamental for religion and religiosity; and in that case implicit arguments via the PEX may well form one of the cornerstones of the religious life.

It is, of course, impossible to *prove* who is right and who wrong in the disagreement over the remarkableness of the world in various of its aspects. Since John Wisdom's 'Gods' and others of his philosophical writings compiled in *Philosophy and Psychoanalysis*,[1] philosophers have become accustomed to the thought that disputes of this kind depend on different ways of seeing

[1] Oxford, 1957.

and noticing things, on differences of sensitivity and attitude, etc. Although I myself believe the world to be remarkable and extraordinary, worthy of wonder and awe, and both have and can point out reasons for thinking so, I cannot prove that it is.[1] Thus one who bases an argument via the PEX for some sort of extraordinary higher being on the assumption of the extraordinariness of the world or of certain aspects of it cannot be as sure of the soundness of his argument as one who attempts to argue something on the basis of such safe assumptions as that New York is a city or that Kennedy was President. On the other hand, he may have strong reason, I think, for believing in the extraordinariness of (certain aspects of) the world, so that his argument may in fact be a sound one—depending, for one thing, on whether the PEX is valid.[2]

Of course, one may argue for the existence of something extraordinary behind things on the basis of certain remarkable dreams, rather than on the basis of the remarkableness of the order and beauty of the world. But the remarkableness of a dream may also come into dispute. And one reason for this, that does not exist in the case of disputes over the remarkableness or extraordinariness of the world, is the fact that dreams are private, are had by only one person. Thus, if x has a dream and tells y about it, it might be true that if y had had an exactly similar

[1] We might someday be able to show that the world was extraordinary or remarkable, despite disagreement among people about this question, on the basis of psychological findings. What if the only people who did not believe the world extraordinary were people whose neuroses could be shown by psychiatrists to be causing this failure of belief? This would surely tend to show that the world really was extraordinary. Similarly, if one could show that the only people who thought the world was not extraordinary were unintelligent, or prejudiced, or totally unaesthetic. The reason for this is, I think, that it is an analytic truth (in which case Firth's Ideal Observer Theory holds true of extraordinariness) or at least a necessary truth that the judgments of the less prejudiced, less neurotic, more sensitive and more intelligent are *more relevant* to and should be given greater weight in deciding what is remarkable or extraordinary.

[2] There are, I think, several basic sorts of reasons that clearly count in favour of something's being extraordinary or remarkable. If we find out that a thing x (a) is statistically rare; (b) cannot be reproduced by us or is in some other way beyond our powers of production or creation; or (c) possesses some valued, or disvalued, attribute to a far greater degree than we do, we have, I think, discovered some reason for thinking that x is remarkable or extraordinary. Certain diseases, meetings of people in far-off places, and body traits exemplify (a); the intricacy of a leaf or rock crystal exemplifies (b); and God (if he exists) and heroes and saints exemplify (c). Even though there are different sorts of reasons for remarkableness or extraordinariness, we need not conclude that 'extraordinary' and 'remarkable' are ambiguous terms. The case is, I think, rather like that of 'morally wrong'. There are many different sorts of reasons for calling something morally wrong, all in the same sense of that expression.

experience, he too would have found it remarkable and extraordinary. But, if *y* has not had such an experience himself, then he may not be able to see that something truly extraordinary has happened to *x*, and so may not be at all inclined to agree with *x* that God is the source of that experience. Furthermore, it may just be impossible for *x* to convince *y* of the extraordinariness of what he (*x*) has undergone. And this will not necessarily be because *y* is unintelligent or distrustful of *x*, but because no amount of description on *x*'s part may be able to convey the power and vividness and force of *x*'s actual experience, that is, convey the very factors that were (found by *x* to be) extraordinary and remarkable about his dream. It may well be, then, that *x* has excellent reason to believe that what he has experienced is indeed remarkable, and yet not be able to communicate that reason to (certain) other people. The fact that one may have reason for believing things that one cannot articulate or communicate has been examined in great detail by Michael Polanyi.[1] And it is clearly a fact of great importance in the area of religion. Perhaps, then, there is some truth in the claim often made by theologians and religious people that no one who has not himself had a religious experience has any right or good reason to deny the truth of those religious beliefs that emerge from or depend on such experience.[2] For, if the PEX is valid, someone who has an extraordinary dream has some reason to believe in some sort of remarkable being as its source; and, since someone who has never had an extraordinary experience of that sort may not be able to grasp or see the remarkableness of that dream, he will simply fail to have or to appreciate the reason possessed by the dreamer for belief in the existence of some sort of remarkable being behind his dream.[3]

In terms of the PEX we can explain why some people on the basis of experiences, events, or things they find extraordinary or remarkable come to believe that something extraordinary is

---

[1] 'Knowing and Being', *Mind* 60, 1951, esp. p. 458.

[2] See Flew and MacIntyre (eds.), *New Essays in Philosophical Theology* (London, 1956), pp. 76 f., 81 f.

[3] Incidentally, I don't think philosophers have given enough attention to the existence of good reasons for beliefs that one cannot share with others. There is even a tendency among philosophers to believe that good reasons *must* be shareable. One might designate as the Fallacy of the Common Denominator the view that reasons for beliefs or statements not available to most people (i.e. not publicly available) are available to no one. This fallacy is, I think, most pernicious in the Philosophy of Religion and in Æsthetics.

behind, is the cause of, those experiences, events, or things. But we cannot in terms of the PEX alone explain why they so often pick out one or another *particular* kind of extraordinary being or thing as the source or cause of that in their experience which they find extraordinary. In other words, one who thinks the universe is extraordinary has, according to the PEX, some reason to think there is some extraordinary force or other behind things. But typically he will not stop there, but will go on to say something about the particular nature of that extraordinary *explanans*. He will perhaps say that it is some sort of god with a personality or with certain virtues, powers, or purposes. And the PEX does not justify such a further move. Similarly, one who has a dream about the Virgin is entitled by the PEX only to conclude that some sort of extraordinary being is responsible for his dream. That principle no more entitles him to say that his dream comes from the Virgin than to say that an amazing green dragon or Satan is the cause of it. Why then do people so frequently go beyond the PEX and posit particular kinds of entities as the extraordinary causes of the extraordinary things they have observed or experienced?

The answer is, perhaps, that, if an event is extraordinary, there is a tendency for people to postulate as the extraordinary cause of it a kind of extraordinary thing or being such that the assumption of its being the cause of the phenomenon in question fits in better with one's other beliefs than does the assumption of any other kind of extraordinary thing or being as its cause. In other words, when one is confronted with an extraordinary phenomenon, one will tend to explain it in terms of that (sort of) extraordinary *explanans* which of all possible (extraordinary) *explanantia* of the phenomenon seems the most likely to be the cause of the phenomenon, given the (truth of the) other beliefs that one has. Thus a good Catholic will say that his extraordinary dream of the Virgin talking to him and telling him to sin no more was sent by the Virgin herself, not by a green dragon, because he already believes in the Virgin and in her occasional appearance to ordinary mortals, and also believes that there are no green dragons. And he will believe that the cause of the dream is the Virgin and not the Devil, even though he believes in the existence of both, if his experience is a moving and a radiantly beautiful one and if in it the Virgin tells him to do things he knows are good and if as a result of having the dream he is happier and morally more upright and more zealous religiously. For he believes that the Devil is not interested in making people happier or more upright morally. But, if the same man has a dream of the Virgin in which she tells him to do things he thinks are evil or appears in a vulgar way or acts in an unholy manner, then he might not be so quick to assume that it was the Virgin, and not the Devil, that was responsible for the dream. For he believes that the Virgin would not act that way, but that the Devil might attempt to make it seem as if she would.

I should like, then, tentatively to propose the following Principle of the Most Appropriate Extraordinary Explanation (henceforth, PMAEX):

'If (one reasonably believes tentatively that) x is an extraordinary observed or experienced phenomenon, one has some reason to think (and it is, other things being equal, reasonable tentatively to think) that it has been brought about by the particular (kind of) thing or being y, if on one's other beliefs, y is the most likely extraordinary *explanans* of x and *if these other beliefs are reasonable.*'

In terms of this principle we can understand why a Catholic might hold that his dream of the Virgin had come from the Virgin, for that explanation of his dream is the explanation (positing an extraordinary *explanans*) that best fits in with his other beliefs, and he, of course, believes that his other beliefs are reasonable and justified. But those other beliefs include belief in the Virgin Birth of Jesus, the belief that the Virgin exists somewhere, and the belief that the Virgin can appear to ordinary mortals, etc. And to the extent that a good Catholic is not rational or reasonable in maintaining these beliefs, the PMAEX does not grant him reason to think that his dream came from the Virgin.[1] And, of course, even if those other beliefs

---

[1] However, we should not assume that, just because we rationalistic philosophers are not justified in believing in the Virgin, etc., good Catholics are not epistemically justified in having such beliefs. For this would be to commit again the Fallacy of the Common Denominator. A good Catholic may have inductive reason to believe in the Virgin, etc., on the authority of his priest, who he knows is reliable in what he says outside the area of religious dogma and much smarter than he. And, if he lives in a backward area, he may not know that morally good, deep-thinking people sometimes do not believe in the Virgin, etc. Given what *we* know, however, *we* are not justified in believing in the Virgin, etc., and cannot have the reason for believing in the Virgin, etc. that the man in question has. So perhaps that man would have reason to explain some dream he had of the Virgin in terms of the Virgin, even though we, if we experienced the same sort of dream, would not.

are not justified, the PEX will at least grant him reason to believe that *some* sort of extraordinary force or being or thing has brought about his dream.

III

Until now we have been assuming that the PEX and perhaps also the PMAEX are valid epistemic principles. Perhaps it is time to say what can be said in support of their validity. Certainly, one thing that can be said in their behalf is that they are principles in accordance with which people do in fact implicitly argue. We have already discussed several examples of the use of the PEX and shall be discussing one or two more examples below. Unfortunately, however, there seems to be no non-circular way of *proving* the PEX or the PMAEX. But then it is well known that there is no way of non-circularly proving the general validity of inductive inferences, or of the principles upon which they are based, and yet we still believe that some such inferences and principles are valid. Perhaps the most that can be said for the validity of some basic principle of inductive inference is that we find it convincing and intuitively correct, that we want to make particular inferences in accordance with it, and that we find the making of such inferences indispensable in our thinking. And perhaps the same sort of thing is all that can or need be said in favour of the PEX or the PMAEX. However, someone of a scientific or anti-metaphysical bent might at this point object that science requires the acceptance of various principles of inductive inference, but can dispense entirely with the PEX and the PMAEX. But do we really have any right to assume that all valid forms of inference are indispensable to or even useful in science and scientific thinking? The PEX and the PMAEX are principles whose primary application and usefulness is within the area of metaphysical and religious thought. But why should there not be valid epistemic principles that are of little or no use to scientists, but which are useful, indeed indispensable, to certain forms of religious and metaphysical thinking?

The PEX has, furthermore, a great intuitive appeal; and not just because it is such a simple and symmetrical principle. If one comes out of a dark house and into the sunlight on a beautiful summer's day, the force and beauty of the day, of the trees, the sky and the flowers, may just strike one as intensely remarkable;

and if they do, one may think softly to oneself that there must be (or may well be) something behind all this, something we don't know, some extraordinary or remarkable power or being we cannot fathom. I have had this sort of experience, and I think many other people have. And for those who have had such an experience—either with respect to the beauty of a summer's day or with respect to the starry heavens or with respect to the phenomenon of a new-born baby—the PEX and the PMAEX will have an immediate intuitive appeal, will make obvious sense. Of course, there are many people who have never seen or felt the remarkableness of the world, of a summer's day, or of the starry heavens, in any intense way. And there are others who have felt this way, but who have not thought, as a result, that there had to be something remarkable behind things. The existence of the former kind of person in no way threatens the validity of the PEX, of course; for the failure of such a person to posit a remarkable *explanans* can be attributed to his failure to find things remarkable.

On the other hand, the fact that some people who feel the extraordinariness of things do not go on to posit the existence of something extraordinary or remarkable behind them also does not vitiate the PEX. For the PEX says only that if (one reasonably believes that) something is remarkable or extraordinary, one has *some* reason to think (and it is reasonable, other things being equal, to think, at least tentatively) that it has been brought about by something remarkable. It would, I agree, be a rather crucial failing of the PEX, if it committed one to believing that there was, for example, some remarkable force or being responsible for the order and beauty of the world, if one merely thought that the order and beauty of the world were remarkable. But in fact it clearly entails no such commitment. According to the PEX, those who find some phenomenon remarkable have and should feel that they have *some* reason to think that something extraordinary lies behind it. And this is, I believe, true, even of many scientists. When a scientist refuses to postulate something extraordinary behind things he deeply feels are extraordinary, it is, I wish to claim, because for him other things are not equal. His reason to posit an extraordinary *explanans* is overridden by other rational considerations, considerations of a kind that I shall be discussing just below. I think, then, that when we understand the PEX in the weak sort of way in which it is stated, the reluctance of scientists and others to postulate extraordinary *explanantia* does not vitiate the PEX, but can, rather, be best accounted for by assuming that such reluctance is the result of the fact that scientists and others allow a certain methodological principle of scientific inquiry, which they accept, to override the PEX, which they also accept.[1]

Let us now consider the crucial question why it is that some people who find the world or various phenomena in it remarkable posit remarkable *explanantia*, while others who find the world or various phenomena remarkable do not. Some scientists and scientific philosophers, for example, Einstein,[2] come to believe in something extraordinary behind things on the basis of the awesomeness or remarkableness of things they find in nature. Others, like J. J. C. Smart, admit the awesomeness, etc. of certain things, but do not seem to want to postulate anything remarkable behind them.[3] The reason why this occurs, I want to suggest, is that such men accept both the PEX and another principle that often comes into conflict with the PEX, and in weighing the one principle against the other, some give greater weight to the PEX and others to the principle that opposes it. But what is this principle that opposes the PEX?

I think one of the reasons why a scientist is loath to postulate a God or some other extraordinary force or being to explain those observed phenomena he finds extraordinary is his reluctance to posit things that do not fit neatly into the scientific theories he already accepts. Science typically seeks not only a greater and greater accumulation of knowledge, but also more and more

---

[1] I am myself *to a large extent*, but *not entirely*, convinced of the validity of the PEX, as I have stated it. But even if the PEX is not valid, it is an important principle to pay attention to, because it seems to be presupposed in certain important areas of human thought. If the PEX is not valid, it is worth asking why people make use of it; and, even if the PEX reflects a basically primitive pattern of thinking, it will still be worth noting the various ways that principle plays a part in areas of thought that are frequently considered not to be primitive.

[2] In his 'Autobiography' (in Schilpp (ed.), *Albert Einstein: Philosopher-Scientist*, N.Y.: Tudor, 1951, p. 9), Einstein says:
'[The development of the world of thought] is in a certain sense a continuous flight from "wonder".'
'A wonder of such nature I experienced as a child of four or five years, when my father showed me a compass. That this needle behaved in such a determined way did not at all fit into the nature of [familiar] events. . . . I can still remember —or at least believe I can remember—that this experience made a deep and lasting impression on me. Something deeply hidden had to be behind things.'

[3] See 'The Existence of God' in Flew and MacIntyre (eds.), *op. cit.*, p. 46.

systematic knowledge. As R. Rudner puts it: 'System is no mere adornment of science, it is its very heart. . . . It is an ideal of science to give an organized account of the universe. . . .'[1] Now to posit a deity or some other kind of extraordinary force behind things, or just to claim that there is some sort of extraordinary force or being behind things, is to postulate an entity that does not fit well into the framework of present scientific theories, an entity whose existence and behaviour are not readily understandable within present systematic scientific thought, nor, it would seem, readily incorporated into some new organized body of scientific thought. For a scientist to posit a mysterious extraordinary being or force as the ground of the world or of particular phenomena in it is thus, in effect, to thwart the inherently scientific aim of systematic unity within scientific theorizing and scientific knowledge. It is to posit an entity whose nature is not well understood, which may operate by different laws from those currently known and whose relation to other entities that are accepted as existing by scientists is not currently understood or likely soon to be understood. Within the structure of current scientific thinking, then, an extraordinary entity behind things, posited either as a result of applying the PEX or for some other reason, would be a sort of 'dangling' entity[2] and to accept its existence would be in effect to accept at least a temporary lessening of the systematic unity of scientific knowledge about the world. I think, therefore, that the following Principle of the Systematic Unity of Science is a valid epistemic principle governing scientific inquiry:

'It is, other things being equal, unreasonable (and there is some reason not) to explain phenomena in terms of entities the positing of whose existence decreases or makes likely a decrease in the systematization or systematic unity of (our accumulated body of) scientific knowledge.'

It should be clear how this principle can come into conflict with the PEX, for in cases where something we have observed seems extraordinary, the PEX gives us some reason to think that

---

[1] 'An Introduction to Simplicity', in *Philosophy of Science*, 28, 1961, p. 112. Also see Eddington's *The Philosophy of Physical Science* (Cambridge, 1949), p. 45; and Kant's *Critique of Pure Reason*, B673–78.

[2] See H. Margenau's *The Nature of Physical Reality*, (N.Y., 1950), p. 86.

there is some extraordinary thing responsible for it, while the Principle of the Systematic Unity of Science (henceforth, PSUS) may give us reason to think that we should not explain the phenomenon in question in terms of this sort of entity.[1] The situation with respect to these two principles and extraordinary phenomena is indeed very much like the situation with respect to moral principles that conflict with respect to a given act. A man may adhere to the (*prima facie*) moral principle that the fact that an act involves helping someone get what he wants gives one some reason (makes it, other things being equal, reasonable) to think that it is morally right, and also to the (*prima facie*) moral principle that the fact that an act involves lying gives one some reason (makes it, other things being equal, reasonable) to think that it is morally wrong. And when a given act involves both lying and helping someone else—lying in order to spare someone's feelings, for example, or lying in order to prevent a would-be murderer from finding his victim—one may find it hard to resolve the conflict between these two principles, that is, to decide whether the act in question is right or wrong. Similarly, when confronted with a situation where the PEX and the PSUS conflict, it may be hard to decide which principle to give greater weight to, and thus to decide whether to posit an extraordinary entity and go against systematic unity or not to posit that entity and preserve that unity. Furthermore, just as people differ among themselves as to which of the above two moral principles they ought to weight more heavily, they also differ as regards the proper weight that should be given the PSUS and the PEX. Thus a philosopher like Kant might always give greater weight to the moral principle about lying, whereas most ordinary people would say that, sometimes, the principle of helping people overrides the principle of not lying, so that it is sometimes right to help someone in a given case get what he wants, even if it involves lying. And similarly, someone like Einstein may feel so strongly about the PEX that he finds it reasonable to posit something extraordinary behind things he finds extraordinary, even at the expense of scientific unity, while many other scientific philosophers and scientists

---

[1] It should be clear that the positing of God or the Virgin to explain a dream goes against the PSUS as much as explaining the (beauty and order of the) world in terms of some extraordinary force or being. It might, incidentally, quite naturally occur to one that positing God or the Virgin might be inquiry-limiting. But this conjecture is not at all easy to substantiate, and, in fact, I am inclined to think it is false.

may find it more reasonable not to posit or believe in the existence of such an extraordinary entity, but to preserve scientific unity instead.

It is an interesting question when it is reasonable and when unreasonable to decide in favour of a particular one of a pair of conflicting moral or epistemic principles. Of course, no such problem arises when there is no conflict of such principles. Just as there is no problem about calling an act morally wrong if it involves lying and no morally favourable qualities (i.e. qualities mentioned in valid moral principles that state which qualities are such that their presence in some act gives one reason to think that act is morally *right* or *good*), so too there is no problem of conflict in cases where either the PEX or the PSUS is not applicable or relevant. Thus, where something is not considered remarkable, conflict is avoided because of the inapplicability of the PEX. More interesting, perhaps, is the fact that for primitive people the PSUS has very little, if any, relevance. Primitive people have presumably no very well developed and unified systematic body of scientific knowledge, so that their positing of a God beating a drum or striking flints does not effect any particular desystematization or disorganization of their systematic (scientific) knowledge of the world. Indeed, at the primitive stage of thought, *greater* system and organization of *their* total knowledge may be brought about by their positing a series of gods and myths about them. If all this is so, we have an explanation of why a primitive man who postulates a deity beating a drum to explain thunder has more reason to do so than anyone who possesses an accumulated body of scientific knowledge. For the latter has definite reason stemming from the PSUS *not* to posit an extraordinary deity to explain thunder.[1]

Of course, the fact that the PSUS does not apply to the thinking of a primitive man is not the only reason why it is more reasonable for a primitive to postulate an extraordinary cause of thunder than it is for us to do so. For we have a scientific understanding

---

[1] Of course, the primitive may *not* be justified in positing the *particular kind* of extraordinary entity he does, but only in positing the existence of *some sort* of extraordinary entity. It is interesting to note, however, that, if the PEX is valid, the primitive mythological view of the world is not as purely fanciful, prelogical, and devoid of rationality as many philosophers and anthropologists have thought. The positing of extraordinary beings to explain extraordinary phenomena is best conceived, perhaps, as the first gropings of rationality, rather than as prerational and purely mythical.

of thunder and there is a tendency for such phenomena to seem at least slightly less remarkable, awe-inspiring and wondrous after they have been scientifically explained.[1] Thus we today perhaps have less reason to find these phenomena remarkable than a primitive man does, and so, consequently, less reason to postulate an extraordinary cause for thunder than a primitive man. Similarly, an ancient who after taking an hallucinogen has an extraordinary dream or other experience has perhaps more reason to believe that something extraordinary has happened to him than someone who thoroughly understands how hallucinogens work and who has the same sort of experience, and so the former will have more reason to posit an extraordinary cause of his experience than the latter.[2]

However, even given scientific knowledge of the causes, effects, and mechanisms of thunder or of thunder and lightning, one might still find such phenomena extraordinary. For, although thunder may not be so remarkable *in the light of* (our understanding of) those things that bring it about, we might still find the whole phenomenon of thunder-taken-together-with-its-causes-effects-and-mechanisms to be remarkable and amazing indeed. One might, that is, still find it amazing that there should be such a phenomenon as thunder (or thunder and lightning) brought about in the way it is and operating as it does.[3] And similarly with other natural phenomena. Even one thoroughly knowledgeable about science may still find it amazing that any-

---

[1] See Heschel, *Man is not Alone*, p. 37.

[2] Perhaps this is why learning that a given mystical or dream experience was partly due to neurosis, hypnotism, or hallucinogens makes us less inclined to feel that that experience supports the truth of any religious beliefs. (If people felt that every religious experience had been thus induced, their faith in God and their religiosity in general would be seriously undermined.) For learning this gives us some reason to think and indeed tends to make us think of the experiences as less amazing and remarkable than we otherwise would. Thus those who say that the 'fact' that those who have come to believe in God through special experiences were all neurotic does not show that the God they came to believe in does not exist are *strictly speaking* right. But they are wrong if they think that learning about the neuroses does not diminish our *reason* for believing in God, *if* we have ever based our religious faith even partially on the fact that saints and others have had special religious experiences. For once we learn this sort of thing, we can no longer so confidently use the PEX to argue (implicitly or otherwise) from the existence of such experiences to the existence of some extraordinary force or being behind them. Cf. C. D. Broad's *Religion, Philosophy and Psychical Research*, N.Y.: Harcourt Brace, 1953, p. 192.

[3] See Heschel, *Man is not Alone*, p. 30, and *God in Search of Man*, p. 45; and also T. Pitcairn's *My Lord and my God*, N.Y.: Exposition Press, 1967, p. 12.

thing exists at all,[1] or that nature is as inexorably lawful as it is.[2] One may find it miraculous that there are no miracles.

Even if scientists and scientifically informed people will consider many things extraordinary or amazing, they will, presumably, also be less inclined than most people to use the PEX, because they are inclined to give greater weight than most people to the PSUS.[3] For a scientist's major interests are usually scientific, and so he is more likely to give greater weight to the PSUS than most other people (who lack those interests) just because by sticking to the PSUS, he tends to further and to serve the fundamental aim science has of explaining phenomena in a unified systematic way.[4] But the fact that something goes against the purposes of scientific inquiry does not necessarily mean that it goes against reason itself. And so a person with less commitment to science or with great aesthetic and/or religious sensitivity and capacity for wonder and awe might not be entirely irrational to give greater weight to the PEX than to the PSUS, and so come to believe in a higher being or force or thing on the basis of some amazing phenomenon.

The argument by which someone, explicitly using the PEX, might attempt to justify belief in some sort of deity can be formally stated as follows:

(a) (It is reasonable to believe tentatively that) the order and beauty of the world (or the fact that there exists something physical, rather than nothing physical at all) are extraordinary, remarkable, etc.

(b) The PEX is valid.

[1] See Smart, op. cit., p. 46.

[2] See Konrad Lorenz, 'On Aggression', part 1, Encounter, August, 1966, p. 29 f.

[3] In his The Structure of Scientific Revolutions (Chicago: Univ. of Chicago Press, 1964, p. 77), T. Kuhn claims that scientists do not discard a theory beset with difficulties until they have another theory to put in its place. They act as if it is better to have some theory, even a faulty and inadequate one, than to have none at all. If the PSUS is valid, we have at least a partial explanation of why this is so. For to give up one's theory in a given area without having a theory to replace it is to give up whatever systematic understanding of the world the first theory provided without getting any new systematic understanding in return. Thus the fact that scientists tend to act this way gives some support to the PSUS.

[4] One result of this chapter is that religious thought and scientific thought can conflict, are not independent intellectual realms, as is sometimes thought. (E.g. by Einstein; see Eddington, op. cit., p. 7.)

Thus

(c) There is some reason to believe that there exists an extra-ordinary force, being or thing that created the order and beauty of the world (or that brought it about that there is something physical).

Two further steps are possible:

(d) The order and beauty of the world (or the fact that there is something physical) are so remarkable, etc. that we should disregard the fact that positing an extraordinary, etc. being goes against the PSUS, and should give greater weight to the PEX than to the PSUS.

Thus

(e) It is reasonable for us to believe at least tentatively that some sort of extraordinary force, being, or thing is responsible for the order and beauty of the world (or for the fact that there is something physical).

This argument differs from most traditional arguments for God in that it does not attempt to prove the *existence* of anything, but at best only the *reasonableness of believing* that something (like a God) exists. Secondly, the proof is not concerned with showing the reasonableness of believing in anything like the traditional all-good, all-powerful Judeo-Christian God. How-ever, the being or thing whose existence it refers to is something very like a God, and is the kind of 'God' most traditional proofs of God's existence are concerned with—as well as being the kind of God most negative theologians want to restrict themselves to talking about. It should be noted, thirdly, that we have above really given two different arguments for God, one from the order and beauty of the world, and the other from the fact of contingent physical existence. And each of these arguments runs parallel to one of the traditional arguments for God's existence.

The traditional Cosmological Argument for God starts with the fact that there is some contingent (physical or other) entity and tries to prove the existence of God as 'First Cause'. We have provided an argument that starts from the fact that there exists some contingent *physical* entity (or from the reasonableness of tentatively believing there is such an entity) and tries to prove that there is *reason* (and that it is *reasonable* at least tentatively) to believe in something like a God.[1] Of course, the argument we have provided proceeds via the notion of the extraordinary and via the PEX and thus differs considerably from the Cosmological Argument. But there is a definite parallel, none the less. We have also provided an argument for some sort of God from the fact of the (reasonableness of believing in the) order and beauty of the world. And this argument parallels the traditional Teleological Argument (Argument from Design) for God's existence, inasmuch as both arguments start from the order and beauty of the world, and try to prove something about the Deity, or about something closely resembling a God.[2] And it is possible to view *our* argument from the order and beauty of the world via the PEX as accomplishing pretty much what the Teleological Argument attempts to accomplish, and as doing so far more plausibly and persuasively than the Teleological Argument itself does. Indeed with respect to both of the arguments presented above, it might be said that what we have done is to take facts that have frequently been adduced as evidence for the existence of a God (by those proposing the Cosmological and Teleological Arguments) and show for the first time just *how* those facts support belief in some sort of God.

The two arguments we have introduced, however, are clearly not beyond criticism. One may question whether the order and beauty of the universe are really so remarkable (or, indeed, whether the world really is so orderly and beautiful). One may question whether it is extraordinary that anything physical exists. One may question the PEX. And, indeed, most people committed to the enterprise of science (myself included) will be particularly unhappy about premise (*d*) and thus about the argu-

---

[1] My argument starts from the fact of physical existence, and not from the fact of contingent existence in general, because I cannot understand the idea of a necessary entity that has causal powers, or thus that is causally responsible for all contingent entities.

[2] In his introductory remarks about the Teleological Argument (which he calls the Physico-theological Proof) in the *Critique of Pure Reason* (B 650), Kant seems to have seen or to have been close to seeing the possibility of an argument from the *extraordinariness* of certain aspects of the world to the existence of some sort of God. But he does not seem to see the argument from extraordinariness as an argument separate and distinct from the traditional Teleological Argument itself, or to recognize the possible validity of a principle like the PEX.

ment from (c) to (e). However, I see no way of showing that (d) is an unreasonable premise, nor thus that the argument for (e) cannot be made to go through. And in any case, the argument(s) we have given will seem plausible to many people, I think, and this fact, if it is a fact, deserves some attention. Furthermore, the argument from (a) to (c) seems to me to have definite appeal and force. For I think we have, at least some of us, definite reason to think certain aspects of the world remarkable or extraordinary, and definite reason to put at least some confidence in the PEX. Thus the argument from (a) to (c) and thence to (e) *may not* entirely overcome scepticism about the Deity or give us rational justification for actually *believing* in God (however tentatively), but it is a more plausible and reasonable argument for the (epistemic) rationality of religious belief than any of the traditional arguments we have discussed or any other arguments for religious belief that I know of. And in the light of the argument(s) presented here for the existence of some sort of God, I think we have at least shown that *thoroughgoing* and *unshakeable scepticism* about the *existence* of God, or, at least, *thoroughgoing* and *unshakeable belief* in the *non-existence* of God, is not entirely reasonable.

IV

We have understood certain problems about whether it is reasonable to believe in some sort of deity in terms of a conflict between the PEX and the PSUS. But there are other intellectual situations we have not yet considered that can be understood in terms of a conflict between these two principles, and that I should like to discuss now.

Consider, for example, the intellectual climate that exists today about the so-called phenomena of Extrasensory Perception. Some people believe in ESP and others do not. But there are, I think, three major stances that can be taken with respect to ESP, and these can be clarified in terms of the PEX and the PSUS. Some psychologists and men of science think that putative ESP phenomena can be explained away as being due to cheating or as merely chance phenomena (i.e. phenomena that could plausibly be thought to have taken place by mere chance). With regard to the ESP card-guessing experiments, on which proponents of ESP place so much weight, it is often claimed that peeking may have occurred, or else that there are purely statistical reasons to expect at least some subjects to perform as well as those few whose performances at card-guessing have been used to support the existence of ESP. Such psychologists and men of science do not, therefore, find the results of ESP experiments particularly remarkable or extraordinary or amazing. So such people have no motive from the PEX to explain the results of ESP experiments in terms of some extraordinary power of Extrasensory Perception.[1]

Others do not think that the results of ESP experiments can be so easily explained away. They think that something quite remarkable is (probably) taking place, but prefer not to jump immediately to the conclusion that there exists a force or power of ESP, because they desire to preserve what they can of the present order and unity of our scientific understanding. For to postulate ESP would be to posit a force or power that cannot readily be understood within the scope of present scientific theories and that is totally different from anything accepted by current science; nor does there at present seem to be any way of incorporating both ESP and the phenomena whose existence physics, biology, etc. now recognize into some new coherent unified body of beliefs. If one really accepts ESP, one opens up the possibility that there are laws unlike any that we have known about and of which we know very little at present. One accepts a lessening of the systematic unity of our scientific knowledge about things, at least for the present. Thus many scientists who find the results of ESP experiments remarkable, refuse to posit an extraordinary power of ESP, because of their allegiance to the PSUS. Instead, they attempt or think one should attempt to understand those results within the framework of current scientific theories and theorizing, think these phenomena can be explained in terms of some perhaps strange or unexpected interaction of forces or entities that are already posited and fairly well understood by science. Such people, then, give greater weight to the PSUS than to the PEX.

Others, of course, (claim to) believe in ESP, and they can perhaps best be understood as people who find the results of ESP experiments remarkable and whose non-allegiance to the PSUS (or whose amazement at the results of ESP experiments)

---

[1] It should be clear that ESP is supposed to be extraordinary even by its proponents, since only a few people at rare moments are supposed to possess it, and it enables them to do things people cannot ordinarily do.

is great enough so that they will give greater weight to the PEX than to the PSUS in current circumstances, and so will posit ESP as the explanation of the results of those experiments. (Unless they are really the charlatans and deceivers some people say they are, those, like Rhine and Soal, who have conducted the ESP experiments belong in this last class. One can perhaps partially explain their extreme readiness to believe in ESP as being a result of their having had the results of those experiments at first hand and thus being more *amazed* by those results than those who only know of them at second hand.)

I am inclined to think it more reasonable not to believe in ESP than to believe in ESP (for most people) at present. First, because of the chance of foul play or faulty experimental design on the part of ESP experimenters, and secondly because I do not think it is rational to rush in and posit an extraordinary *explanans* for every extraordinary new thing that one observes or hears about. Respect for the 'old truths' and for the preservation of previously won scientific *system* makes it reasonable, I think, to refrain from positing something that does not fit in well within the current organized body of scientific knowledge (like ESP) and first to make every attempt to fit the remarkable phenomenon in question into already existing patterns of scientific explanation, to explain it, that is, in terms of some interrelation of things, forces and laws already posited and investigated.[1] However, if such attempts persistently fail, then, perhaps, the PSUS should give way and one should posit an extraordinary *explanans*. At present, I think, we have not done all we can to explain the results of ESP experiments in terms of existing ideas and theories. So I think positing ESP is premature. That is, I think that in present circumstances we ought to give greater weight to the PSUS than to the PEX with respect to ESP experiment results. But this may not always be so in the future.

Whether or not it is reasonable to believe in ESP at present, the current existence of disagreements among scientists and others with respect to putative ESP phenomena can be explained in terms of our two principles, the PEX and the PSUS. And these principles can be used to explain other scientific or intellectual disagreements as well. Current disagreements about flying saucers or ghosts can be understood in much the same way as we explained current

[1] As is suggested by M. Scriven in 'Modern Experiments in Telepathy', *Phil. Review*, 65, 1956, p. 249.

disagreements about ESP, as the reader can quite easily verify for himself. And, inasmuch as many phenomena of intellectual life can be very plausibly understood in terms of our two principles, we can see the prevalence and pervasiveness of those principles in human thought, and this in turn is *some* sort of reason additional to those given earlier for thinking that those principles are valid and for thinking that the argument(s) given above for the existence of some sort of God, which depended on the PEX in particular, has (have) some force.

In recent decades, religious thinkers and philosophers have often claimed or held that, if religious belief and thought are not rational by scientific standards, have no justification of the sort that scientific hypotheses or theories have, they are not rational at all. Since there does not seem to be any available way to verify religious beliefs in the manner of scientific hypotheses, they have tended to conclude that religious belief is irrational and blind or that religious 'belief' is really just an attitude, emotion or *'blik'* that is cognitively meaningless—neither of which is a very pleasant prospect for religionists to have to face.[1] If the argument of the present chapter is correct, however, there is a middle way out of this predicament; and there is more to religious belief (in the existence of God, at least) than sheer emotionalism and/or irrationality. There are some epistemically rational grounds for religious belief, but these are not essentially *scientific*. Rather, there is a rationality *sui generis* to religious thought that is not encompassed by science, or by purely scientific standards of the reasonable acceptance of hypotheses, a rationality whose nature and significance are only now beginning to be understood.

[1] For clarification of the notion of a *'blik'*, see 'Theology and Falsification' (especially the section by R. M. Hare) in Flew and MacIntyre, *op. cit.*

CHAPTER 7

CONCLUSION

We have argued for the *reasonableness* of belief in an external world that is very much as it appears (to us) to be, in other minds, and in objects that are not in our presence and are presently unobserved by us (even indirectly). We have also argued that there is *some reason* to believe in some sort of deity or extraordinary force or being behind things. We have not, however, considered the reasonableness of believing in the sorts of physical, chemical, and biological theories, etc., that the ordinary man knows about, if at all, only at second hand. Quite possibly, principles like those we have used here could be used by scientists possessing empirical data to justify many of the conclusions of the special sciences on the basis of the sorts of assumptions we here have shown how one can justify. Or perhaps quite different principles would be needed for such a task. We have also for the most part ignored scepticism about values and value judgments in the present work. Such scepticism deserves extensive treatment, but not, I think, in a book like the present one, whose major emphasis is on forms of epistemological scepticism.

All through the present work, we have talked about experiences, physical objects, physical processes, persons, God, etc. without defining any of these notions in any explicit and complete way. But, of course, it is legitimate to use notions that one cannot define in the doing of philosophy, as long as one understands those notions in an implicit way. And I think we do understand the notions I mentioned above, and the distinctions among them, in an implicit way. In a future work, however, I shall attempt to discuss and define the sorts of notions we have mentioned above, and that we have been using throughout the present work. Correct definitions of those notions are, I hope to show, consistent with everything said here in applying those notions, and, indeed, even support the approach taken in the present work to scepticism and to the Theory of Knowledge in general. But all this must, unfortunately, remain in the form of a promissory note, for the time being.

I have in the present work been tacitly assuming the analytic validity of at least one form of the Causal Theory of Perception, have been assuming, that is, that it is an analytic truth that perception, whether direct or indirect, of the external world or of objects and processes in it logically requires having experience that is caused by something physical. Construed in this way, the Causal Theory is, I think, compatible with Phenomenalism. However, I have *also* been assuming (on the basis of arguments given in Chapter 1 and in other works than the present) that physical notions are *not* to be defined phenomenalistically (or idealistically). And I have used these analytic or definitional assumptions to give an argument for (what we can call) *traditional* Causal Realism, that is, for the view that physical objects cause our experiences of sense and memory, even though physical notions cannot be defined phenomenalistically (or idealistically), that is, in terms of actual and/or possible experiences.

One reason, I think, why Phenomenalism has been held to by so many philosophers despite the numerous objections that have been raised against it as a theory of the *meaning* of physical notions is that Phenomenalism seems to offer the possibility of justifying claims about the external world, etc. in a way that certain of its most plausible alternatives (in particular, traditional Causal Realism) do not. For most philosophers are not sceptics and believe in an external world, etc. that can be reasonably believed to exist. And so it is natural for them to seek in Epistemology for a theory that allows for and accounts for justified belief about (objects and processes in) the external world. Phenomenalism seems to many philosophers to allow the possibility of justifying belief in an external world and of accounting for how such justification is possible. For if statements about physical entities *reduce* to statements about actual and possible experience, then presumably statements about our actual experience can serve to *verify* such statements. (Though I do not think the matter is as simple as some Phenomenalists have thought.) On the other hand, many philosophers have felt that traditional Causal Realism *cannot* give any plausible justification of claims about the external world.[1] And this seems a not unreasonable view to take of the matter, in the light of the total failure of such traditional Causal Realists as Descartes and Locke to offer any plausible justification for beliefs about the (present and past nature of) the external world.

[1] E.g., A. Quinton, in 'The Problem of Perception', in Swartz (ed.), *op. cit.*, p. 498, and Price in *Perception*, ch. 4.

Thus Phenomenalists are reluctant to abandon Phenomenalism even in the light of strong criticisms of it as a theory of the meaning of physical object terms, because it seems to them that if they do, they will be left with no argument for or account of the reasonableness of beliefs about the external world. And as Kuhn points out in his *The Structure of Scientific Revolutions* (and as we have emphasized in Chapter 6 in our discussion of the Principle of the Systematic Unity of Science), it is perfectly understandable that scientists (or, presumably, philosophers) should refuse to give up a theory that can account for certain things they consider important, in spite of serious criticisms of that theory, *if* they possess no other theory that can account for those things. And so it is understandable that Phenomenalists should until now have continued to hold on to Phenomenalism (usually in weaker and weaker versions), since the most plausible leading alternative to Phenomenalism, namely, traditional Causal Realism, has always seemed to offer no possibility of justifying beliefs about the external world. (Phenomenalists have usually felt that Berkeleyian, or Hegelian, or Bradleyian Idealism was, if anything, *less* plausible than traditional Causal Realism.) If the argument of the present work is correct, however, it is no longer possible to fault old-fashioned Causal Realism in the way so many philosophers have or to hold on to Phenomenalism *as a last resort.* For we have shown that a traditional Causal Realist can give arguments for his position, that is, can show the reasonableness of belief in an external world as the cause of his experiences while assuming that physical objects are not analysable into actual and possible experiences of them. Standards and/or principles of scientific thought and methodology can be used to justify believing in physical objects, processes, etc., so that we can *at least* be justified in believing in physical entities (on the basis of our experiences) in something like the way that physicists are justified in believing in subatomic particles (on the basis of experimental and other data). That is not to say that there are no important differences between the way one can be justified about macroscopic physical entities and the way one can be justified about subatomic particles. Presumably our justification for the former is much stronger and more unshakeable than our justification for the latter since our justification for the latter seems evidentially to depend on our justification for the former. Also, our justification for believing in material objects, processes, events, etc., as well as for believing in other minds and unobserved objects, etc., is obviously much greater than we have attempted to argue in this book. Presumably, we have overwhelmingly good reason to believe in external objects and other minds, etc., but we have here only attempted to show that (tentative) belief in these sorts of things can be reasonable. But, inasmuch as we have shown even this, and have done so via the sorts of principles we have, I think Phenomenalism can no longer reasonably be maintained. There are just too many telling criticisms around of Phenomenalism as a theory of meaning, and there is another theory available, namely, traditional Causal Realism, that is not subject to the criticisms that have been levelled at Phenomenalism, as a theory of meaning, and that can argue for and account for the reasonableness of belief in an external world pretty much the way we think it is (and was) in a more thoroughgoing and plausible way than Phenomenalism has ever been able to do.

INDEX OF PRINCIPLES

Principle A, 74 (stated), 76, 77n., 80, 83, 84n., 90, 103, 108n., 179

Principle A (of Plantinga), 115 (stated), 116–17, 125

Principle A' (of Plantinga), 116–17 (stated), 125

Principle B, 76 (stated), 77, 80, 90–1, 98, 101–3, 107n., 108n., 111, 134, 161–2, 179

Principle B'', 102 (stated), 103n., 111, 134, 161

Principle C, 76–7 (stated), 78, 80, 90–1, 98, 101–3, 107n., 108n., 111, 134, 161–2, 179

Principle C', 91n. (stated), 101–2

Principle C'', 102 (stated), 103, 184

Principle D, 80 (stated), 91, 103, 173, 176, 180, 184

Principle E, 104 (stated), 108n.

Principle of Extraordinary Explanation (PEX), 192–3 (stated), 194ff.

Principle of First-Person Verification, 42 (stated)

Principle of Illusion and Evidence (PIE), 99–100 (stated), 101–4, 108n., 110, 179–80

Principle of the Most Appropriate Extraordinary Explanation (PMAEX), 201 (stated), 202–3

Principle of the Systematic Unity of Science (PSUS), 205 (stated), 206ff.

Principle of Unlimited Inquiry (PUI), 66–7 (stated), 68–9, 74–5, 80, 86, 91, 103, 108n., 175, 179

Principle Y, 129–30 (stated), 131–2, 134–5, 157, 165

Principle Z, 149–50 (stated), 151–2, 156, 162, 165, 182

Principle Z', 155–6 (stated), 157, 162, 165, 182

Principle Z'', 161–2 (stated), 163, 165, 171, 173, 175–6, 179–80, 182–4

Strong Principle of Induction, 119–20 (stated), 121–5, 131, 152–3, 157–60, 163–5, 174–5, 176n.

Weaker Version of the Strong Principle of Induction, 120 (stated), 121, 123–5, 158, 164, 174–5

GENERAL INDEX

accident, see chance
Acton, H. B., 122
alikeness, see likeness
analogical-inductive argument, see Argument from Analogy
analyticity, 167n.
a posteriori truth, 50
Appearance, 171–3
a priori principles, 88n.
Argument from Analogy, 111–18, 126, 128, 133, 153
argument from contingent existence, see contingent object
Argument from Illusion, 185
argument from order and beauty, 197f., 202f., 209–11
argument from orderliness and coherence, 95f.
Aristotle, 88n.
Austin, J. L., 19, 29, 57n.
avoidance of error, 78f.
'A-words', see Nowell-Smith
Ayer, A. J., 32n., 36n., 42n., 119, 181f.

Barker, S., 146n., 157n.
Bennett, J., 27, 92n.
Berkeley, 36n., 178, 218
Berkeley's God, 63, 178; see also God
Blanshard, B., 22
body, see external world
Bosanquet, 22
Bouwsma, O. K., 63f.
Bradleyian Idealism, 218
Braithwaite, R. B., 92n.
Brandt, R., 92n.
Broad, C. D., 24, 45n., 208n.

Carneades, 177n.
Carnap, R., 63f.
Cartesian demon, see demon
Cartwright, R. L., 49n., 51n.
Causal Realism, 180–3, 186, 217; see also traditional Causal Realism
Causal Theory of Perception, 216f.
certainty, 19–21, 29, 45, 47, 55, 60n., 72, 81f., 88, 119

chance, 35, 60f., 63, 77–9, 83f., 91, 103, 107n., 173, 175f., 184, 190, 212
Chisholm, R., 32n., 35n., 40n., 85f., 92n., 177–9
Coherence Theory, 22, 92n., 138
common sense, 18f., 29, 41n., 46, 61, 63f., 97f., 105f., 108, 111, 114n., 121, 124, 170–6, 183f., 188
confirmation, 131; see also induction, sample class
conscious being, 17f., 27, 160f., 176n., 183, 192n., 216
contingent identity, see identity
contingent mind-body identity, see mind-body identity
contingent object, 189–91, 195, 209–11
continuity, see spatio-temporal continuity, experience
Cornman, J., 56n.
Cosmological Argument, 188–91, 210f.

Davidson, D., 146n., 166n.
deception, see experience, veridical, hallucination, illusion
demon (spirit), 17, 22, 28–40, 48, 58–84, 90–2, 96, 103, 107n., 111, 124, 172f., 179n., 180f.
Descartes, 32, 35, 60n., 84n., 95, 101n., 160, 178, 217
Deutscher, M., 185n.
Dewey, J., 37f., 40n.
differential property, 140–5, 148, 164, 167f.
dis-, unembodied being, 37, 40–55, 58f., 110
dreaming (dreaming-scepticism), 17, 25, 32f., 36f., 60f., 94ff., 185f., 194, 198f., 206n., 208
dualism, see mind-body identity

Eddington, Sir A., 205n., 209n.
Einstein, A., 204, 206, 209n.
élan vital, 65f.

Emotivism, 196
entrenched predicate, *see* New Riddle of Induction
enumerative induction, *see* induction, enumerative
epistemic possibility, 50*n*.
epistemic principles, 179–81, 191*f*., 202, 205, 207
epistemic reasonableness, 21*n*., 85–7, 92, 101, 173, 183, 201*n*., 212, 215
epistemological present, 90, 109
epistemological priority, 19–29, 38
Epistemological Realism, 121*f*.
epistemological reconstruction, *see* reconstruction of knowledge
exact likeness, *see* likeness
experience, 18–20, 47*f*., 109, 117, 158, 170, 173, 192–5, 199, 203, 208, 216–19
  continuity of, 45–7
  immediate, 19–24, 27–30, 38, 40*n*., 159
  past, *see* memory-impressions
  religious, 199, 208*n*.; *see also* religion
  sense (outer), 21–40, 58–64, 67–110, 159, 170–2, 175, 177–85, 217
  veridical, 18, 31*f*., 57*f*., 76, 91, 94*f*., 98–110, 171, 173*n*., 179, 182–6
external world (external-world scepticism), 17–64, 67–76, 80–101, 106–11, 117–28, 133, 157–9, 170–89, 216–18
  past existence of, 43*f*., 56, 90–2, 108–11, 176*n*., 183, 185
extraordinariness, 191–216
Extrasensory Perception (ESP) 212*f*.

Fallacy of the Common Denominator, 199*n*., 201*n*.
Feigl, H., 53*n*.
Firth, R., 34*n*., 38, 87, 178*n*., 198*n*.
Foot, P., 97*n*.

Geach, P., 49*n*., 110*n*.
genera, 155*n*., 156

God (the Deity), 17*f*., 32, 37, 40, 121*n*., 188–94, 198–200, 204–12, 215*f*.
Goodman, N., 103*n*., 121*n*., 132*ff*.
Grice, H. P., 35*n*.

hallucination, 25, 57*f*., 95, 100*f*., 105, 183, 185*f*.
Hare, R., 169, 215*n*.
Harman, G., 106*n*., 124
Hegelian Idealism, 218
Heidelberger, H., 177*n*.
Hempel, C., 131
Heschel, A., 195*n*., 208*n*.
Hintikka, J., 50*n*.
Hume, 24*n*., 166, 174*n*., 178

Ideal Observer Theory, 198*n*.
identity, 49–55, 160, 164; *see also* mind-body identity
illusion, 69–79, 84*n*., 90*f*., 94*f*., 99–107, 171, 173, 175
imaginability, 53–6
immediate experience, *see* experience, immediate
incorrigibility, 19*f*., 29
indirect observation, 186, 216*f*.
indubitability *see* incorrigibility
induction (inductive argument, generalization), 37, 64*n*., 92, 109, 114*f*., 117–19, 121*f*., 127–34, 137–9, 147–9, 151*f*., 154, 156–8, 160, 162–7, 169*f*., 202
  analogical-inductive argument, *see* Argument from Analogy
  enumerative, 111, 120–4, 130, 134, 138*f*., 155, 157, 162, 166*f*., 170, 175, 182, 189
  justification of, 82*n*., 166
  simple inductive argument, 113–18, 127
  inductive validity, 168–70, 173, 175
innate ideas, 22
innate knowledge, 23*n*.
inquiry-limitingness, 66*f*., 75–84, 98, 111*f*., 168, 206*n*.
intelligent design, 189–91
'is' of identity, 49*n*.

James, W., 67n., 79n.
Jevons, F. B., 192n.

Kalish, D., 101n.
Kanger, S., 50n.
Kant, 23, 178, 205n., 206, 209n.
Kaplan, A., 80n.
kind (of thing), 155–7, 161f., 164–6;
    see also differential property
Kneale, W. and M., 50n.
Kripke, S., 50n., 56n., 174n.
Kuhn, T., 209n., 218

law (lawfulness), 38–40, 80n., 122f.,
    195, 209, 213f.
Lazerowitz, M., 59n.
Leibniz, 50n.
Lewis, C. I., 24, 90, 92n.
Lewis, H. D., 96n.
likeness, 43, 140ff., 161ff., 182
Locke, Don, 23n.
Locke, John, 24, 26, 178, 217
Logical Behaviorism, 112
logical positivism, 40
'looks as if' statements, 34n., 38–40
Lorenz, K., 209n.

Malcolm, N., 56–8, 95–7, 112
Margenau, H., 205n.
Martin, C. B., 143n., 185n.
material objects, see external world
memory, 17f., 31, 81, 100, 105,
    108, 183, 185f.
memory-beliefs, 92f., 177n.
memory-impressions, 47, 89–110,
    118, 158f., 176n., 179f., 184f.,
    217
'Method of Hypothesis', 178
mind, 160f.
mind-body identity, 47–9, 52–6;
    see also identity
Moore, G. E., 25n., 33, 37n., 141n.,
    186n.
Moral Argument, 188
moral principles, 206f.
Morgenbesser, S., 80n.

Nagel, T., 52n.
necessary a posteriori truth, 50n.
New Riddle of Induction, 103n.,
    132–54, 157, 166–70

nominalization, 51–3; see also pure
    proper name
non-observational predicate, 140,
    147; see also unobservable
    entities
Nowell-Smith, P. H., 196
null-explanation, see chance

occult power, 121; see also élan
    vital
Ockham's razor, 106
O'Connor, J., 142n.
Ontological Argument, 188–91
ordinary language, 33, 59, 143
other minds, 17–20, 27–9, 31, 87,
    89, 106, 109, 111–28, 132–4,
    153f., 157–61, 174–6, 216, 219

pain, 113–15, 118–20, 125–8, 132,
    153f., 158f., 161
Paradigm-Case Argument, 58,
    166n.
Penelhum, T., 44
perception, 17f., 31, 57f., 105, 108f.
    177f., 183, 185f., 217
person, see conscious being
Phenomenalism, 36f., 182, 217–19
physical object, see external world
Pitcairn, T., 208n.
Planck, M., 182n.
Plantinga, A., 59n., 62n., 112–17,
    124, 126f., 154, 188–91
Polanyi, M., 199
Price, H. H., 32n., 178f., 181, 217n.
primary qualities, 106
primitive thought, 192f., 204n.,
    207f.
Principle of Confirmability, see
    Price
private language, 58f.
projectibility, see New Riddle of
    Induction
pure proper name, 49–53
Putnam, H., 49, 52n., 96, 112n.

Quine, W. V. O., 17n., 50n., 141,
    155n., 182n.
Quinton, A., 217n.

Ramsey, F. P., 64n.
Rationalists, 22

Reality, 171*f.*
reconstruction of knowledge, 20*f.*, 40, 48
religion, 191, 194, 197, 199*ff.*, 215
remarkableness, *see* extraordinariness
Rhine, J. B., 214
Rudner, R., 205
Rundle, B., 49*n.*
Russell, B., 24*n.*, 32*f.*, 37*n.*, 62*n.*, 88*n.*, 93, 160, 185
Ryle, G., 57*f.*

sample class, 115, 119–22, 125, 131–3, 150, 152*f.*, 158, 190
sceptical hypothesis, 17, 68*n.*
Scheffler, I., 163*n.*
Schopenhauer, 193
science, nature and goals of, 65, 67–9, 79*f.*, 100, 145, 204*f.*, 209
scientific methodology, 18, 30–2, 37, 178, 191, 218
scientific practice, 19, 87*f.*, 101, 159*f.*
Scriven, M., 214*n.*
secondary qualities, 105*f.*
sense datum, 35*n.*, 185
sense experience, *see* experience, sense
Shaffer, J., 27
Shoemaker, S., 92*n.*, 112
Shope, R., 84*n.*
simple inductive argument, *see* induction
simplicity, 46, 62, 64, 80*n.*, 124, 146–8, 150*f.*, 156*f.*, 159, 161, 163, 165, 175, 191, 202
Sleigh, R., 128–31, 154
Slote, M. A., 19, 58*n.*, 186*n.*, 196*n.*
Smart, J. J. C., 182*n.*, 204, 209*n.*
Soal, S., 214
species, 155*n.*, 156

Stace, W. T., 121–3
Stedman, R. E., 122
Stocker, M., 59*n.*
Strawson, P. F., 43, 112
subatomic particles, 41, 66*n.*, 80*n.*, 160, 181*f.*, 218; *see also* unobservable entities
Subjectivism, 196
Swinburne, R. G., 142*n.*
systematic unity, 204–7, 209, 213*f.*

Teleological Argument, 188–91, 211
third-person verification, 42, 46*ff.*
traditional Causal Realism, 217–19: *see also* Causal Realism

Unger, P., 23*n.*, 43, 90*n.*
unlikeness, *see* likeness
unobservable entities, 159*f.*, 181*f.*; *see also* non-observational predicate, subatomic particles
unobserved objects, 18, 109, 111, 113, 121–3, 127*f.*, 133*f.*, 153*f.*, 157–9, 163, 176*n.*, 181, 192, 195*n.*, 216, 219

value judgments, 195*f.*
verifiability, 40–7, 61–4, 96

Wallace, J., 166*n.*
Whitehead, A. N., 93
Williams, B., 45
Williams, D. C., 62*n.*, 172*n.*
Wilson, K., 58*n.*
Wisdom, J., 160, 197
Wittgenstein, L., 24, 26, 58*f.*, 112

Yost, R., 101*n.*

Ziff, P., 124, 137